Breaking the Shell

Breaking the Shell

**Voyaging from Nuclear Refugees to
People of the Sea in the Marshall Islands**

Joseph H. Genz

University of Hawai'i Press
Honolulu

Publication of this book was supported by University of Hawai'i at Hilo.

24 23 22 21 20 19 18   6 5 4 3 2 1

Library of Congress Cataloging-in-Publication Data

Names: Genz, Joseph H., author.

Title: Breaking the shell : voyaging from nuclear refugees to people of the
    sea in the Marshall Islands / Joseph H. Genz.

Description: Honolulu : University of Hawai'i Press, [2018] | Includes
    bibliographical references and index.

Identifiers: LCCN 2017009433 | ISBN 9780824867911 (cloth ; alk. paper)

Subjects: LCSH: Navigation—Marshall Islands. | Canoes and canoeing—Marshall
    Islands. | Marshall Islands—History.

Classification: LCC GN440.2 .G46 2018 | DDC 306.09968/3—dc23

LC record available at https://lccn.loc.gov/2017009433

Cover illustrations: (*front and spine*) photographs courtesy of Mark Peterson/Redux;
(*back*) *Wapepe*, constructed by Isao Eknilang

Dedicated to the navigator Captain Korent Joel,
who dreamed of returning by canoe to his
ancestral home island, and to Ben R. Finney,
who championed the renaissance of voyaging through
his sincerity of heart.

Captain Korent Joel, 1948–2017   Ben R. Finney, 1933–2017

Contents

Acknowledgments

I CANNOT sufficiently convey here the depths of my gratitude to Captain Korent for allowing me to accompany him on his heroic quest to become a navigator. To his surviving elders who worked with us to make this a reality, I am so thankful: Isao Eknilang, Thomas Bokin, Anno Aisaia, Francis Livai, and Mejohn River. To the families of the late Lijon Eknilang, Willie Mwekto, and Alton Albious, I am equally appreciative and hope this book provides a loving memory and testament to their heartfelt efforts at safeguarding their most precious knowledge.

In the Department of Anthropology at the University of Hawai'i at Mānoa, I had the honor of being Ben Finney's last graduate student and immensely benefiting from his mentorship and friendship. This story of Captain Korent reclaiming his ancestral identity as a person of the sea would not have happened without Ben's pioneering vision, clear guidance and oversight, culturally sensitive facilitation, and unwavering support. I also received sage advice and direction as a graduate student from Geoff White, David Hanlon, Nina Etkin, Mark Merrifield, and Terry Hunt.

I am indebted to Alson Kelen and Dennis Alessio for inviting me into their family of canoe enthusiasts and for their cofacilitating the voyaging revival effort. Long-standing administrative and logistical support from the community organization Waan Aelōñ in Majol is gratefully credited to Jill Luciano, Rachel Miller, Jessica Brandt, Lezil Gana, and Tolina Tomeing. The recent canoe voyage to Aur was accomplished by navigation apprentice Alson Kelen, master canoe builder Binton Daniel, and sailors Sear Helios, Elmi Juonraan, Ejnar Aerok, and Jason Ralpho, and I am grateful for their dedication to the canoe *Jitdaṃ Kapeel* and sharing their stories. Mantel Laik built the canoe model used as an illustration.

Chiefly permission to conduct the first phase of the project came from Iroijlaplap (Paramount Chief) Imata Kabua and Iroij (Chief) Mike Kabua, and permission to sail to Aur came through Iroij Jackious Boklon. Permission to travel to Bikini and Rongelap as well as to have access to their sea transport came from Bikini mayor Eldon Note and Rongelap mayor James Matayoshi. Working with Alton Albious on Namu was facilitated by land manager Christian Leyman. I cannot adequately express my gratitude in allowing me to enter into familial relationships with these esteemed individuals and to share the proprietary knowledge of navigation beyond family lines of inheritance for the sake of preservation and revitalization.

I would like to thank my host family for welcoming me as one of their own, from the villages on Ailuk and Botkan village in Majuro to distant Honolulu. Especially helpful from the entire Ailuk community were the late Kilon Takiah and his wife Kanji Alfred, their daughter Alimi Alfred and her husband Tem Alfred, and sons Russell Takiah and the late Kajima Takiah. To the other atoll communities of Aur, Namu, and Ujae as well as the construction workers on Rongelap, I am appreciative of their hospitality, especially to Bollon Boklon, who formally welcomed me and the sailing crew to Tabal islet on Aur.

On Majuro I would like to acknowledge the archival assistance of the Alele Museum through the successive guidance of Clary Makroro, Ingrid Ahlgren, and Carol Curtis. The Marshall Islands Environmental Protection Agency also helped to locate satellite images of wave patterns. The Marshall Islands Marine Resource Authority supplied the escort vessel, M.S. *Jebro*, and the Marshall Islands Fisheries and Nautical Training Center, under the direction of Joel Clinton, provided an air-conditioned classroom for us to conduct our talk-story sessions and meetings.

In Hawai'i, I benefited from the mentorship of several individuals for introductory Marshallese language training and an awareness of the nuances, sensitivities, and complexities of Marshallese culture. A heartfelt thanks to Laji John, Byron Bender, Julie Walsh, Monica LaBriola, and Rachel Miller.

The oceanographic field study was facilitated (and salvaged!) by the assistance of University of Hawai'i graduate students Jerome Aucan and Oliver Vetter. Chris and Richard Barrie graciously used their trimaran, *Windswept*, for one series of wave buoy deployments. Eric Nystrom and Priam Kanealii also allowed Captain Korent to guide their yacht, *Mali*, between Kwajalein and Ujae. Harvard University physicist John Huth and Delft University of Technology oceanographer Gerbrant van Vledder provided a fresh perspective of the wave patterns, and they, as well as *New York Times Magazine* writer Kim Tingley and photographer Mark Peterson, provided the canoe revival with a surge of excitement that enhanced the most recent voyage between Majuro and Aur.

The research, approved by the University of Hawai'i Institutional Review Board and permitted by the Marshall Islands Historic Preservation Office, was funded by several grants over the course of more than a decade. The first phase of the project (2003–2009) to document the wave patterns through a blending of anthropology and oceanography was funded by the University of Hawai'i Sea Grant College Program under Grant No. NA05OAR4171048, the National Science Foundation under Grant No. 514594, the Wenner Gren Foundation for Anthropological Research, Inc. under Grant No. 7282, the U.S. Ambassador's Fund for Cultural Preservation, and Mobil Oil Micronesia. The second phase of the project (2010–2015) to use the wave patterns for canoe voyaging and begin to transfer the knowledge to a protégé was funded by the United Nations Educational, Scientific, and Cultural Organization (UNESCO) Participation Programme, the U.S. Ambassador's Fund for Cultural Preservation, the National Geographic Society's Genographic Legacy Fund, and a seed grant from the University of Hawai'i at Hilo. The Department of Anthropology at UH Hilo also funded the video documentation of the recent canoe voyage to Aur.

Technical assistance in the production of the book came from the scanning assistance of University of Hawai'i at Hilo librarian Mary Louise Haraguchi and graphics coordinator Darin Igawa, and from the digital rendering of black-and-white photography by Dino Morrow. The base map of Oceania was produced by Nathan Stephenson of the University of Hawai'i at Hilo's Spatial Data Analysis and Visualization Lab. I am also grateful for the helpful advice of Craig Severance, Trent Woodworth, and Fa-Tai Shieh in their reviews of the manuscript and the valuable suggestions by three anonymous reviewers.

My family has been extremely supportive of this project, which has now spanned the last sixteen years of my life. My parents, Tom and Scherry, and my stepmother, Judy, fostered my adventurous spirit that led to my journeys in the Pacific, and the actual focus on traditional navigation was fueled by my father's impassioned intellectual curiosity for the wonder of science and mathematics. My brothers, Will and Tom, and their families have been incredibly supportive from their respective corners of the globe, Argentina and Wisconsin. Above all, my wife Ayesha has been by my side this entire time, supporting my many excursions to the Marshall Islands, living with me for a year in Majuro and visiting Ailuk, providing critical research assistance and help in designing the graphics, carefully reviewing the manuscript, and raising our two lovely boys during my absences. Thanks as well to my sister-in-law, Afsheen Siddiqi, for being the other parent when I have been away.

Notes on Orthography
and Names

I FOLLOW the modern orthography of the Marshallese language as depicted in the *Marshallese-English Dictionary,* but I revert to older spellings of place names for ease of recognition. Following the expressed wishes of my Marshallese collaborators, I use their full names, often attributing their contributions and voices by their more familiar first names.

Introduction:
From Nuclear Exodus to
Cultural Reawakening

A boy of eleven years by the name of Korent Joel stands at the edge of a coral island gazing out to sea in an area of the Pacific Ocean his ancestors once called Aelōñ Kein Ad, or simply "these islands of ours." Instructed by his maternal grandfather, he watches the waves of a rolling swell break on the outer reef and reform as smaller wavelets that spread toward him. Glancing at an image sketched in the sand by his grandfather, the boy remembers to look in the opposite direction for similar waves that are coming across the wide lagoon. He knows that shortly his grandfather will blindfold him, place him lying down in a small outrigger canoe, and tell him to feel with his body how these two sets of waves interact with each other, as one day his life and the lives of his sailing crew will depend on it. This is the start, in 1959, of the boy's formal training to become a *ri-meto*, a "person of the ocean" who would one day navigate at sea by the waves. However, this path to attain one of the most highly coveted and respected positions within this atoll society comes to an abrupt halt.

The grandfather suspects but could never get verified that they are living on a nuclear wasteland. Five years earlier, in March of 1954, the United States detonated a hydrogen bomb, code-named Castle Bravo, at neighboring Bikini atoll as part of its nuclear weapons testing program. An unprecedented explosion—equivalent to the force of fifteen million tons of trinitrotoluene (TNT) going off—obliterated several islets on Bikini, sending pulverized radioactive coral into the atmosphere in a mushroom cloud that stretched twenty-five miles in diameter. The radioactive fallout not only contaminated Bikini but also Korent's family living downwind on Rongelap; they had been evacuated by military personnel only after two days of direct radiation exposure. In addition to immediate radiation burns, inhalation and ingestion of radioactive fallout, and contamination of resources, the Rongelapese would experience several waves of forced relocations, treatment as unwitting human subjects in biomedical experiments, and intergenerational birth defects. The community returned to Rongelap three years later, being informed by scientists that the land and its resources were safe. But now, at the start of Korent's navigation training, his grandfather and other residents believe that every savory coconut crab they catch and eat, every sweet pandanus key they chew, and every breadfruit they allow to deliciously ferment is slowly, painfully killing them.

Korent studies navigation for five years, but then his grandfather, suffering from radiation-related sickness, decides that the teenager, sixteen years of age, should leave. Much later, completely distrustful of scientific reports claiming the land was suitable for life, the community resettles on distant islands. Living in near-permanent exile with great uncertainty about the possibility of returning to his ancestral homeland, Korent and his family effectively become nuclear refugees. The cessation of his and others' navigational training is one of the myriad tragic consequences of the nuclear testing. Living in exile from the home of his ancestors, he yearns to somehow reclaim his identity as a navigator. But he cannot tell anyone of his partial abilities and guides government transport ships for the next four decades in silence.

~   ~   ~

Sitting on a woven pandanus leaf mat placed over the coral rubble floor in the shade of a small thatched house in 2006, a much older Korent, approaching sixty years of age, watches as the last reputed titled navigator in Aelōñ Kein Ad constructs a model. The elder has just stripped four coconut fronds bare of leaves and begins to weave the spines through the sitting mat, creating a pair of arches that intersect at the ends to outline a rounded diamond shape, and then adds a similar pair of arches perpendicular to the first. Within this symmetrical design, the elder places a series of coral pebbles. He begins to instruct Korent—by now honored with the title of captain for his growing reputation of navigational prowess—on the meaning of the curves.

The elder navigator, too old to embark on an ocean voyage, uses his hands to imitate how a canoe would travel along the length of one set of curves, feeling a balancing motion as the canoe rocks from side to side. This is a variation of the "stick charts" that had captured the cartographic imagination of early European explorers, missionaries, and ethnographers. Captain Korent's uncle, Isao Eknilang, had previously constructed and explained a similar model out of lashed thin sections of pandanus roots, but the elder navigator now offers a different interpretation, explaining his ideas under the glow of a kerosene lantern as night approaches. Armed with these two teachers' models of how islands disrupt the flow of swells and currents in distinctive ways, Captain Korent finally puts his knowledge to the test. Because he still cannot fully explain the wave formations that he has been experiencing at sea since leaving Rongelap in his youth, this voyage serves to prove his ideas, continue his learning, and finally catapult him to the status of navigator.

~　　~　　~

Standing in front of the helmsman on a thirty-five-foot, sloop-rigged yacht in 2006, Captain Korent scans the starboard horizon, waiting patiently for a wave shaped like a fishhook to disrupt the rhythmic motion. We are sailing toward a western atoll, having covered the vessel's compass. It is the afternoon of our second day of sailing into the remnants of a westerly storm system, constrained in the timing of our voyage by military restrictions. Convinced that the atoll lies to our starboard or right side, Captain Korent begins to signal to tack through the wind and adopt a different course. At that exact moment, I glance to the opposite side and see a faint shape on the horizon appear and then disappear. Captain Korent retracts his command as we watch it slowly drop back from us. Considering the possibility that it is an island, Captain Korent orders the crew to fall off the wind, rather than tack, and sail toward it. I discretely check my handheld global positioning system (GPS) and realize this is a tiny atoll close to our target—we are actually right on course! But I cannot share this knowledge with Captain Korent without jeopardizing the purity of his navigation test.

Dawning enlightenment is the way this moment has been described to me. The difficult task of finding land with only reference to the waves during one's navigation test is like "breaking the shell" of a sea turtle—an intellectual and social transformation of an apprentice into a navigator. Instead, with a sinking feeling in the pit of my stomach, I see confusion wash over Captain Korent's face. A sense of panic seems to envelope Captain Korent as he once again tells the helmsman to set another course, which I silently know is the wrong way. That path will take us clear out of the archipelago's western seas into open ocean. I do not dare speak of the story that Captain Korent had previously shared with me, of another navigator who had lost track of his position, fell into a crazed state of mind, and continued sailing until he died at sea. Illumination will hopefully come soon to Captain Korent, but his unnerving search for the waves that never appear makes me feel like all is lost.

~　　~　　~

In this book, I present the story of how Captain Korent Joel voyaged from be-ing a nuclear refugee to a *ri-meto*—a "person of the sea," or navigator—in the Marshall Islands. After his forced exodus from his home atoll of Rongelap, Captain Korent has reconnected to his ancestral maritime heritage and forged a new, unprecedented path toward becoming a navigator, the first time this has happened in living memory and a testament to efforts of cultural revital-ization in the Marshall Islands and throughout greater Oceania. Captain Ko-rent is like a blend of the renowned Satawalese navigator Mau Piailug and his Hawaiian protégé Nainoa Thompson—grounded in traditional beliefs and ideas while blazing an uncharted route toward becoming a navigator. Blend-ing Western and Marshallese scientific knowledge systems, resolving ambiv-alence in nearly forgotten navigational techniques, and deftly negotiating cul-tural protocols of knowledge use and transmission characterize Captain Korent's quest to become a navigator. Ultimately, the efforts by Captain Ko-rent and supportive family members would inaugurate not just a return to their maritime heritage for the Rongelapese navigators but also a reforging of identity for the greater Marshallese nation as a people born to the rhythms of the sea. The resilience of this community to revitalize their nearly lost voyag-ing traditions in the wake of nuclear trauma considerably substantiates Epeli Hauʻofa's vision of Pacific Islanders' deep affinity with the ocean.[1]

Steeped in tradition but facing the realities of the modern world, Cap-tain Korent attempted to guide a yacht between two low-lying coral atolls using wave piloting techniques. In the vast seas of the Marshall Islands, lo-cated in the central equatorial region of Oceania, a long line of Captain Ko-rent's ancestors observed how islands disrupt the flow of various wave phe-nomena and developed a comprehensive system of navigation. More accurately, Marshallese "wave piloting" involves remotely sensing land by detecting how swell and gyre currents transform in the vicinity of an island. Navigators differentiate between locally generated wind waves from swell—a series of smooth waves that propagate with long wavelengths far away from distant weather systems that created it—and gyre, a system of looping ocean current streams caused by the Coriolis effect. The Marshallese language en-compasses these and other wave phenomena within the single word "wave" (*ṇo*), affording cultural attachment to the term "wave piloting." The concep-tual basis of wave piloting is represented cartographically in the stick charts that show island-induced swell and current transformations, but in practice the embodied knowledge of the sea is indispensable—feeling slight variations in the canoe's movement as it pitches down a wave or rolls sideways across a wave.

At the dawn of the millennium, Captain Korent's goal in voyaging out of sight of land using the ancient wave piloting techniques was to *ruprup jọkur,* a nautical expression and proverb in Marshallese roughly translated as "breaking the shell." A navigational trial at sea marks the end of a navigator's apprenticeship; passing the test simultaneously affords intellectual growth, a ritualistic social transformation, and chiefly sanctioning of becoming a navigator. The main argument of the book is that through his own *ruprup jọkur* navigation trial, Captain Korent and a small group of surviving mariners from Rongelap and Bikini are, against one of the darkest hours in human history, "breaking the shell" of their prime identity as nuclear refugees to begin recovering their most intimate of connections to the sea.

Between 1946 and 1958, the U.S. government detonated sixty-seven atomic and thermonuclear bombs in the Marshall Islands as part of its Cold War–era nuclear weapons testing program, and those events sent a series of environmental, biological, social, and psychological shockwaves throughout the islands, from which the residents and their descendants are still trying to recover.[2] This amplified militarization of the islands resulted in forced relocation and consequential loss of cultural attachment to ancestral homeland, community fragmentation and an alteration of the very fabric of the Marshallese culture, direct radiation exposure followed by unmatched levels of cancers and intergenerational birth defects, biomedical experimentation without consent, contaminated marine and terrestrial resources with half-lives in the thousands of years, nuclear waste dumping, and, more recently, missile testing. Compounding these largely overt damages to the Marshallese have been highly symbolic ways in which their horrific experiences have been diminished, altered, or erased by others and the structural ways in which their voices have been silenced at home and abroad.

The research and development in the early 1940s that led to the testing of nuclear weapons in the Marshall Islands has profound consequences not just for the Marshallese but for all of humanity. Anthropologist Barbara Rose Johnston argues that the new radioisotopes generated by these explosive forces have fundamentally and irrevocably altered the composition of our atmosphere and generated pathological processes in our physiology. In Johnson's view, the radiotoxicity and chemical toxicity released from this time period marks the beginning of the Anthropocene, a time period characterized by a human-induced downward, degenerative arc in the cycle of planetary life.[3] Against this looming tipping point and the seemingly never-ending dark chapter in the history of the Marshall Islands, waves of resistance and cultural revitalization are building like the front of a storm. And throughout the island communities of Oceania, it is the outrigger canoe that has played a central role in this resurgence and process of regaining control.

Using the canoe also as a metaphor for island histories, communities throughout Oceania are navigating unknown courses to recover highly specialized and powerful knowledge systems that have been lost, forgotten, and fragmented. In this sense, "voyaging" in the book's title is meant literally as Captain Korent's trial sea voyage to authenticate his status as a navigator and metaphorically as the forging of new routes of knowledge reclamation. Captain Korent symbolically embodies the long decline and recent resurgence of voyaging traditions in the Marshall Islands, but the story is much larger than him. And the process of community-driven heritage management and knowledge recovery is never without complications and setbacks.

The term *jǫkur* specifically refers to the dense shell of a sea turtle—the hardest material for a Marshallese to break. The metaphorical "breaking" of tradition to open the knowledge of navigation beyond secretive lines of family inheritance appropriately captures Captain Korent's courageous journey. He has drawn from his elders, reached out to academics for guidance, and begun to pass on the knowledge to an apprentice. There are other surviving individuals steeped in navigational expertise who similarly faced the nuclear exodus from Rongelap after the radiation exposure from the apocalyptic Bravo shot of 1954, including Isao Eknilang. This group of supporting Rongelapese elders, led by Isao, contributed to Captain Korent's growing knowledge in preparation for his *ruprup jǫkur* test. During this time, a junior relative named Alson Kelen, from neighboring Bikini where many of the nuclear tests were detonated, observed and felt the waves that Captain Korent pointed out as his informal protégé. Alson also listened to the stories and chants performed by Isao's group, as well as the explanations of the stick charts. Alson soaked in this Rongelapese navigational knowledge while a team of anthropologists (including myself) and oceanographers helped to provide Captain Korent, at his request, a non-Marshallese perspective of the wave dynamics. But to get experience on the water to one day lead a new generation of navigators, Alson would have to call upon other atoll communities armed with traditional canoe building and sailing skills, as the Rongelapese and Bikinians had entirely lost their social infrastructure to build canoes as an unintended consequence of their forced displacement. This comradery of once-disconnected communities ultimately led to the undertaking of two canoe voyages under extraordinary protocols of the sharing and use of navigational knowledge.

The opening story with three distinct scenes—the young Korent on Rongelap in 1961 and the teaching of the stick chart wave models that was intertwined with the navigation test of 2006—are remarkable moments in this story of friendship, navigation, and perseverance. When I tell my version of this story, these are among the most revealing episodes, and I enjoy attempting to narrate them as *bwebwenato*. This Marshallese word can mean a particular way of holding a conversation as well as telling a story, partly captured in Hawai'i-centered English as "talking story," in which the narrator holds the listener's attention with the craft of a talented storyteller. A more complete definition of *bwebwenato* includes "talk, conversation, story, history, article, episode, lore, myth, and tale." Slight derivations of the term can also refer to legends (*bwebwenatoon etto*), chatting (*bwebwenato bajjek*), and biography (*bwebwenatoun mour*), all of which can be seamlessly interwoven within the overarching telling of a grand story. The Marshallese storyteller (*ri-bwebwenato*) served as a living repository of traditional Marshallese culture and history. As deceased Bikinian elder Kilon Bauno once stated, "We stand firmly on the stories of our elders."[4] My Marshallese host-father, a master canoe builder named Kilon Takiah, was a storyteller, recalling at twilight inside his cement-walled home some old memories of sailing canoes as his family listened before bedtime. Isao Eknilang is a storyteller from a nearly bygone era, enrapturing his audience with legendary voyaging heroes and guiding spirits. And navigation apprentice Alson Kelen is a gifted storyteller who can move his audience to jovial laughter, providing minute-by-minute details of canoe voyages that he undertook twenty years ago.

In this book, I share a series of broadly defined *bwebwenato* (stories, conversations, histories, legends, biographies) about Captain Korent and the remarkable saga of mariners from Rongelap and Bikini who, while living in exile from their irradiated homelands, have begun to return to their heritage as a people of the sea. My inspiration for narrating this story as a series of Marshallese *bwebwenato* comes from Katerina Teaiwa's portrayal of the consumption of Banaban land, in which she presents "many stories around the kava bowl" to capture the voices and perspectives of people whose lives have been transformed by the ravaging of their island for phosphate.[5] The *bwebwenato* are expressed in part by Captain Korent himself. My treatment of Captain Korent thus parallels to a degree the genres of life history, biography, and memoir as practiced in Oceania. In Lino Olopai's reflections as a Saipan Carolinian who had journeyed back to Satawal to learn navigation, for example, anthropologist Julianna Flinn attempts to keep Lino's narrative style close to his oratorical style that had produced recorded testimonies.[6] Yet Captain Korent is quite taciturn, and his deep reticence eluded a similar autobiographical storytelling and required other voices.

Some of the *bwebwenato* about Captain Korent and the multiple histories and meanings of voyaging are expressed in interviews by his close elder Isao Eknilang and his navigation protégé Alson Kelen. This is resonant of Sam Low's telling of the key individuals who built and sailed *Hōkūle'a*, the

1975 replica of an ancient Polynesian voyaging canoe that, with the initial navigation by Mau Piailug and later under the leadership of Nainoa Thompson, would ignite a renaissance of Hawaiian culture.[7] Recounted experiences from these individuals in their own words converge on a nuanced understanding of the challenges and various cultural meanings attached to the inaugural voyages of this experimental moment in Oceania. As exemplified in Low's methodology, story is a means to give voice to the marginalized by building trusting relationships between the researcher and research participants without fragmenting their knowledge.[8] Indeed, developing respect, creating relationships, and sharing stories with Captain Korent, Isao Eknilang, Alson Kelen, and other Marshallese individuals are the heart of this book. That they were able to entrust their most prestigious knowledge to me testifies to the importance and responsibility I now bear as an ethnographer among their indigenous community to serve as a guardian of their stories.

Aware of my heightened responsibility to safeguard knowledge that has been placed in my trust, I draw from history and anthropology to situate their voices in broader historical and cultural contexts. Stories and histories of voyaging in the Marshall Islands are performed through songs and chants, embedded in proverbs, inscribed in tattoos, carved into canoes, retraced through the woven cartographic latticework of the stick charts, deciphered from ancient discarded fragments of giant clam shell adzes and other archaeological artifacts, and generated and reenacted during ocean passages on outrigger voyaging canoes.[9] Some of the stories are also my own experiences from my particular vantage point as an ethnographer and sailor, while other stories emerge from satellite images, three-dimensional data on waves, virtual simulations of the wave dynamics, and other oceanographic techniques. And some stories have come before, recorded diligently by inquisitive anthropologists and before them by intrepid explorers and dutiful missionaries. Writing in the wake of exemplary ethnographies, documentary films, and studies of voyaging and navigation such as Thomas Gladwin's ethnography of Polowatese navigation and Ben Finney's chronicling of the genesis of *Hōkūleʻa,* my holistic approach follows the productive tension in ethnography between the cultural insider and outsider perspectives, as well as between detached Western scientific observations and the postmodern turn of self-reflexivity.[10]

At the heart of this productive tension are the epistemological foundations of a plurality of knowledge systems. Dichotomous rhetoric between Western scientific and indigenous knowledge has been predicated on a relativistic debate about science from the standpoint of epistemology—a branch of philosophy concerned with theories of knowledge. A philosophically narrow positivistic-reductionist view of science emphasizes external evidence, hypothesis testing and falsification, and universal laws of generalizability that contradicts a more integrated, holistic, and contextualized indigenous approach to knowledge. Yet a more broad minded perspective espoused through the lenses of anthropology, sociology, and the philosophy of science have deconstructed this division to show that it is produced by presumptions of substantive, methodological, theoretical, and contextual differences. In a comparative study in the sociology of Western scientific and indigenous knowledge, David Turnbull demonstrates how Oceanic navigation and Western science are both ordered, systematic bodies of knowledge embedded in practical activities and everyday experiences that really only differ in how the knowledge is assembled and moved beyond its site of production. Turnbull highlights that canoe builders develop ways to harness the power of the wind to move across the sea, weather forecasters and astronomers observe the heavens to time the voyages for optimal sailing conditions, and navigators employ elaborate mental representations of space and embodied knowledge to guide their canoes toward unseen islands. Other studies have illuminated the ways in which island communities in Oceania construct and theorize about knowledge, and in doing so have recognized multiple types of knowledge with varying but equally valid ways of knowing.[11]

Despite my attempt to interweave *bwebwenato* from a variety of voices and sources with different underlying epistemologies, what follows is my impartial understanding and representation of the story of Captain Korent and others reclaiming their identity as a people of the sea. Considering Captain Korent's recent passing, another version of this story could appear as a collaboratively written ethnography with the fully integrated voice of his protégé Alson Kelen. Collaborative, community-based approaches to research—from the research design and fieldwork through the writing process and toward community advocacy—are both necessary and difficult throughout Oceania today. Researchers must consider the collapsing distinction between cultural outsider and insider and their multiple and shifting fieldwork practices, obligations, responsibilities, and audiences.[12] I am also hopeful that Alson and the surviving custodians of navigation will write or find other ways to share their own versions of these events, telling the story in their own styles, their own voices, in their own language, for their own audience, and in their own time. Alson's rendition, which he already shares orally as *bwebwenato* with his family on the island of Ejit in Majuro under the shade of the palm trees and while fishing at sea in his small aluminum outboard skiff, is solidly a Marshallese perspective. I have glimpsed such a worldview from the time I have spent in the Marshall Islands and attempt to emulate it in this book, but my roots lie elsewhere.

Through a series of serendipitous events, I stumbled onto anthropology and eventually to navigation in the Marshall Islands. I was born and raised in a small farming community in western Wisconsin. With my father's occupation as a pilot, I was afforded the luxury of frequent travel growing up, tramping through Europe, for instance, with my two brothers upon finishing high school. During the spring of my sophomore year at the University of Wisconsin at Madison, I was sitting in a German language class when an instructor bolted into the room and announced that the application deadline for a study abroad program in Freiburg, located in the Black Forest of southwestern Germany, had just been extended by one day. Anyone who signed up would likely go. Inspired by my older brother, who had also participated in this program, I impulsively ran home to put together my application, and by the end of the day I knew I would soon be setting off on a year-long adventure.

I could not have imagined then that my burgeoning comprehension of the German language would allow me to one day translate some of the first written documentation of Marshallese navigation! Attaining a degree of fluency in the language afforded me my first look into the worldview of another culture, but it was a single conversation with a fellow student that changed my life forever. Sitting in a small local brewery in Freiburg, he talked about the Peace Corps, of serving for two years in another country to help build up their local capacity and sustainability. Charged with this idealism, when I returned to Madison my first priority was to search out a Peace Corps recruiter. I was regaled by stories of living in mud-dung huts in Nepal, and I signed up instantly. A year later, when I opened up an official-looking letter from the U.S. government, I realized I would be experiencing something quite different from what I had envisioned. I would be spending the next two years teaching high school science and math in a small village at the base of a secluded waterfall on the outskirts of Apia, the capital of Samoa. I lived with a wonderful Samoan family headed by a woman named Tupe Lemalu, who patiently guided me through the nuances of the Samoan language and customs. I relished this cultural immersion, tearful upon my departure as I left behind a newfound family. After another year abroad teaching English in a small village in Japan, I realized that I could follow this passion professionally as an anthropologist. I had devoured David Lewis' classic book on traditional navigation, *We, the Navigators: The Ancient Art of Landfinding in the Pacific,* and my thoughts began to converge on the anthropology of voyaging.[13]

My first meeting with Ben Finney in the gentle breeze of Waikīkī was nothing short of the most intimidating encounter in my life. The premiere academic on Pacific voyaging and navigation, Ben had the pioneering vision to co-construct *Hōkūleʻa* and was instrumental in locating Mau Piailug to guide her inaugural voyage of over 2,400 miles from Hawai'i to Tahiti in 1976. The resulting synergistic Hawaiian renaissance of voyaging had since gathered momentum and sent waves of inspiration outward to other indigenous voyaging communities, including the Marshall Islands. With a humbleness regarding these accomplishments that mirrored his gentle demeanor, Ben talked of his connections with Captain Korent and invited me to pursue with him the emerging Marshallese voyaging revitalization as my PhD project at the University of Hawai'i. Cofacilitating a cultural revival of voyaging would be unique among anthropological dissertations and deeply rewarding, but it would also likely be a lifetime endeavor fraught with unforeseen challenges, he warned me. Soaked in a naïve idealism as a new graduate student, I gulped, and then with resolute affirmation, launched my budding career as an anthropologist toward the Marshallese navigation project.

My involvement with Ben Finney, Captain Korent, Alson Kelen, Isao Eknilang, Kilon Takiah, and many others spans sixteen years, and this story of opening what was once the most severely restricted realm of knowledge in the Marshall Islands is also about our comradery, friendship, and enduring bonds of family. I have conducted fieldwork in the Marshall Islands for about two years in total, starting during the summer of 2003, with intensive work from the summer of 2005 through the fall of 2006, and then for shorter stays in the summers of 2007, 2009, 2014, and 2015. This companionship started at my first meeting with Kilon Takiah, the aging master canoe builder, who sat on a partially built outrigger canoe in Majuro with his cane spread across his lap, waiting patiently for me to show up. With heartfelt compassion, Kilon adopted me into his Ailuk family with the same expectations and responsibilities as if I were Marshallese. With a few boxes of peanut butter and biscuits, we journeyed to his island where no English was spoken. I have since watched a host of babies and toddlers grow up into teenagers who now call me in Hilo using video Skype.

My growing experiences and connections with key individuals partly shape the structure of this book. I began my journey in 2003 with Kilon sharing *bwebwenato* of canoes, learning from him how to make the sennit rope used for their lashings, and learning from his family demonstrating how to build and sail them. As the navigation project unfolded in 2005, Captain Korent invited his elders to share their expertise in voyaging. This eventually led to his *ruprup jọkur* navigation test in 2006, with subsequent voyaging attempts in an outrigger canoe in the following summers. I documented the ways in which Captain Korent and Alson expanded their understandings of the guarded, highly regulated, still sacred knowledge of weather forecasting, astronomy, and navigation.

When thinking about the enduring value attached to the various forms of voyaging knowledge, I imagine a cone, with the apex pointed upwards. The circular disk on the bottom represents the largely public, accessible, and interconnected forms of knowledge such as canoe building, sail weaving, fishing, and rope making. A slice in the narrowing of the cone midway up represents the increasing restrictions of such elevated fields of knowledge as the ability to predict the weather and strategize about voyaging with seasonal observations of the stars. The apex—navigation—subsumes everything in the cone, and this is the most carefully guarded realm of knowledge. The book, then, roughly begins with canoe building and sailing, moves to weather forecasting and astronomy, and ends with navigation. This is the process by which I slowly learned increasingly secretive knowledge as our rapport and trust matured. However, the thrust of Captain Korent's quest is navigation, and his search for deeper comprehension of the waves occupies the majority of the book's technical focus.

The cone imagery is also helpful in thinking about the flow of time and how a Marshallese storyteller would narrate Captain Korent's journey, and this partly informs the structure of the book. If the apex of the cone, still pointed upwards, represents the present moment in time, the widening of the cone underneath represents the historical past as recounted in memory, texts, and artifacts, and the base of the cone represents the mythical past and the origins of time itself. In retelling the pivotal moments that led to Captain Korent's *ruprup jọkur* test and Alson Kelen's courageous canoe voyages, a grand Marshallese storyteller would start from the beginning—*the* beginning. This would not even start with the beginnings of navigation in the Marshall Islands but with the dawn of our humanity and even as far back as the origins of the cosmos. This would not, however, be a linear extension back in time encompassed by a singular narrative.

The structure of the book is thus a reflection of the way a Marshallese storyteller might enrapture his audience, a statement about the shifting prestige, power, utility, and sacredness of nautical knowledge and my own journey and fellowship of the waves. The first section of the book moves forward in time from origins through the precontact era and into historic and contemporary times, simultaneously beginning with an extremely large spatial reference (our world), quickly narrowing to Oceania and then the twin island chains of the Marshall Islands (Ratak and Rālik), with a detailed examination of one atoll (Rongelap) within a small voyaging sphere (the sea of Adjokḷā). With this place of Rongelap as the focus of nuclear exodus, the book turns to the process of reviving the voyaging traditions. Here, the discussion traces the deterioration and loss of knowledge as well as its resurgence. With the development of the collaborative navigation project, the last section of the book shifts to Captain Korent's process of remembering, gaining knowledge, and relearning from his elders the wave piloting techniques through maps, models, and simulations. Unlike canoe building, such esoteric information of navigation has not generally been disseminated beyond family lines of inheritance under chiefly regulations until now. The book concludes with Captain Korent's *ruprup jọkur* experiential navigation test to launch him to the status of navigator and offers a glimpse into the future ways outrigger canoe voyaging may shape the destiny of the Marshallese.

Bwebwenato can shift style depending on what the storyteller wants the reader to understand and remember. In the style of telling a story through *bwebwenato*, I dramatically open each chapter with a vignette to bring certain moments alive. These narrations are based on my direct experiences and reconstructed scenes from listening to others' stories. They generally shift in content throughout the book from my early experiences with canoe builder Kilon Takiah to my heavy involvement with navigator Captain Korent to my recent work with navigation apprentice Alson Kelen. After the introductory vignettes, my narrative voice switches to a more conventional narrative tone, interweaving archival material, my experiences, and the voices and sentiments of Captain Korent, Isao Eknilang, Alson Kelen, and other individuals from a deeper history whose voices have been preserved.

Chapter 1, "Born from the Sea, Coming across the Sea," introduces the beginnings of the Marshallese and sets the stage for the complementarity of knowledge systems. From a traditional perspective, the seas of the Marshall Islands are part of the fabric of the cosmos at the dawn of time upon which deities created the islands and eventually the first people. I situate this and other origin stories alongside archaeological evidence of exploratory seafaring, serendipitous landfalls of discovery, and eventual settlement of the myriad previously uninhabited islands of Oceania. Several Marshallese *bwebwenato* navigate between these seemingly opposed worldviews, encapsulating the notion of multiple, simultaneous histories—migratory canoe travel involving the discovery or "fishing up" of atolls mixed with generative acts of island creation. The Marshallese stories and anthropological perspectives on voyaging converge on the epistemological foundations of different but equally valid ways of knowing about the past, whether conceptualized as born from the sea or coming across the sea.

With the first people inhabiting Aelōñ Kein Ad, or "these islands of ours," chapter 2, "Sailing in the 'Sunrise' and 'Sunset' Islands," provides background information on the archipelago, focusing on local conceptions of the islands and seas, shifts in canoe technology and interisland patterns of

communication during the precontact era and early historic times, and encounters with non-Oceanic navigators and their vessels from across the horizon. Historian Paul D'Arcy, in his survey of Pacific Islander's connections to
the sea, states that despite a trove of sources on voyaging and navigation,
"there has been no comprehensive investigation of variation in navigational
practice across time, space, and community."[14] In response, this chapter begins a focused maritime history of navigation in the Marshall Islands. Whether
from divine origins or voyaging ancestries, it is clear that the first inhabitants
were, and continued to develop into, a people of the sea through their wave
piloting traditions.

Chapter 3, "Exodus from a Stronghold of Navigation," moves forward
in time to the late historic period to characterize what I believe was one of two
last bastions of navigation in the Marshall Islands. Until the societal, biological, and environmental damages wrought by the U.S. nuclear testing program
from 1946 to 1958, canoe building, weather forecasting, astronomy, and navigation survived on Rongelap and neighboring atolls, and strict protocols on
the dissemination of knowledge still governed its use at a regional training
center. These restrictions exacerbated the decline of voyaging that had begun
earlier with various efforts by the German, Japanese, and American colonial
administrations—and even by the Marshallese themselves!—to diminish the
importance of this knowledge, but the era of U.S. nuclear testing most severely impacted the continued existence of Rongelapese navigation. In this
chapter, I introduce Captain Korent's navigator ancestors and living relatives,
share his youthful training on Rongelap, and describe the community's self-
exile. I highlight local experiences of the nuclear testing and its fallout for
voyaging as well as the continuing forms of sacredness that surround navigation. Here I also introduce my prime collaborator and navigation apprentice,
Alson Kelen, whose family was similarly displaced from Bikini—the ground-
zero site of the Bravo detonation that resulted in the radiation of the Rongelapese. It is this history that led to a virtual cessation of voyaging in the postnuclear era, eclipsed only by one other small, relatively isolated region where
the knowledge of navigation remained in the minds of a few navigators. These
last strongholds of navigation also reveal the continuing significance of
women in the navigation traditions.

A stark gendered dichotomy usually characterizes descriptions of maritime activities in Oceania: women manage the land, whereas men preside
over the sea.[15] However, *bwebwenato* in the first three chapters reveal that the
two genders are profoundly intertwined in the Marshall Islands. Women are
more prominent than men in the genealogies and histories of navigation. For
instance, a creator goddess raised a vaulted dome toward the heavens in the

genesis of our world, demarcating the cardinal directions and calling forth the celestial objects, wind-generated swells, and flowing currents that would prove critical for the development of wave piloting (Jineer ilo Koba, chapter 1). Another deity, the mother of the stars, invented the first sail to be attached to the outrigger paddling canoes that would eventually allow for vast networks of communication across the archipelago (Lōktañūr, chapter 2). And it was a woman who first learned how to navigate by reading the waves (Litarmelu, chapter 3). Lijon Eknilang, the younger sister of Isao Eknilang, learned navigation as a young girl on Rongelap until the Bravo event of 1954, sharing her retained knowledge just prior to her passing. However, it is two men—Captain Korent and Alson Kelen—who have today come to increasingly represent the renewal of the navigation traditions.

Using the canoe as a metaphor for island histories, chapter 4, "Navigating the Cultural Revival of Voyaging," chronicles the complexities of the resurgent canoe building, sailing, and voyaging in the Marshall Islands near the end of the twentieth century. I discuss the complicated nature of revitalizing such powerful knowledge as canoe building, weather forecasting, astronomy, and navigation within community and academic initiatives. Here I reflect on my own role as an outside academic researcher in the process of cultural revitalization and the potential for unknown impacts on traditional structures of power and authority. By chronicling the shifts over time in how a community organization moved from salvage documentation of canoes to a resurgence in canoe sailing and then to a rediscovering of navigation, this central chapter in the book speaks to broad issues of culture change, the cultural politics of knowledge, and the management of maritime heritage.

With the navigation project firmly underway in 2005, chapter 5, "Maps, Models, and Simulations," explains the concepts, teaching devices, and techniques of wave navigation that Captain Korent was attempting to reconstruct in terms of Western science and Marshallese theories of the ocean. I highlight the process by which Captain Korent remembered and learned some of this knowledge from his elders. Continuing with D'Arcy's charge to investigate variation in navigational practice across time, space, and community, I compare ambiguities of navigational knowledge among surviving experts with previously documented ethnohistoric information across the region.

Captain Korent's application of the oceanographic knowledge at sea during an interisland voyage in 2006 is the focus of chapter 6, "Breaking the Shell." The journey simultaneously served as Captain Korent's chance to become a navigator in a distinctive rite of passage, an opportunity for him to verify his rediscovered knowledge and subsequently question and learn from a more experienced navigator, and a teaching moment for Alson Kelen to begin to internalize the sensations of movement of the waves. After this voyage of rediscovery, his governing chiefs conferred the title of navigator, but the fallout from Captain Korent's rise in status placed all of our revitalization efforts in jeopardy.

Chapter 7, "Rise of the Apprentice," concludes the book with a glimpse into the future of the cultural revitalization of wave navigation in the Marshall Islands, focusing on the highly unprecedented but surely needed determination and courage of the apprentice Alson Kelen to complete two canoe voyages in 2010 and 2015 by following the waves without Captain Korent's guidance. This chapter, with its practical engagement of sailing at sea, highlights the reestablishing of ancestral connections to the ocean through the revitalization of the outrigger canoe voyaging culture under shifting protocols of the use of navigational knowledge. The story has moved beyond Captain Korent's *ruprup jǫkur* test to become a navigator. With Alson at the helm as Captain Korent's modern apprentice, momentum is gathering. He is voyaging not only for the Bikinians and Rongelapese but for all the Marshallese to return to living as a people of the sea.

What is at stake in this journey is nothing short of cultural survival. As if the impacts and legacies of the nuclear testing and other forms of militarization were not enough, the Marshallese face yet another imminent threat to their continuing existence as an ocean people. Even the most conservative estimates of how climate change will impact the Marshall Islands are deeply alarming. It is not a matter of if, but rather of how long it will take before rising seas salinate the underground freshwater lenses—the only source of fresh water other than rainfall—and then completely inundate the low-lying atolls.[16] At a time when the Marshallese and others throughout Oceania are examining their options to search for adaptable ways to stay or migrate to higher land in another country, Alson Kelen's vision is to confront this potentially apocalyptic future by seeking and reclaiming ancestral wisdom. Bringing back the sleek outrigger canoes that once gracefully plied through the ocean for sustainable wind-driven sea transport might just give the Marshallese an edge in their battle against the rising ocean and allow them to celebrate their existence as people born to the rhythms of the sea.

Chapter 1

Born from the Sea, Coming across the Sea

Long, long, long ago there wasn't any land at all, only the ocean, but there was a god named Lōwa who came down to an island. This god made a command followed by a magical sound, "Mmmmmm," and all of the islands were created.

—Ebon navigator and storyteller James Milne[1]

Countless voyages "on the road of the winds" underwrote the discovery and settlement of the myriad Oceanic islands.

—Archaeologist Patrick Kirch[2]

~   ~   ~

Instinctively, I crawl farther out along the planked deck of the canoe as its outrigger float lifts upwards, breaking from its submersion in the water. A burst of wind penetrates through a gap between closely spaced coral islets and fills the sail, raising the outrigger clear out of the water. The canoe, tilting sideways, slices through the small waves, racing northwards along the atoll's protected lagoon of some thirty miles in length. My slight movement alters the canoe's balance and sends the outrigger gently back down to the surface of the ocean. My Marshallese brother smiles approvingly, and I enjoy my sole job as the canoe's wet human ballast.

We are sailing a twenty-five-foot outrigger canoe across the lagoon of Ailuk in the northeastern region of the Marshall Islands to reach a burial site. We are passing an islet called Bawojen that marks the completion of a third of the journey. My Marshallese father Kilon Takiah, a master canoe builder and storyteller of seventy-five years of age, had directed us earlier this morning to go to the uninhabited, distant islet of Enejelar, where his maternal ancestors are buried. He had been sitting on a manicured section of white, bleached-out coral fragments outside his cinder-block home when he halted his morning's work to discuss the day's activities (Figure 1.1). Setting down his mallet that he had been using to pound the fibers of a coconut husk to prepare cordage for the lashings of a canoe, Kilon told me about the meaning of Bawojen. Maintaining the burial site and clearing debris are important tasks—upon his death, Kilon will also rest here. From the silent reverence of the sailing crew as we now sail toward Bawojen, I know this islet is special for Kilon, and I wonder what events had taken place there and what stories had been told.

Back on the atoll's main residential islet, I had previously asked Kilon, now too old to sail, whether he could share a story about the beginnings of the Marshallese. His brow had tightened in fierce concentration for several moments before he told me that such stories had not been passed on to him. Later I would also ask Captain Korent and the surviving elders steeped in navigation lore, but they too replied that their teachers had not shared such stories

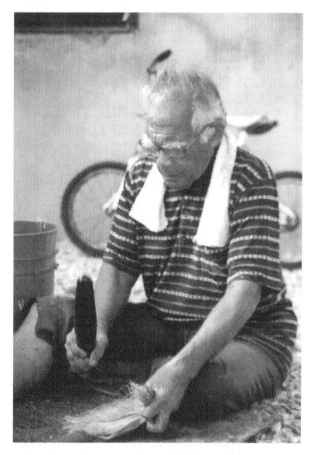

Figure 1.1. Storyteller and author's adopted Marshallese father Kilon Takiah, preparing cordage from coconut husks outside his home on Ailuk, 2003.

with them. I wondered why such stories were no longer remembered. Were they lost to time, or did they survive with a reluctance to share with me or for some reason I could not yet comprehend? Was there a conflict perhaps between Christian theology and traditional belief in gods of creation?

As we sail toward Kilon's eventual resting place, I think about his telling of stories. In the twilight of his cinder-block home, Kilon, stretched out on the concrete floor, would reflect on the day and occasionally share his coveted *bwebwenato*. I imagine that the telling of such a grand story or series of stories as the genesis of the Marshallese, if known to him, would require a more profound place than his concrete home. Although Kilon is not on the canoe with us, I imagine that in his younger years he would have filled the sailing crew with stories as they journeyed to Enejelar and likely enamored them with stories long into the night with such close proximity to his ancestors.

How would Kilon have narrated the story of Captain Korent's quest to become a navigator in the wake of nuclear testing? If Kilon had sailed to his ancestral islet with his close family members, perhaps he might regale them with such an incredible story. As a gifted storyteller, Kilon would likely not start with the navigational prowess of Captain Korent, which is memorialized in song. He would likely not even begin with the life of Captain Korent nor of his navigator ancestors on Rongelap. He would, I believe, journey back in time to a deep ancestral past of seafaring with multiple stories of how the first canoes appeared. But without his narrative voice or that of the surviving navigation elders, my construction of this story of origins primarily rests on archival material, including ethnographically documented stories from a prior generation of storytellers.

As in many other island cultures of Oceania, the accounts of the beginnings of the Marshallese as skilled navigators are paramount for a sense of place and identity today. The numerous oral traditions of the Marshall Islands focus almost exclusively on generative acts of creation. These stories are cosmogonic—they speak not only of the creation of the first humans but also of the genesis of our world and the origins of the universe. In one version, the very fabric of the cosmos at the dawn of time was the watery expanse of an ocean. According to some accounts, as noted earlier, the first people simply referred to their world as Aelōñ Kein Ad, or "these islands of ours." Oral traditions also include vague references to northward migrations from the atolls of Kiribati, a path that generally aligns with current archaeological tracing of likely voyaging routes of discovery and settlement of the Marshall Islands about two thousand years ago.

Accounting for the beginnings of the Marshallese, with their deep ties to the ocean, is a quest that thus requires attention to stories both of procreation and the anthropology of voyaging.[3] Such an approach blends mythological connections to the sea with the canoe as a tangible artifact of ancestral voyages of discovery. In this chapter, I demonstrate how the various stories of cosmogonic origins and migratory traditions converge on the ocean as the central element: the ocean is the fabric of the cosmos at the dawn of time; the islands penetrating the ocean are the center of the world; and the waves on the surface of the ocean were the guideposts for precocious seafarers to discover "these islands of ours" in their canoes. From a Marshallese perspective, these views of the ocean in connection to their ancestral past as a people of the sea are complementary. They are different but epistemologically equivalent. Neither perspective is necessarily championed over the other, ultimately forging a manifold understanding of the beginnings of the Marshallese—born from the sea and coming across the sea.

Cosmogonic Origins

Storyteller (*ri-bwebwenato*) Jelibor Jam shared the following opening lines of the longest recorded Marshallese origin story, "The Beginning of this World," with anthropologist Jack Tobin in 1975:

> In the beginning there were four posts. They remained there. And the post in the east fell down and made the sky in the east. And it was given the name Ḷōkōṃraan. It remained a short while, and the post in the south fell down to make the sky in the south. Its name was Ḷōrōk. A short while later, the post in the north fell down to make the sky in the north. Its name was Ḷajibwināṃōn. It remained a short while, and the post in the west fell down to make the sky in the west. Its name was Iroojrilik.
>
> The sky was very foggy. It remained there, and two men appeared from the sky. The names of these men, Ḷowa [also spelled Lōwa] and Ḷōṃtal. And Ḷowa made the islands with his voice. He said, "Ḷowa and reefs." And there were reefs. And he spoke again, "Ḷowa and rocks." And there were rocks. And he spoke again, "Ḷowa and the islands." And there were islands. And he spoke again, "Ḷowa and human beings." And there were human beings.
>
> The sky remained foggy. One could not see afar.
>
> Now Ḷōṃtal. He made the sea. He said with his voice, "Kick out in the depths of the sea and make it flow to the east. It flows to the east." And he again said with his voice, "Kick out in the depths of the sea and make it flow to the south. It flows to the south."
>
> And he spoke again, "Kick out in the depths of the sea and make it

flow to the north. It flows to the north." And he spoke again, "Kick out in the depths of the sea and make it flow west. It flows west."[4]

Starting with Ḷōkōṃraan, or the very first dawn of the eastern sky, this *bwebwenato* of the past is a cosmogonic narrative that describes, from an ancient Marshallese worldview, the fabric of the cosmos, the creation of our world, the divine origins of humankind, and—extremely relevant to the story of Captain Korent's quest to become a navigator—the genesis and movement of the seas (Figure 1.2). This story, with its many variants, points to the ocean as a core aspect of the cosmos and as born from the cosmos. As articulated by Jelibor Jam, Ḷōṃtal seems to be creating the flow of four dominant swells or other movements of the ocean waters, but in other versions of this story the sea had been part of the cosmos prior to the generative acts of Ḷowa, who existed as a lone, uncreated spirit in the sea. The German Catholic missionary and longtime resident August Erdland recorded in 1914, for instance, that inhabitants in different regions described the sea as a low-rising reef or a marshy area.[5]

During the first moments of creation, the four posts, or gods, harnessed their unique powers when they fell from holding up the sky: Ḷōkōṃraan of the east created light; Ḷōrōk to the south grew food and controlled the winds; Iroijrilik from the westward land of Eb sent forth the first people and established their first matrilineage; and Ḷajibwināṃōn of the north had the ability to kill people.[6] The boundaries of the horizon, now divided into northern and southern hemispheres demarcating sunrise and sunset, kept expanding during this time of cosmic origins.[7] Jelibor Jam's narration of the *bwebwenato* continues with Ḷōṃtal creating coral atolls by "kicking out" the lagoons. In another version, a deity named Wūllep arranged the islands in two nearly parallel chains: the "Sunrise" or Ratak in the east and the "Sunset" or Rālik in the west.[8] These forms of island creation ultimately led to the birth of an atoll world, today referred to as the Marshall Islands (Figure 1.3). After the calling up and naming of all living things by Ḷowa and Ḷōṃtal, two other gods, Lewoj and Lanij, called forth and painted the fish and other animals to bestow their individual differences and then incised the marks of tattooing on the humans to similarly differentiate them. This was the creation of our humanity.

Against these primal male deities, a goddess named Jineer ilo Koba is credited with raising up a vault toward the heavens in the continuation of Jelibor Jam's origin story.[9] After becoming pregnant, she gave birth to a ripe coconut and began exploring its many uses. She discovered how to make a braided sennit line from its sea-soaked fibers and ensnared a flying sooty tern. The sky cleared when the bird fell, enlightenment dawning on each person.

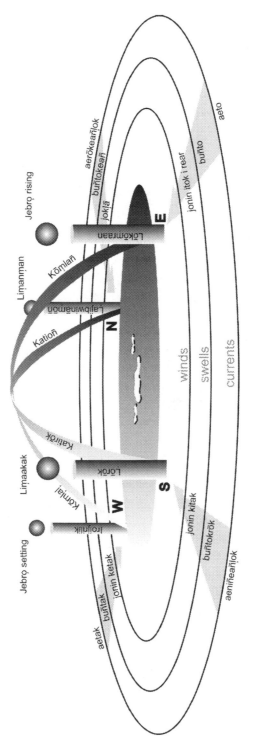

Figure 1.2. Cardinal directions and spatial orientation derived from wind, currents, swell, and stars, based on the story of the creator goddess Jineer ilo Koba as narrated by Jelibor Jam (Tobin 2002, 11–17).

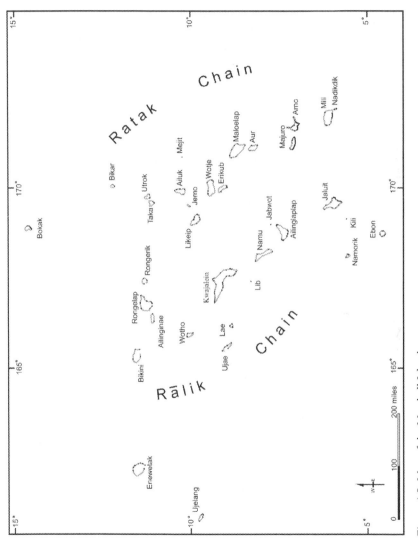

Figure 1.3. Map of the Marshall Islands.

Eventually, this creator goddess would call forth the sun and the seasons, the moon with its various phases and tidal movements, the winds and rains, and wind-generated swells and flowing current streams, but not before she continued to separate the earth and sky and in the process delineate the four cardinal directions:

> Now she saw the light was better. The woman brought two supports and placed one at the east and bent it and extended it to the west. Now she again brought the other stick and placed it at the south and bent it and extended it to the north.
>
> And the name of the support at the north: Katioñ. And the name of the support at the south: Katirōk. And the name of the support at the east: Kōṃlañ. And the name of the support at the west: Kōṃlaḷ. And it is like this to this day.
>
> Now the sky could not fall down (because there were supports).[10]

Jineer ilo Koba's arched supports demarcating the horizon and the sky into four quadrants form the basis of spatial orientation from a traditional Marshallese perspective. Encoded in the Marshallese language are terms for east (*rear*), west (*rilik*), north (*eañ*), and south (*rōk*); the terms for north and south derive from the posts Katioñ and Katirōk, respectively. Most of the winds, swells, and currents generated by Jineer ilo Koba similarly derive their names from the cardinal directions either toward or from which they flow.[11]

Anthropologist Laurence Carucci observed that in the traditional Marshallese worldview, articulated by the residents of Enewetak, the atolls are affixed to the ocean floor on "house posts" and that the dome of heaven similarly rests on posts that are affixed to the earth. Either four or six posts, depending on the narrative, divide the sky according to the rising and setting positions of celestial objects. For instance, Liṃanṃan (Polaris) remains fixed on the celestial dome to always indicate north (0°), and Liṃaakak (an asterism in the shape of kite, or the Southern Cross) marks south (180°). The rising and setting positions of the star Jebrọ (η Tauri in the Pleiades) demarcate east (90°) and west (270°); in alternate narratives, other "posts" are located equidistantly from the north and south poles (60°, 150°, 210°, 300°).[12]

Cosmogonic narratives that explain the origins of the universe and origin genealogies that situate the ancestral emergence of the first humans are widespread throughout Oceania, with several points of convergence with the Marshallese story of Ḷowa as expressed by Jelibor Jam. For instance, a lengthy cosmogonic, genealogical prayer chant in Hawai'i known as *Kumulipo* similarly divides the genesis of the world into two periods, with a continuous birthing of the lower life forms to sea life, plants, and eventually mammals in the period of darkness, and the first gods and people appear in the period of the opening of light.[13] One version of the *Kumulipo* also tells of how the union of Wākea, or Sky Father, and Papahānaumoku, or Earth Mother, resulted in the premature birth and subsequent burial of Hāloa, from whom the first taro grew, while their second born, also named Hāloa, became the first Hawaiian.[14] This theme of genealogical ties to the land in Hawai'i is partly played out in the Marshall Islands through the birth of the first coconut by Jineer ilo Koba, a woman sometimes referred to as the mother of the Marshallese.[15]

The raising up of the "vault of the heavens" and its subsequent support by posts or pillars also comprise a common motif throughout much of Oceania, but two distinct pictures emerge from the Marshall Islands. Theologian and anthropologist Jay Dobin, in his synthesis of traditional religious systems, emphasizes that the conception of the universe among the western Rālik chain of atolls resembles the shape of an inverted bowl above the surface of the ocean, characteristic of ancient Chuukese concepts to the west. However, the eastern Ratak chain of atolls invokes imagery of prying open a giant cosmic clamshell for the first acts of creation.[16] This is closer to the Polynesian elements of mythology found in Kiribati to the south. In particular, one story recorded by Erdland in 1914 from the Ratak chain tells of Wūllep (Ullip) and Lejmaan, supernatural worms, who lived in a shell in the depths of the ocean. Their raising of the upper part of the shell became the sky and the lower part became the earth: "The shell, in which they found themselves, expanded itself and Ullip widened it with a staff until it reached the height of the heavens and the expanse of the ocean."[17] In the Rālik version, Wūllep emerged and fell from a boil on Ḷowa, suggestive of descent from above. Dobin suggests that these different views of the universe within the Marshall Islands may reflect its geographic bridging of ancestral ideas, as well as reflecting the distinctive mythology of the Ratak and Rālik island chains.

An alternate cosmogony comes from beyond the main islands of the western Rālik chain. Stories from distant Enewetak, located several hundred miles west of the Rālik atolls, emphasize primordial travel through both the heavens and the seas. From his collected legends and stories from Enewetak, Carucci describes how ancient supernatural beings with incredible powers came from Kapilōñ, or the "back side of heaven." They moved through Ujelang, or the "middle of heaven" (and also the name of a neighboring atoll to the south), to emerge on earth at Enewetak, or the "island opening to the windward." From Enewetak, these beings created other early places, starting with the northern islets of Enewetak, followed by the eastern seas and the islets of Bikini, and proceeding down to the central Rālik chain, referred to as Kapinmeto, or "the back side of the ocean."[18]

The basic story of Ḷowa's creation of the world is known today throughout the Marshall Islands, with key elements of this cosmogonic story embedded within place names of particular atolls. According to Ebon storyteller James Milne, as told to anthropologist William Davenport in 1951–1952, the meanings of island names derive from the generative acts of Ḷowa, starting with the creation of the islands as depicted in the opening epigraph. The expansion of the four gods who held up the sky to the limits of the directions east, west, north, and south started from one place, Ailinglaplap, which means "large island" for its cosmic significance. Ḷowa dispersed and arranged the islands, which he had kept in a plaited coconut leaf basket. After he placed Ebon, which was named after the bountiful land of Eb to the west governed by the god Iroijrilik, Ḷowa threw away this basket (*kilok*), which turned into and served as the basis for the name of the small island Kili. In another example, the coconut, stemming from the birth by Jineer ilo Koba, first grew on Bikini, which means "sand for coconut."[19]

The cosmogonic narratives and origin genealogies of Ḷowa—whether descending from above or ascending from a watery cosmos, and whose descendant gods either raised an inverted bowl-shaped vault or opened a giant clamshell to separate the earth from the heavens—are traditional forms of knowledge (*bwebwenato*) that account for the creation of the world and its people. Complementing these histories is a different kind of origin story. As Patrick Kirch so eloquently states in the second epigraph, it is a history based on migratory traditions of travel "on the road of the winds."

Migratory Traditions

The narrations of the various *bwebwenato* center on creation stories but also describe some canoe migrations from the neighboring archipelago of Kiribati to the south. A holistic anthropological account expands this perspective by incorporating archaeological, genetic, linguistic, and ethnographic information to understand those migratory traditions. This complementary approach moves backwards through time and space to understand the various canoe trajectories that would have led to the first landfall in the Marshall Islands. This is a history of two very distinct movements of people, starting with our very first movement across the sea and ending with long-distance voyaging routes, one of which eventually led northward from Kiribati to the southern atolls of the Marshall Islands about two thousand years ago.

The penetration of humans into the Pacific Ocean marked the crossing of a great threshold in our cultural development. When our first *Homo sapiens* ancestors evolved and then spread out from Africa approximately 130,000 years ago, we were a terrestrial species, foraging for food. During this time of the late Pleistocene epoch, when colder global temperatures induced lower sea levels to expose the shallow continental shelves, the area now configured as island Southeast Asia was part of the Asian mainland, referred to as Sunda. Between 60,000 and 40,000 years ago, the world's first mariners left their terrestrial world of Sunda and made a series of short water crossings to reach the landmass of Sahul, which once connected Australia, New Guinea, and Tasmania. The descendants of this wave of mariners, speaking Papuan-family languages, kept island-hopping to reach the Bismarck Archipelago and the Solomon Islands.[20]

How the first Pleistocene water crossing and subsequent voyages happened remains largely conjecture. The consensus view is that the earliest watercraft were rafts made of lashed giant bamboo or logs, but it is unclear if these vessels simply drifted with the ocean currents or were intentionally paddled or sailed. Experimental voyages with a large bamboo raft rigged with square sails showed that long crossings, from Timor to Australia for example, were possible by sailing downwind.[21] Based on evidence of transported materials by twenty thousand years ago, archaeologist Geoffrey Irwin suggests that seasonal and predictable reversals of the monsoon and trade winds enabled people to move throughout this corridor, an area that served as a voyaging nursery for the development of seafaring skills with outrigger canoes.[22] With the rising of sea levels during the early Holocene about ten thousand years ago and the reconfiguration of present-day island geographies, there would have been an imperative to refine such technology.

Then, about 4,000–3,500 years ago, a completely separate community of mariners speaking Austronesian-family languages left their known coastal waters of southern China or the island of Taiwan, or even possibly the Philippines, and began at least three distinct waves of migration that would eventually result in the discovery and settlement of every inhabitable island in the Pacific Ocean and beyond (Figure 1.4). One wave of migration extended west, likely traversing the already inhabited Indian subcontinent until discovering the uninhabited large island of Madagascar off the eastern coast of Africa. Another migration ventured to the southeast, moving through island Southeast Asia into New Guinea and the Bismarck Archipelago, where they developed pottery and other culturally diagnostic features known as the Lapita complex. These Lapita seafarers sailed throughout this region of closely spaced, almost entirely intervisible islands until they reached the eastern section of the Solomon Islands as far as Makira (San Cristobal). Along the way, they interacted with the descendants of the much earlier Pleistocene voyages.

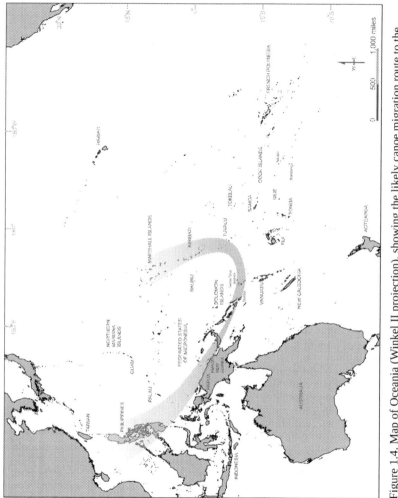

Figure 1.4. Map of Oceania (Winkel II projection), showing the likely canoe migration route to the Marshall Islands (base map by Nathan Stephenson of the University of Hawai'i at Hilo's Spatial Data Analysis and Visualization Lab).

The term "Near Oceania" captures the closeness of the islands in this region and marks a significant time depth of human settlement compared to the rest of the Pacific, which is referred to as "Remote Oceania" for its vast inter-archipelago distances.[23] A final wave journeyed directly east into the region referred to as Micronesia to make landfall on the islands of Palau and the Marianas.[24] Those Austronesians who sailed along these two latter routes faced both an unprecedented and unknown flat horizon. For the first time in human history, there was no land to see.

Voyaging throughout the corridor of intervisible islands extending from island Southeast Asia to this unknown world near the eastern edge of the Solomon Islands (Makira) rested on the origins and development of the outrigger sailing canoe.[25] The long lever arms of an outrigger float or companion hull to the windward side of a vessel provide buoyancy or weight, stabilizing the rolling effect of the main hull when under sail by producing a righting moment. Determining the design of this first outrigger canoe and its sailing rig, along with subsequent modifications, is fraught with archaeological evidence that is insufficiently diagnostic, traditional lore that is not detailed, and the nonspecificity of historical linguistics.[26] The sailing canoes observed and sketched by Europeans, starting in the sixteenth century, consisted of various types of outriggers and sailing rigs.[27] Based on the premise that the basic forms of canoes and rigs were more alike in the remote past than at European contact and that changes in style and function occurred in different island contexts, the overarching consensus is that the canoes of the initial Lapita expansion in Near Oceania were single-outrigger canoes with a dugout hull and raised freeboard (the portion of the hull above water) with sewn-on planks, sailed with a simple woven triangular sail framed by two long spars, or booms, that may have changed direction by some mode of tacking and that had some upwind capability. In its simplest form, this two-boom triangular sail, called a spritsail, would resemble a modern windsurfer design: tilting the sailing rig front (fore) and back (aft) would control the direction of the craft relative to the wind. Refinements to this basic design would have involved steering the canoe by adjusting ropes (sheets) attached to the trailing or lower spar, allowing these early mariners to sail downwind, across the direction of the wind where the wind is blowing perpendicular to the hull (a beam reach), and slightly upwind.[28] Observations by Europeans between the early seventeenth and eighteenth centuries of east Polynesian spritsail-rigged tacking canoes indicate moderate speeds of about five knots.[29]

It will likely remain forever unknown how the first Austronesians and their Lapita descendants in Near Oceania guided their canoes. Ethnographic accounts of surviving navigational traditions among these closely spaced, intervisible islands suggest the Lapita mariners used a form of piloting, where coastal landmarks, reefs, shoals, and other signs of land would have been used as reference points to sail across small water gaps between islands.[30] Predictable seasonal reversals of winds and currents would likely have enabled them to refine their voyaging skills as they piloted their canoes up and down this voyaging corridor. Reaching the eastern section of the main Solomon Islands ending at Makira, these coastal pilots faced a different world. Here, looking out to the direction of the rising sun, they would have gazed upon only blue water spreading out to the horizon.

The Lapita seafarers who reached the last of the intervisible string of islands would have had no way to know what, exactly, lay beyond the horizon and how far they would have to travel to find land. Imagining this moment—looking out toward an uncharted, unknowable horizon—conjures an analogous moment right now with the imminent approach of human space exploration beyond our familiar solar system, albeit exploration with a third dimension of space! It would be a water crossing of about 230 miles before those precocious seafarers sighted the Santa Cruz group, marking a transition to sailing in Remote Oceania where the island groups are no longer intervisible. Distances increasing from several hundreds of miles to thousands of miles of open ocean would have required considerable improvements in canoe technology, deep-sea navigation, and long-distance sailing strategies.

One trajectory of the Lapita seafarers led to the eventual discovery of the far reaches of Polynesia, with the development of double-hulled canoe technology. Waves of migration through New Caledonia and Vanuatu led to landfall on the Polynesian ancestral homelands of Samoa, Fiji, and Tonga, where a cessation of island expansion ensued for nearly two thousand years. The expanded range and cargo capacity of the double-hulled canoe would have facilitated the exploration and discovery of eastern Polynesia.[31] The settlement of the Society Islands between a thousand and nine hundred years ago was followed by an extremely rapid and unprecedented burst of settlement of the most remote islands and archipelagoes of Hawai'i, Rapa Nui (Easter Island), and Aotearoa (New Zealand) between eight hundred and seven hundred years ago.[32] Mounting evidence strongly suggests that this eastern expansion, which entailed voyages of thousands of miles, led to pre-Columbian landfall and cultural contact in the Americas.[33] Intrepid explorers also employed extreme southern latitude sailing, with Aotearoa as the base, to reach the subpolar, iceberg-riddled Auckland Islands.[34]

Another route of the Lapita expansion pushed northward from the region of the Santa Cruz group in the eastern Solomon Islands as well as Vanuatu and New Caledonia into the seas of what is now Tuvalu, Kiribati, the

Marshall Islands, and the central Carolinian atolls to discover and settle the distant volcanic high islands of Pohnpei and Kosrae. Slightly higher than current sea levels would have inundated the low-lying coral atolls; Pohnpei and Kosrae would have penetrated this otherwise empty region of eastern Micronesia. The submerged coral atolls, likely visible under the surface of the water, may have been an enticement to keep exploring. Voyagers' first sightings of the Marshall Islands may have been from the deck of a canoe skimming over its submerged landscape.

It remains unknowable how the Lapita sailors transitioned from nearshore pilotage to deep-sea navigation and what techniques and sailing strategies were employed on the first exploratory probes that eventually led to the discovery of distant regions such as the Marshallese seas. European explorers, ethnographers, archaeologists, and others have investigated Pacific navigation, but the surviving knowledge is predicated on known island geographies, whereas the pioneering seafarers facing the flat horizon unpunctuated with islands would sail into entirely uncharted seas. However, results from experimental and simulated voyages, combined with oral traditions and actual voyages guided by traditional navigators, converge on the idea that intentional, two-way voyaging enabled the systematic exploration, discovery, and settlement of the farthest reaches of Oceania.[35]

Starting in the late 1960s, detailed ethnographic investigations of surviving navigational traditions in diverse regions of the Pacific revealed that islanders share a common system of wayfinding with regional variations and that this information could offer a window into the ancient transition from pilotage to blue-water navigation. Of note is David Lewis' survey of navigation techniques, Thomas Gladwin's ethnography of Polowatese navigation, Steven Thomas' reflective study of Satawalese navigation, and Richard Feinberg's ethnography of Anutan navigation.[36] For ease of comprehension, these and other researchers analytically divide what is a fluid, integrated noninstrumental system of navigation into techniques for setting and maintaining a course, estimating position once out of sight of land with consideration of leeway and currents, and honing in on the target island.

Traditional navigators throughout Remote Oceania use the progression of stars or other celestial objects across the night sky or the directions from which characteristic winds blow during various seasons to form a conceptual compass for setting and maintaining course. Star orientation is based on guiding the bow of the canoe toward a rising or setting star along the horizon that has the same bearing as the destination island. The rising of a star in the east and corresponding setting in the west occurs four minutes earlier each day due to the earth's orbital motion around the sun, and the nightly movement across the sky traces an arc that limits each star's usefulness to point to the destination island. Navigators thus recall a nightly progression of stars, called a "star path," for each destination island for various voyaging seasons throughout the year. Navigators calibrate the fading star field at dawn to the direction of ocean swell and the rising position of the sun on the horizon. Since the earth's equator is tilted with respect to its orbit around the sun, the angular distance of the sun north or south of the celestial equator (declination) shifts annually from 23.5 degrees north to 23.5 degrees south; navigators' calibration of the sun to the star field must make adjustments for these daily shifts in the sun's rising and setting positions. Navigators in the central Caro-linian atolls, part of the Federated States of Micronesia, developed these ce-lestial ideas into a star compass that conceptually divides the horizon into thirty-two points arranged symmetrically about a north-south axis. The stars provide the names for abstract segmentations of the horizon that can be used to indicate the direction of surrounding islands.[37]

Once out of sight of land, navigators maintain course and estimate their progress through dead reckoning procedures, while taking into account the displacement effects of currents and winds (leeway). Two surviving systems illustrate how certain island groups focused on particular environmental phe-nomena. Navigators in the central Carolinian atolls estimate their progress with a celestial-based concept described as a "moving reference island." From this perspective, islands move around a canoe that seems to be fixed in place—the destination island appears to approach the canoe, while islands ly-ing off to the side appear to fall behind. The reference island, or *etak*, lies off to one side of the sailing course and is not visible at any time during the voy-age. The navigator envisions how the reference island "moves" along the ho-rizon in terms of shifting star bearings. Cognitive anthropologist Edwin Hutchins argues that the navigator is not concerned with the length of each voyaging segment but rather how much time has elapsed before he asserts that the reference island lies under the next star bearing.[38] Misjudgments of current streams and the sideways force of wind on the sail can result in sailing too far off the course line and missing landfall. When starting a voyage, navi-gators typically face astern and take a back bearing on their home island in order to check and compensate for the direction and strength of the current and the effects of leeway. A second system, exemplified by navigators in the Santa Cruz Islands, is based on the winds but incorporates stars as well. Te Nohoanga Te Matangi, loosely translated as "the Wind Bearing System," con-ceptually divides the horizon into thirty-two equidistantly arrayed positions from which the wind blows. The navigator uses this wind compass to corre-late the named positions with the rising and setting positions of celestial bodies, wind seasons, calendrics such as equinoxes and solstices, and interisland voyaging routes.[39]

Closer to land, navigators expand the range at which islands can be detected through various remote-sensing techniques. Observations of birds, clouds, swell patterns, sea animals, currents, tides, and shoals are common land-finding techniques, but they vary according to island geography and local environmental features. Carolinian navigators developed an elaborate inventory of marine life that extends out to sea from an island along each of the star compass directions.[40] They also observed the flight patterns of specific birds that nest on land but fly out to sea during the day to fish. Observations in the morning as the birds fly toward their fishing grounds or in the evening when they return home inform the navigator about the direction and distance to land. Navigators also pay attention to cloud formations that can be seen for considerable distances: high volcanic islands interrupt the flow of trade winds and produce distinct cloud effects, and shallow lagoons of coral atolls reflect their greenish colors on the undersides of clouds. Another common remote-sensing technique involves feeling the movement of the canoe in response to swell and current patterns that are disrupted by islands, as exemplified in the Marshall Islands. Through these techniques, low-lying atolls can generally be detected about thirty miles away and high islands about fifty miles away.[41] A less well known light phenomenon can be detected more than one hundred miles from an island, affording the exact direction toward land. Navigators from the Santa Cruz Islands describe *te lapa* ("the flashing") as instantaneous bolts of light that emanate from land.[42]

The advancement of navigational techniques—perhaps similar to those described by anthropologists in the latter part of the twentieth century—coupled with strategic use of weather patterns enabled the systematic exploration and expansion into Remote Oceania. Computer simulations of thousands of voyages setting out from various home islands have demonstrated that while one-way accidental drift voyages or navigational errors certainly contributed to the inadvertent discovery and settlement of some islands, such a scenario cannot account for settlement of all of Oceania. These simulations have converged with historic accounts, oral traditions, and insights from experimental voyaging to largely support Irwin's thesis of systematic exploration strategies.[43] Irwin, an archaeologist with extensive blue-water sailing experience, argues that these mariners safely searched upwind against the direction of the prevailing easterly trade winds by either tacking back and forth against the winds or by exploiting seasonal westerly wind shifts and, whether they found uninhabited land or not, returning home with the resumption of the trade winds to then set out on future colonizing expeditions. This is much safer than first sailing downwind and, in the case of not finding land, tacking back and forth against the trade winds or returning by a different route through different weather systems.

The idea of waiting for the seasonal alternation from the easterly trade winds to westerly winds in order to sail and search in an upwind direction for land is also referenced in historic accounts and oral traditions, demonstrated in experimental voyages, and implied in the navigational techniques. Captain James Cook learned such a strategy from a navigator in Tahiti named Tupaia in 1769, and an oral tradition in Fiji describes searching upwind for uninhabited islands.[44] The experimental voyaging canoe *Hōkūle'a* exploited westerly wind shifts when sailing through the Cook Islands between Aitutaki and Rarotonga in 1986 and when searching for the lone island of Rapa Nui in 1999.[45] Finally, the documented navigational technique of zenith stars and windward landfall is suggestive of upwind sailing and searching upwind for considerable distances. With this technique, navigators guide their canoes to arrive at the windward latitude of an island based on the appearance of a particular star rising directly overhead (the zenith) and then turn downwind with the trade winds to make landfall.[46] Making inferences from these historic-era observations about how the early seafarers crossed the threshold to deep-sea navigation remains problematic, but it is still suggestive that such an event was possible.

Inhabiting "These Islands of Ours"

With the navigational penetration into the longer inter-archipelago distances of Remote Oceania, made possible by the development of the spritsail-rigged outrigger canoe, refined navigational techniques, and strategic use of weather patterns, a northward migratory trajectory ensued that resulted in the discovery and settlement of the Marshall Islands. Upon the reconfiguration of sea levels back down to current conditions about two thousand years ago, the arc of newly exposed coral reefs—Tuvalu, Kiribati, Marshall Islands, and Caroline Islands—became habitable once again as atolls, and in very rapid succession these archipelagoes were discovered and settled. Excavations of taro swamps in association with earth ovens and a range of artifacts, such as shell adzes, gouges, chisels, fishing gear, and food scrapers from several atolls in the Marshall Islands, have been radiocarbon dated to approximately two thousand years ago.[47] Yet a combination of a paucity of preserved archaeological sites and the likelihood of continuing interaction after settlement blurs the quest to pinpoint the exact timing and sequence of the migratory origins that led to the settlement of the Marshall Islands. Anthropologist Glen Peterson argues that the Santa Cruz group in the eastern Solomon Islands, where high islanders would have first become accustomed to atoll resources once the sea levels dropped, is a key place from which eastern Micronesia was settled, but he also suggests that several waves of colonists from different locales likely brought with them a range of cultural practices and languages.[48] Archaeologist Paul Rainbird suggests that precolonization "seeding" events may have helped to prepare the newly emergent atolls for settlement.[49] A reconnaissance group could locate such an island with virtually no flora and fauna and prepare it for future occupation by seeding it with crops that require little maintenance once established such as coconut trees, banana plants, and breadfruit.

The mariners heading northward to discover and possibly seed the Marshall Islands possessed an oceanic view of the world. As a people of the sea, these mariners likely knew that if they continued to sail, they would discover uninhabited coral atolls and islands that they could claim as their own, fueled by the ambitions of younger siblings to circumvent the constraints of primogeniture—the rights of succession belonging to the firstborn child. Stories of cultural heroes and demigods such as Māui fishing up or discovering islands with powerful hooks abound throughout Oceania. Storyteller Jelibor Jam introduced such a story in his cosmogonic narrative of the Marshall Islands, and a navigator named Jowej from the northern Ratak chain elaborated this imagery within a chant for anthropologist Jack Tobin in 1952.[50] The chant speaks of two demigods named Bukonmar and Lañinperan who fished up the atoll Mili in the southern Ratak chain with a special hook from the atolls of Kiribati to the south after the demigod trickster Etao had overturned and sunk it:

> Bukonmar gathered Mile [Mili] up
> The released Mile [Mili]
> Bukonmar is lowering (the fishing line) O, It is calm
> Lady North of the sheet cleats O-yell
> Climb aboard Lañinperan
> Hello.
> It shall not be the hook of the north
> The hook of the south
> The hook of Nabu
> Beg for that Gilbertese [Kiribati] hook
> O, lower it.
> It is taut
> Because of Mile's [Mili's] great resistance on the line
> Let us try hard
> Try hard to reach it

That land of Mile [Mili] it is
Your land and my land
Our land
And that is all
On top of this reef, O, lower our sails.

In an elaborated version of this story documented by anthropologist William Lessa, Etao overturned Mili in order to trick its inhabitants when they had searched, at his prompting, for an unknown reef. Lañinperan, from the spiritual island of Eb, instructed the Mili islanders to haul it up with the special hook, but it was so full of water that they had to punch a hole in the island to drain it. Its unusual lagoon is not navigable in rough weather, according to the story.[51] Other stories describe the purposeful exploration northward from Kiribati to discover and settle the southeastern atolls of the Marshall Islands, starting with Mili. One story describes how Lijebake, the wife of the deity Wūllep, swam north from Kiribati in the form of a turtle with her granddaughter, Limaninbit, on her back under the guidance of Wūllep, who could fly overhead as a frigate bird. They first reached Mili and continued northward up the Ratak chain until they discovered the small coral island of Jemo.[52]

Jowej's chant of fishing up an atoll from the bottom of the sea, combined with narratives of exploring northwards, encapsulates the notion of multiple, simultaneous histories. The use of a southern Kiribati hook by two supernatural Marshallese implies either a northwards journey from Kiribati toward the Marshallese southern islands or previously established links between these two archipelagoes. Both scenarios are suggestive of migratory canoe travel with the discovery, or metaphorical fishing up, of atolls and islands, or even the transformation of island environments through time as indicated by Lessa's narrative. The story of Lijebake's journeying northward from Kiribati also describes the first settlement of the islands by people—her granddaughter Limaninbit stepping ashore on Jemo. Alternately, the idea of pulling islands out of the sea resonates with Ļowa's generative acts of island creation, especially because in some oral traditions the sea is part of the fabric of the cosmos and the bottom of the sea is the place of Ļowa's dwelling.

Whether the Marshallese invoke one or both of these worldviews or the many variations within each worldview, it is clear that the first islanders to inhabit this atoll world conceived of themselves in a distinctive way. Like most places in Oceania, those people indigenous to the islands would have identified themselves according to their particular islet and larger atoll, to regions or entire chains within the archipelago, and as a collective people. The name "Marshall Islands," however, is an artifact of a late eighteenth-century European mapping and naming process. According to some accounts and embracing both divine and migratory origins, the ancient Marshallese may not have felt the imperative to distinguish themselves from other cultural groups.

Living on "these islands of ours," the first inhabitants of Aelōñ Kein Ad held a veritable oceanic perspective of the world. They settled throughout the archipelago, conceptualizing and naming the islands and seas in distinctive ways, including the two main island chains—Ratak and Rālik. And while they established and maintained links with neighboring groups, the Marshallese also advanced the development of their canoe technology and refined their wave-based navigational methods, which led to some of the most extensive seafaring in all of the Pacific Ocean. It was from one of the last strongholds of these Marshallese voyaging traditions that Captain Korent emerged to lead the revitalization of wave navigation and ultimately reconnected with his oceanic heritage by leading his community in their return to identifying themselves as a people of the sea.

I would like to imagine how Kilon Takiah, my adopted Marshallese father from Ailuk, may have narrated an interwoven version of these various origin stories and canoe traditions while sailing across the lagoon to his ancestral islet of Enejelar. Suspended at the edge of the outrigger float to counter the stiff trade winds blowing on the sail, I talk with the sailors—Kilon's children—for several more hours as we continue on our northern tack. They point out their familial islets, the canoe serving as an intimate space for storytelling. Just as sailing canoes and the expanse of the ocean are featured in the origin stories, so too is this canoe on which we are journeying part of a deeper story of placemaking, technological ingenuity, long-distance networks of communication, and cross-cultural encounters.

Chapter 2

Sailing in the "Sunrise" and "Sunset" Islands

[We are] born to the rhythm of waves that tumble on this reef.
—Rongelapese navigator Lapedpedin Lakabol[1]

The canoe has always been the vehicle of life for us, the water people.
—Bikini navigation apprentice Alson Kelen[2]

~   ~   ~

We are sailing past Bawojen. I sit now on the outrigger complex near the base of the mast with Kilon Takiah's daughter, Alimi, as my friend Kumrik pulls in the main sheet. We quickly accelerate with the mild fifteen-knot trade wind coming across our beam, or perpendicular to the length of the hull. From an easterly direction, this wind enables us to sail directly north toward the distant islet of Enejelar, still unseen below the horizon. While I watch the water race past the painted black lower and upper hull sections, I cannot but marvel at the outrigger complex. Its main structure is a series of strong primary outrigger booms that extend outward from the hull and curve upwards to end just above the outrigger float. Flanking secondary outrigger booms also extend outward and curve down to lashing points on the outrigger float. I had read about how the outrigger "lift" works as a shock absorber, but it is incredible to see. The sticklike lift is lashed above the outrigger float at the ends of the outrigger booms, and ropes connect it to the midpoints of the outrigger float. Like a toggle mechanism, the outrigger lift allows the float to ride up and down the waves without disturbing the flow of the canoe through the water.

When I had awoken this morning, there had been a buzz of excitement in the house. Kilon had directed his son, Russell, to take me with him and his sister, Alimi, to Enejelar. We would later bring back the canoe laden with fish, burlap bags of coconut husks for fire making, and bundles of dried pandanus leaves for handicrafts. But the main reason for the trip was to maintain Kilon's ancestral burial site. My usually solemn Marshallese brother Russell caught my eye and smiled in a rare moment. I was ecstatic to be called down to the beach. "Hurry up!" Russell called out, and I had just enough time to grab my hat and lather on a coat of sunscreen before the crew assembled on the shore and got to work.

To prepare the beached canoe, Russell had carefully released the back stay to cant the mast forward, which rested on a step in the center of the canoe, and his friend Kumrik had tightened the opposite front stay so that the mast was securely angled toward the bow. The side-to-side positioning of the mast was already in place, with the windward shroud attaching the mast to the outrigger complex and the leeward shroud connecting the mast to the leeward platform. From the rafters of the house, Russell and Kumrik had carried out the rolled sail, a heavy, white plastic, tarplike material sewn along the length of the two booms called the upper "male" boom and the lower "female" boom. Kumrik had placed the lashed section of the two booms into a notched step at the extreme end of the bow, and after attaching the upper boom to the halyard that traveled through the top of the mast that served as a block, Russell hoisted the sail so that the upper boom angled sharply from the bow to the top of the mast and the lower boom remained roughly parallel with the hull. They had attached the rudder to the stern with locking pins and secured the sheet to the lower boom with a detachable pulley before signaling Alimi and myself to climb aboard.

We pass islet after islet on our right. Alimi tells me the names of each islet and points out those to which she and her family have matrilineal-inherited use rights. After we pass the slight wind shadow of each islet, the canoe starts to heel with the gusts that get channeled through the gaps. Russell motions for me to sit farther out on the outrigger complex, past the main support, to sit directly on the crossbeams. When the canoe heels over, the outrigger float rises out of the water. Kumrik massages the tension on the main sheet so that the outrigger is just barely skimming the surface of the water. Once in a while the wind suddenly reduces in intensity, and the outrigger crashes into the water. A few times we encounter a large wave despite sailing in the protected lee of the islets, and the wave seems to devour the canoe. The bow becomes submersed. As our speed diminishes, the wave seems to engulf the rest of the deck. It is almost as if the canoe is a submarine. We are drenched in an instant.

We travel so fast—about thirty miles in two hours, or thirteen knots—that it seems almost anticlimactic to reach Enejelar. After we beach the canoe, Russell, Kumrik, and I prepare the canoe for the return trip through the shunting or "changing ends" process. Because the northward journey uses a single point of sail—a beam reach—there was no need to shunt while sailing. Instead we change ends at the beach on Enejelar. Russell and Kumrik first release and tighten the opposing stays to re-center the mast. Russell walks the base of the lashed booms down the length of the hull, staying to the leeward side of the mast until he can set it in the other end's boom step. This maneuver flips the sail from one end of the canoe to the other. They cant (tilt) the mast the other way to the end that has now become the bow. This shunting would have normally taken place on the water if the course had to be changed with relation to the direction of the incoming wind. Russell and Kumrik lower the halyard just enough that the upper boom rests on the lower boom and roll up the sail to prevent it from flapping in the wind. Russell throws out an anchor so that the rising tide will not carry the canoe away.

Kilon had watched our canoe depart, but, too old to sail, he had remained behind to plait a three-hundred-foot length of sennit, the two-stranded coconut-fiber rope for the lashing and rigging of the canoes. Seventy-five years of age, Kilon represents an older generation of surviving master canoe builders that grew up in the early 1900s. The knowledge, skills, stories, and protocols passed on to him from a line of canoe builders—and now embodied in his son Russell—trace back several generations to the mid-1800s. This was a time when social changes were sweeping through the Marshall Islands, while the traditions of canoe building and sailing as well as people's connections to the sea remained strong.

Paul D'Arcy's appropriately titled *The People of the Sea* examines the oceanic connections of Pacific Islanders from the late eighteenth to late nineteenth centuries. Of note are the islanders—usually atoll dwellers—who were known for their canoe-borne raids and unmatched sea power and referred to by others as "sea people." For the Tongan people of Tongatapu, these were the raiding *kakai me tahi* (people from the sea) of Ha'apai. In other island groups, small communities harbored ferocious sea warriors. For the Samoans of Upolu and Savai'i, these were the *'aiga i le tai* (family in the sea) of Manono; for the Fijians, these were the *kai wai dina* (sea people) of Bau; and for the Tahitians, these were the islands of Bora-Bora, known as, among other titles, "Porapora of the muffled paddle" in reference to the barely audible paddling of their raiding fleets.[3] Although not named for such exploits, Marshallese warriors used grappling hooks to lock their canoes together and engage in hand-to-hand combat at sea. Of course, naval power is only one facet of being recognized by others as a people of the sea. At least one cosmogonic origin story of the Marshallese places the ocean as part of the very fabric of the universe itself (especially Ebon navigator James Milne's *bwebwenato* of Ḷowa), and the migration histories rest on firm evidence that the ocean was more of a highway than an impediment for exploration, discovery, settlement, and spheres of communication.

Whether originating from the primordial depths of the sea or across the sea through voyaging ancestries, the first inhabitants of the islands were, and continued to develop into, a people of the sea. While the Marshallese were not known in their vernacular or among neighboring groups as a collective "sea people," their connections to the ocean manifested in other aspects of the language as well as conceptions of islands and seas. In this chapter, I establish the various ways that the Marshallese elaborated their associations with the ocean as they sailed throughout and beyond the "Sunrise" (Ratak) and "Sunset" (Rālik) island chains. Of particular relevance, the navigator—the quintessential figure of an ocean people—is called *ri-meto*, or "person of the ocean."[4] Lapedpedin, a navigator from Rongelap, described one of his ancestors in the opening epigraph as born to the rhythms of the ocean. Such an oceanic worldview rests solidly on the canoe as the foundation of life for such "water people," as expressed by Captain Korent's navigation apprentice Alson Kelen in the second epigraph. Refinements of the lateen-rigged outrigger sailing canoe had led to widespread interaction within the archipelago for nearly two millennia when the geographical knowledge of navigators caught the attention of European explorers in the early nineteenth century. The recent canoe journey to Enejelar on the atoll of Ailuk by Russell and the technical skills that he learned from his father Kilon represent a twenty-first-century continuation of these deep ancestral connections to the ocean.

Outrigger Sailing Canoes

The outrigger sailing canoe was fundamentally important to the early Marshallese, fluidly merging the realms of the living and the dead. It facilitated movement across the ocean for communication, transportation, subsistence, and a host of other daily activities, and it guided the paths of souls in the afterlife. The canoe also mediated these two worlds by serving as the vessel to carry commoners out to sea upon their death. Whereas chiefs and lineage heads were traditionally buried near house sites, the lack of available land for earthly burial led to the custom of sending corpses of commoners out to sea on old canoes or rafts to known currents that would flow away from the island.[5]

Meļaļ, a novel written by Robert Barclay, poetically captures the multidimensional aspect of canoes in the traditional Marshallese worldview.[6] An archaic word translated as "playground for demons," *Meļaļ* is set in the postnuclear reality of living on the severely overcrowded islet of Ebeye, juxtaposed against the fully militarized mindset and control of neighboring Kwaja-

lein islet. Based on contemporary practices and grounded in the early
ethnographic studies of Marshallese culture, Barclay develops a simultaneous
fantasy and reality of the past and then-current Marshallese culture of the
early 1980s. In this narrative, the canoe becomes a symbol of traditional culture through the adventures of a teenager, Jebrọ, and his younger brother,
Nuke. The boys sail to their ancestral homeland in defiance of military restrictions, as their lagoon is being used as a target for the testing of intercontinental ballistic missiles. A parallel story unfolds in the spiritual realm, with the
demon Kwōjenmeto and his beast, Ṃōñāḷapeṇ, paddling their canoe from distant islands to devour the last heroic ṇooniep, a magical dwarflike being, who
is trying to save the young Jebrọ. When the ṇooniep takes his final breath, he
journeys through the spirit world in his own canoe toward the land of Eb, the
final resting place.[7]

Jineer ilo Koba, the goddess credited with cosmogonically raising up
the vault toward the heavens, continues in Jelibor Jam's *bwebwenato* to unite
the first people together after the building of the first canoe.[8] In this story, the
original people cut down several breadfruit trees to fit together the planks of
the canoe, but they were unsuccessful. Finally, one man carefully used the
discarded pieces from the previous failed attempts to build the canoe. An-
gered at his success, the others left, and this division of the first people explains, from a Marshallese perspective, the origins of the matriclans in Marshallese society. Jineer ilo Koba, in her speech to reunite the men, tells them
that the canoe lies at the heart of what it means to be Marshallese in the following proverb: "*Wa kuk, wa jiṃor. Waan kōjipañ koj, waan kọkkure kōj.
Waan jokkwier,*" or "Canoe to bring us together, canoe belonging to everyone.
Canoe to help us, canoe to destroy us. Canoe to give meaning to our lives."[9]
To help placate their jealousy, she continues to explain that while the canoe
belongs to everyone, only certain people have access to that knowledge:
"Some knew the work and thus it is that the canoe is completed."[10] This important phrase encodes the partitioning of family-based specialized canoe
knowledge.

Jelibor Jam's story of the creation of the world continues with the building of a second canoe on Bikini, while other oral traditions describe Bikini as
the site of the invention of the first canoe. Collected by several ethnographers,
different versions of this common *bwebwenato* similarly place Bikini as the
site of the first canoe that initially lacked human propulsion. Ḷowa, the creator god, sent two men, Leoa and Ḷōṃtal, from the heavens with measurements.[11] Prior to the development of sailing technology, this inaugural vessel
was first towed by fish and then, after being consumed by a giant, paddled by
Leoa and Ḷōṃtal to the neighboring atolls of Ailinginae and Rongerik and fi-

nally south to reach Ailinglaplap.[12] It is here on Ailinglaplap that, according to other oral traditions, the technology of the paddling canoe was enhanced by the innovation of the sail.

The refinement of outrigger sailing canoe technology to the localized seas of the Marshallese archipelago would have been a critical postsettlement development to foster lines of communication among the dispersed atolls. Following the routes of the descendants of the Lapita seafarers, it is quite likely that a push northward from the Santa Cruz group ultimately led to the discovery of the Marshall Islands with fore-and-aft spritsail-rigged outrigger canoe technology about two thousand years ago. At some point in time after settlement, the Marshallese, as well as neighboring island communities, developed an extremely efficient lateen-rigged shunting outrigger canoe design that was well suited for inter- and intralagoon travel (Figure 2.1). Based on historic records, the advanced sail and hull design would have likely allowed for sustained speeds of fourteen knots.[13]

One of the most striking features of this new design was the development of a triangular-shaped lateen sail. In simple lateens, as documented in other regions of Oceania, the upper boom supporting a triangular sail rested in a crotch on a short mast mounted midway along the hull. In the Marshall Islands and neighboring archipelagoes, this triangular sail is suspended from a halyard from a mid-hull mast that is canted downward toward the bow and stepped at the extreme end. In order to change directions when sailing upwind, the mast is repositioned in the center of the canoe, the upper boom is unstepped and moved to the stern—which, identical in shape, now acts as the bow—and finally, the mast is canted downward toward the new bow. This process of changing the position of the mast from the ends of the symmetrically shaped long axis of the hull is called shunting. While the tacking of spritsail-rigged outriggers induces drag due to the switching of the outrigger from the windward to leeward side of the vessel, the more advanced shunting lateen rig always retains the outrigger to the windward side of the vessel. The outrigger complex, with its outrigger float working as a toggle mechanism, provides roll stability by counteracting the force of the wind on the sail. In addition to the lateen rig, symmetry of the long axis of the hull, and outrigger, the hull design included other innovations. The V-shaped hull slices through the water rather than slowly riding over the waves, as characteristic of more rounded hulls. The deep hull redirects the force of the wind on the sail, allowing the canoe to propagate in a forward direction. The hull is also asymmetrical from side to side, with a flattened lee side of the hull. Water flows past the more curved windward edge faster than the straighter leeward edge, inducing a hydrodynamic pull to windward. In effect, this minimizes the leeway drift

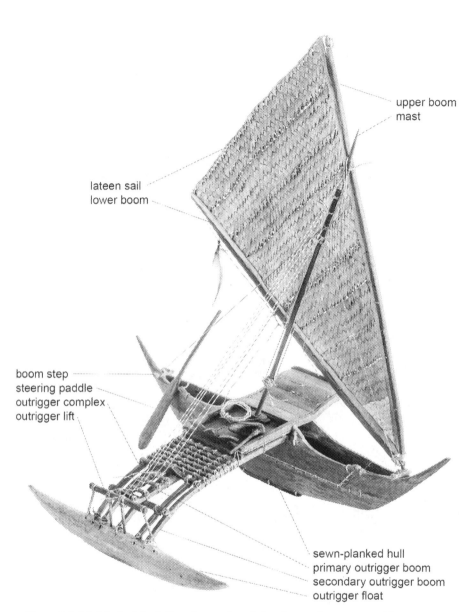

upper boom
mast

lateen sail
lower boom

boom step
steering paddle
outrigger complex
outrigger lift

sewn-planked hull
primary outrigger boom
secondary outrigger boom
outrigger float

Figure 2.1. Model of a Marshallese lateen-rigged shunting outrigger canoe with sewn-planked hull construction, constructed by Mental Laik (photograph courtesy of Dino Morrow).

that typifies most sailing vessels. In addition, a lee platform enables a large amount of cargo to be transported.[14]

A complementary development of the distinctive sail design of the Marshallese sailing canoe is contained within legendary *bwebwenato*. The story of how a mother named Lōktañūr introduced the sail to the paddling canoes of Ailinglaplap is arguably the best-known legend in the Marshall Islands today, with representations in a range of contemporary performances such as cultural festivals, political speeches, songs, and formal storytelling. Rongelapese elder Isao Eknilang highlights the main aspects of the story, which articulate well with Kapinmeto navigator Jelibor Jam's 1975 rendition:[15]

> After the introduction of the canoe to the people of Bikini from the demigods Leoa and Ḷōṃtal, the islanders paddled southward to Ailinginae to acquire tattoos from other demigods, and there the inhabitants of Ailinginae learned how to build and advance the design of the canoe. Lōktañūr was a woman from the large atoll of Ailinglaplap in the western Rālik chain who raised twelve boys. When they became young men, they planned to each build a paddling canoe and race each other across the lagoon. The first to arrive at the eastern point of the atoll would become the ruler. As they were preparing to depart, their mother came and requested that she ride with them. She was carrying a large bundle so her eldest son, Tūṃur, rejected her request. She asked her other sons in descending age to assist her but was similarly denied each time. Finally, her youngest, Jebrọ, agreed. Tūṃur ordered the race to start, but Jebrọ waited while his mother unfolded the bundle. She helped him to erect and understand how to use a sail. He quickly caught up to the others by harnessing the power of the wind, but Tūṃur commanded him to hand over the sailing canoe. Jebrọ obediently switched canoes, but Lōktañūr had quietly told Jebrọ to take the forward cleat with him. As Tūṃur could thus not adequately control the sails he sped away in a southerly direction, while Jebrọ paddled to shore at Je islet to win the race. Realizing that his youngest brother beat him to the finish, Tūṃur conjured violent seas. This caused harm to his other brothers still on the water, so Jebrọ calmed the seas. The sibling rivalry ended with Tūṃur sailing back to the west, far from his youngest brother.[16]

The continuation of the story provides a cosmological explanation of the stars and their relation to the seasons as markers of the annual cycle of time and illuminates a celestial view of the canoe. Jebrọ, Tūṃur, and the other ten children of Lōktañūr became deified as stars, and their locations in the night sky mark the onset and shifts in the seasons. Traditionally, Marshallese astronomers (*ri-jedjed iju*) observed the timing of the disappearance of asterisms and single stars to mark annual weather patterns. The stars become significant when they "fall down" (*wōtlọk*) toward the sea and are not seen again for another six months. When Jebrọ (η Tauri in the Pleiades cluster located in the constellation Taurus), the youngest son of Lōktañūr, dives under the sea, his disappearance during the summer months signifies the calm, plentiful season known as *rak*. Close to Jebrọ in the celestial dome is Lōktañūr (Capella in the constellation Auriga) and several canoe-based asterisms, including an outstretched sail and a boom step. The "falling" of Tūṃur (Antares in the constellation Scorpius) in the winter heralds *añōneañ*, the season of strong easterly trade winds associated with drought and famine.[17] Jebrọ's regeneration of life is associated with an intangible force that allows him to "tow" or "reveal" the Milky Way galaxy in the first half of a new year, creating a sweeping sky of stars as Jebrọ sets. This celestial force is a kind of "wind." The Marshallese word for large wind (*lañ*) also means "heaven" or "sky," and it is a similar force that powers the winds that propelled Jebrọ's fast sailing canoe.[18]

The swiftness of the Marshallese canoe is captured in the stories of the legendary demigod Etao (also called Letao), who uses its speed for his own pursuits of trickery. In a story documented by the German ethnographers Augustin Krämer and Hans Nevermann in the twentieth century, Etao's deception of a Majuro chief about the type of wood of his canoe resulted in the petrification of the chief as a coral head. The chief of Majuro asks Etao to trade canoes, as Etao's canoe is very fast. Etao convinces the chief that the wood, actually very appropriate for carving canoes, should be replaced with the smooth and shiny wood of a very hard tree. Thinking that the sleek wooden panels would render the canoe even faster, the chief agrees, and at Etao's suggestion, he lashes himself to the canoe so that he would not fall off. The chief, sailing a canoe built from this heavy wood, sinks off the leeward side of Majuro to become memorialized in coral, while Etao escapes his pursuers to continue his next adventures in deception.[19]

With the advancement to a more efficient shunting lateen rig and hull design, the Marshallese diversified three classes of canoes based on their size and function: the *walap, tipñōl,* and *kōrkōr.* The *walap* was a large voyaging canoe, reaching one hundred feet in length, designed for ocean voyaging. These vessels could carry up to fifty people and supplies. The proverb "*waan kōjipan kōj*" (the canoe to help us) expresses the idea that long-distance voyaging on the *walap* was essential for survival.[20] The midsized *tipñōl,* with lengths ranging from twenty to thirty feet, could carry about ten people for quick travel and fishing in the protected lagoon waters and on the open ocean in close proximity to land, including short intervisible water crossings. The smaller *kōrkōr,* varying from twelve to eighteen feet in length, was designed to be paddled or sailed by a few people in the protected lagoon for fishing and local transportation. Differences in the design of the depth and shape of the hull, as well as the construction process, led to regional variations; however, the hulls were generally hollowed out from a carefully groomed breadfruit tree, and cut breadfruit planks were then sewn with coconut fiber sennit onto the sides of the dugout and caulked with breadfruit sap to heighten the hull.[21]

The canoe and its components have deep cultural meanings embedded in the Marshallese language. *Wa,* the basic term for canoe, is also a possessive classifier (*wa-*) for an entire class of objects that can be steered, starting with *wa eo waam* (your canoe) but extending to modern equivalents, such as *bicycle eo waaō* (my bicycle). More significantly, the Marshallese use extraordinary stories called *waanjonak* to measure their accomplishments. Glossed as "example," *waanjonak* literally means "a vehicle or sailing-class thing with which to measure." A core understanding of *wa* thus rests on the idea of people metaphorically sailing through life on particular courses.[22]

Beyond the grammatical meanings of *wa,* the parts of the canoe extend meaning to core aspects of Marshallese culture that strongly resonate with people today. From interviews with canoe builders, Rachel Miller explains the cultural meanings bestowed on several canoe components: the lower hull section (*jouj*); the upper and lower booms; and a combination of the main sheet, bailer, and steering paddle, known collectively as the "mother of the canoe" (*jinen wa*).[23] "*Jouj eo mour eo, lāj eo mej eo*" ("Kindness is life, hate is death") is a common proverb that is linked to the canoe. As the lower hull section, the *jouj,* which also means "kindness," is the first component to be built, carrying the weight of the canoe during construction and the weight of people when sailing. The connection between these two meanings of *jouj* is that selfishness and kindness, demonstrated by the function of the *jouj* component, together comprise a virtuous trait. The upper "male" and lower "female" booms work in tandem to harness the power of the wind. The cultural extension of this dualism relates to marital relationships—the harmony of husband and wife provides for a successful life. "Where is the outrigger?" is another commonly used expression that may be asked of a man in reference to the location of his wife as a stabilizing force. The main sheet, bailer, and steering paddle are used for steering the boat, and this composite term, "mother of the canoe," relates to the relationship between a mother and child. As the rudder of the canoe, the mother guides her children properly. Overall, the names and functions of these and other canoe parts express meanings of kinship and lifestyle.

Islands and Seas

The original peoples of Aelōn̄ Kein Ad dwelled in an environment where the ocean permeated every aspect of life. Spread out over 750,000 square miles of sea in the central equatorial Pacific Ocean, the recognized boundaries of the archipelago today, officially designated as the Republic of the Marshall Islands, circumscribe twenty-nine coral atolls and five raised limestone islands concentrated mainly in two parallel island chains spread over five hundred miles along a slight southeast-northwest axis. The size of the islands, totaling about seventy total square miles of land, fluctuates daily depending on the tidal movements. The individual islets average about seven feet above mean sea level, but the smallest of the country's 1,225 islets become awash at high tide.

Coral atolls comprise the last phase of volcanic island formation, and this geology is linked to particularly few terrestrial resources that would have been available to the first inhabitants. Tectonic plate motion away from an area of rising magma leaves behind an island with a growing fringing reef. Increasing subsidence of this reef-encircled island is accompanied by upward growth of the coral that results in a smaller volcanic island surrounded by a higher barrier reef and intervening lagoon. The final submersion of the island forms a coral atoll, which will also eventually subside entirely beneath the surface of the sea. The larger islets can sustain freshwater through the accumulation of percolating rainwater in a subsurface lens that floats above the heavier salt water. People would have been drawn to these potentially habitable islets.

The ancestors that first inhabited the archipelago of Aelōn̄ Kein Ad forged a relatively homogenous community with a single language among its low-lying coral atolls and islands, as expressed in their identification as "people of these islands" (*armij aelōn̄ kein*). Yet with an oceanic area so large, the ancestral Marshallese differentiated themselves in part through geography, which is reflected in the place names of island groups and their localized seas (Figure 2.2). The eastern chain, from Mili in the south to Bokak in the north, is called Ratak or "Sunrise," and the western chain, from Ebon in the south to Bikini in the north, is named Rālik, or "Sunset." Two atolls—Ujelang and Enewetak—are located some two hundred miles to the west of the main Rālik chain, and an atoll located six hundred miles to the north—Enen-kio—has strong cultural and archaeological ties to the Marshallese but, better known as Wake Island, is currently a territory of the United States managed by the U.S. Air Force. According to ethnographic research by Krämer and Nevermann, the area north of Majuro within the eastern chain was called Ratak En (north-

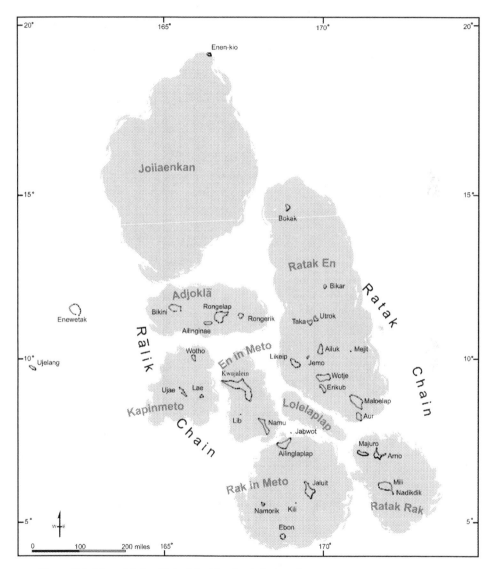

Figure 2.2. Map of Aelōñ Kein Ad with island chain and sea names.

ern Ratak) and from Majuro southward was Ratak Rak (southern Ratak). Similarly, the area north of Ailinglaplap in the Rālik chain was En in Meto (northern ocean) and south of Ailinglaplap was termed Rak in Meto (southern ocean).[24] These older names are no longer spoken. Today, the northern Rālik chain is sometimes referred to as Kapinmeto (bottom of the ocean), but it can also more narrowly refer to only the central Rālik atolls of Ujae, Lae, and Wotto, or the "western atolls."[25] The sea between Rongelap, Ailinginae, and Rongerik was once referred to as Metodikdik, but Rongelapese elder Isao Eknilang shared with me the name Adjokḷā for the northern Rālik atolls of Rongelap, Rongerik, Ailinginae, and Bikini, which he translates as "our northern wind."[26] Other ethnographic studies indicated that the Marshallese called the central sea bounded by these four quadrants Lolelaplap or Lolui-laplap, and the sea north of Bikini and Bokak was named Joiiaenkan.[27]

Archaeological evidence from Majuro indicates that the precontact settlement patterns favored the larger islets, with house sites and coconut trees near the lagoon side well above the high tide mark. Past the cooking facilities and rubbish dumps, the middle of the islet, with the greatest concentration of subterranean freshwater, contained zones of breadfruit, artificial depressions for the cultivation of taro, and protective screens of pandanus. The ocean side of this gardening center contained some habitation sites that extended to salt-resistant shrubs and broadleaf forest along the ocean shore. The traditional land division ran across these ecological zones to ensure access for each household.[28]

Other islands exist in other dimensions that do not allow for simple cartographic mapping and description. A mythical island home to the deities in the Marshallese pantheon is well known. This is the land of Eb, which lies somewhere to the south or west of the archipelago. According to narratives collected by Erdland in the early 1900s, Eb is the spiritual home of the god Wūllep.[29] The ethnographers Krämer and Nevermann described that the souls of the dead dwelled on two islands in the west. Tormented souls of evil people were condemned to suffer on Eb (Laulib), while those of good people rested on Juirik.[30] A soullike entity arising from a deceased person would move in the form of a sailing canoe to this island of the dead after passing through the small island of Nadikdik near Mili.

Interisland Communication

The advancement of the lateen-rigged outrigger canoes of the Marshall Islands, coupled with the canoe's symbolism and ties to spiritual dimensions, led to widespread patterns of interisland and extra-archipelago communication.[31] The clearest indication for extensive communication networks is language. Linguistic homogeneity in the Marshall Islands extends farther than anywhere else in Oceania. Regular social interaction among the inhabitants of the atolls, which are generally separated by single overnight voyages of less than one hundred miles, helped to maintain mutual linguistic intelligibility, and slightly longer distances with lesser degrees of communication worked to forge regional dialects. The islanders of the Ratak and Rālik chains speak with different dialects. Some dialect differences also occur within each chain, such as Mejit in the far eastern quadrant of the Ratak chain, and beyond the main two chains, including distant Ujelang and Enewetak.[32]

Within this high degree of cultural homogeneity, it remains difficult to construct an archipelago-wide cultural historical sequence and interisland voyaging networks. This is mostly due to the limited number of adequately dated archaeological sites. Archaeologist Marshall Weisler conducted excavations on Utrok, which lies at the most marginal edge of permanently inhabited atolls in the northern Ratak chain, to begin to characterize precontact voyaging networks. The Marshall Islands encounter an extreme rainfall gradient, running from about 900 millimeters (35 inches) of rain per year in the arid north to about 4,000 millimeters (157 inches) of rain in the wet south. In the dry north, Utrok is subject to long-term interannual variability of rainfall and drought, and distant, uninhabited Bikar is so dry that it cannot sustain coconuts. This, in combination with typhoon damage and seasonal inundation of salt water, led to environmental buffering mechanisms that alleviated the impact of variability in periodic food shortages, such as drawing from the freshwater lens for cultivation of giant swamp taro and the use of subterranean pits for storage of breadfruit paste. In historic times, the dry northern atolls exchanged finished goods and some food, such as pearl fishhooks, woven pandanus mats, turmeric, and arrowroot, for food in the wet southern atolls, including breadfruit and various fruits. Weisler, who has uncovered evidence in eastern Polynesia for a precontact interaction sphere between the ecologically diverse high volcanic island Mangareva and the resource-poor outlying islands of Henderson and Pitcairn, suggests that Utrok may have been linked in a voyaging network with surrounding atolls and islands (Taka, Ailuk, Mejit, Jemo, and Likiep) and perhaps an atoll even more distant (Kwajalein).[33]

Interatoll alliances provided some relief for environmental catastrophes such as typhoons. Particularly damaging, typhoons can generate sustained wind speeds of at least seventy miles per hour and wave heights of at least thirty feet. Typhoon waves can inundate entire islets, disrupting the freshwater lens and suspending the vital topsoil. For instance, about 800 people of Ebon's 1,300 inhabitants temporarily moved to Jaluit after massive damage sustained by a typhoon in 1857, and the people of Mili, after a typhoon of

1905, moved to Arno while supplies of coconuts, pandanus, and breadfruit were sent from neighboring Majuro to Mili.[34]

The quest to obtain special bird feathers for tattooing may have been a strong imperative to sail to the northern atolls, such as Bokak and distant Enen-kio, and the variations of the tattoo designs also speak to older patterns of voyaging. The traditions of tattooing were practiced widely among men and women, with the motifs drawing spiritually and conceptually from the marine environment. Called *eo* after the exemplary lines of the blue-striped or regal angelfish, the full-body tattoo of the men is laid out in a series of ornamental zones that describe the seafaring nature of the Marshallese. A heavily marked triangle in the upper chest symbolizes a canoe, and a lower-chest triangle depicts waves reflected from the land. These are both bisected by a line reaching the navel, which bears the name of a canoe's mast. Other ornaments, some of which were restricted to those of chiefly rank, signified such environmental features as clouds. A large triangle on the back shows the ocean, and a series of flanking bands arranged in "posts" (*jur*) represents wave features used in navigation. One of these, *jur in dilep,* or the "spine post," is the most significant wave pattern identified today by surviving navigation experts. The similarities of the tattoo motifs at the time of their documentation by the traders and ethnographers of the late nineteenth and early twentieth centuries suggest widespread interaction, but oral traditions suggest that the tattooing designs of the Rālik and Ratak chains were noticeably different. Documented stories also indicate travel to Enen-kio to obtain the bones of albatross or frigate birds to use for tattoo chisels. These nesting seabirds remain largely airborne over the rest of the archipelago and would have been nearly impossible to catch, but they bred on the northern atolls. Easily caught on Enen-kio, the short-tailed albatross was prized for its large-diameter wing bone that produced a very straight chisel.[35]

In addition to resource extraction and exchange to offset periodic shortages in food supplies and environmental disasters, voyaging occurred for obligatory payments to higher-ranking chiefs. Patterns of this redistribution of wealth come from the early contact period and early German colonial period. The German sailor Otto Eisenhardt became shipwrecked on Ailuk in 1871, for example, and wrote that the people of Ailuk voyaged once a year to an atoll 150 miles distant—possibly Aur to the south—and this was likely for providing annual tribute of arrowroot starch, pandanus mats, and dried pandanus paste.[36]

The sea also served as a zone of conflict for chiefly challenges to authority and rights to land and marine resources. Lineage tenure of marine resources centered on inshore waters and only extended to the depth where people could fish with a pole.[37] With only vague claims farther offshore, confrontations occurred about rights to reefs and fisheries, and such contestations extended to entire atolls. Warfare was actually characteristic of the island chains. In 1817, Lemari, a chief originally from Arno, had killed the chief of Aur and thus assumed command of the powerful center of the Ratak chain. Lemari had extended his northern military reach to Wotje and, with the aid of introduced European hatchets, established power on Majuro to the south.[38] The entourage for this battle consisted of forty vessels with about four hundred warriors, with two ranks of men and women fighting a particularly bloody battle on Majuro for six days.[39] This extensive warfare is suggestive of earlier precontact patterns of interatoll conflict.

Insular geography and interisland distances may have affected the patterns of long-distance voyaging. When David Lewis conducted his survey of surviving navigation traditions throughout Oceania in the late 1960s, he demonstrated that swell patterns and other land-indicating environmental features can be detected about thirty miles away from low-lying atolls. Overlapping thirty-mile radii around closely spaced islands means that arrival is navigationally certain.[40] The close proximity of the atolls in each island chain reveals, with thirty-mile radii circles drawn around each atoll, a near continuum of overlapping swell patterns. Navigators may have strategically sailed among these closely spaced atolls and their zones of detectable wave patterns to reach farther destinations. Ethnographic observations in the late nineteenth and early twentieth centuries describe particular moments when Marshallese navigators steered toward an intermediate atoll to locate its disrupted wave patterns before changing course for an island that lay farther away.[41] The German naturalist Hernsheim also reported that extensive voyages were made with ten to twelve canoes extending in a V-shaped configuration thirty to forty miles across with the apex pointing toward the destination.[42] Heading the flotilla of canoes was the navigator of *junmeto* status. The bestowal of the *junmeto* title by the chief was reserved for the most experienced navigator to lead a fleet of canoes.[43]

The pattern of sailing between closely spaced islands is also suggested by star courses and specific words for voyages between particular atolls. Observations by Erdland are revealing, as he recorded the names of sixty-six stars for particular sailing courses. Rather than forming an elaborate celestial compass as had developed in the neighboring Carolinian atolls, the Marshallese at the time of Erdland's visit used only a single star for basic orientation toward each destination island upon departure. A basic celestial axis drawn between Polaris and the asterisms associated with the Southern Cross (such as the kite Limaakak) would allow a line of orientation to use star azimuths to approximate courses to islands. Navigators sailing a northern course from Kwajalein to Rongelap, for instance, would initially direct their canoe toward the direction of Polaris, whereas the return trip would align toward the Southern Cross.[44] In 1938, Krämer and Nevermann also recorded named courses between relatively closely spaced atolls, such as from Jaluit to Ailinglaplap or from Rongerik to Kwajalein.[45]

Patterns of interisland movement can also be discerned through the cartography of the so-called stick charts that were first observed and collected by missionaries and ethnographers in the late nineteenth century. In one class of such teaching devices, navigators mapped the relative locations of atolls in relation to wave patterns in an intricate latticework of lashed splines of pandanus or midribs of palm fronds. German ethnographers based on Jaluit collected many of the stick charts from this time period, which likely skews attempts to discern archipelago-wide voyaging patterns. But of those collected, most provide the locations of atolls in the southern portion of the Rālik chain, the northern Rālik chain, or along the entire corridor of the Rālik chain.[46] However, Carucci recorded from Enewetak mariners that their isolated location obviated the reliance for learning through such stick charts; the devices instead showed the sailing conditions of the more frequent courses in the Rālik and Ratak chains.[47]

Sailing courses were also remembered and reenacted through the observations of particular features of the seascape. These seamarks, typically of a spiritual nature, resided in the form of waves, currents, marine life, and other environmental phenomena near specific islands or in association with particular seas. Their locations are informative to patterns of long-distance communication. The Enewetakese, for instance, recalled for Carucci the names of waves, seas, and coral heads navigators would encounter when sailing to Ujelang, Bikini, and distant Enen-kio.[48] The German ethnographer Paul Hambruch recorded the name of a particular sea state enclosed by wave shadows of Aur, Arno, Jaluit, and Ailinglaplap.[49] A navigational chant remembered today among Rongelapese navigators chronicles the seamarks discovered by their famed ancestor as he had voyaged throughout the archipelago. Other seamarks extend well beyond the close proximity of the atolls. These seamarks, documented from early ethnographic accounts, are arranged in arcs around the northern atolls reaching as far as Enen-kio, to the southwest of the southernmost Rālik atolls, and to the southeast of the southernmost Ratak atolls, beyond which lay the worlds of other peoples.[50]

The Marshallese were in contact with islanders beyond their seas. Oral traditions mention intentional voyages in all directions. The Marshallese sailed west to Kosrae and Pohnpei, the central Carolinian atolls including

Mwoakilloa (Mokil), Sapwuahfik (Ngatik), and Pingelap, and possibly farther to Yap. In one instance, sailors from Majuro journeyed to Kapingamarangi around 1870, killing most of the original inhabitants and leaving a settler colony behind. Different versions of the story describe fifty canoes either intentionally setting out to devastate the Kapinga or the scattering of the fleet during a storm and drifting to Kapingamarangi.[51] The Marshallese also likely sailed to Johnston Atoll to the east and central Kiribati and Banaba to the south.[52] In addition, reports of Marshallese storm-drift voyages from the late nineteenth and early twentieth centuries come from as far south as Nauru, as far west as Guam, and as far southwest as New Ireland in New Guinea. In the opposite direction, drift voyages from the central Carolinian atolls and distant Yap as well as the central atolls of Kiribati to the Marshall Islands would have prompted further knowledge of the outside world to the Marshallese.[53]

Encounters from across the Horizon

The Portuguese explorer Ferdinand Magellan, who sought a trade route to the Spice Islands (the Moluccas) of Southeast Asia, missed the Marshall Islands and virtually all the islands between South America and Guam during his voyage across what he named the "Pacific" in 1521. Spanish explorers plying this route in their galleons were the first non-Oceanic navigators to sight the islands, make landfall, and meet the inhabitants. Contact along the galleon route would have been in the northern atolls of the Marshall Islands, away from the more populated centers of chiefly power in the south. The first sighting of land occurred with García Jofre de Loaísa's voyage past Bokak in 1526. The first outside contact with the Marshallese was documented by the Spanish explorer Álvaro de Saavedra Cerón, who sighted the northern atolls of Utrok, Taka, Rongelap, and Ailinginae in 1528 and then went ashore on the return trip at either Bikini or Enewetak in 1529. But this moment, and occasional brief visits in the sixteenth century by other Spanish explorers for resupplying their long voyages, do not seem to have left memorable impressions on either side, nor had they significantly altered traditional patterns of voyaging. In 1594, the Treaty of Tordesillas gave Spain ownership of the Marshall Islands and other island communities extending westward to Guam.[54]

In 1778, British merchant navy captains John Marshall and Thomas Gilbert sailed their double-decked, three-masted, copper-sheeted vessels *Scarborough* and *Charlotte* through the southern region of the archipelago while charting a less treacherous easterly route from Australia to the Mariana Islands en route to China. The captains were not trained in making ethnographic observations, and their terse journal entries likely reflect their constant fear of running aground on the uncharted reefs as well as the need to take on fresh provisions. Their published accounts briefly mention a few encounters at sea with Marshallese sailors. While none of the names they bestowed on particular atolls endured, the name "Marshall Islands" began to appear on European maps.[55]

The next substantial encounter from non-Oceanic mariners intruding from across the horizon came with the scientific expedition of the German explorer Otto von Kotzebue. Inspired by Captain James Cook's early cartographic discoveries of extensive Tahitian spheres of voyaging, Kotzebue led the first documented inquiry into Marshallese patterns of voyaging and navigation in his mapping of the archipelago. In the era of eighteenth- and nineteenth-century Enlightenment in Europe, Russian nobleman and statesman Count Romanzoff funded the expedition of the brig *Rurik* between 1815 and 1818 to increase geographical knowledge of the north circumpolar regions, particularly the existence of a supposed subarctic navigable passage across the North American continent, and a second expedition followed aboard the larger *Predpriatie* between 1823 and 1826. Count Romanzoff chose Kotzebue, then a lieutenant employed in the Russian navy, to lead the expedition. The relatively young Kotzebue—twenty-eight years old—had already voyaged around the world with Adam Johann von Krusenstern, who had led the first Russian circumnavigation. He also demonstrated great enthusiasm to Count Romanzoff for making new discoveries of navigation and geography. Inspired by the journals of Captain Cook, who had befriended the Tahitian navigator Tupaia and mapped the extent of his geographical knowledge, Kotzebue sought to similarly investigate traditional navigation and chart new islands.[56]

In 1817, over the course of two and a half months, Kotzebue traveled throughout much of the eastern Ratak chain, visiting nine atolls. He made meticulous astronomical observations in order to determine longitude and latitude. He, the French-born naturalist Adelbert von Chamisso, the German-Russian painter Louis Choris, and other scientists and officers befriended the inhabitants of several atolls by presenting gifts of food and valuables, particularly iron, and learned the rudiments of the Marshallese language. Over time and with much patience, Kotzebue was able to discuss and record with several Marshallese their geographical knowledge of the nearby islets and surrounding atolls, which also informed Kotzebue on the extent of Marshallese voyaging and effectiveness of their navigation. Kotzebue also charted some of the atolls and islands of the present-day Marshall Islands that were previously unknown in Europe. His production of two charts—a regional map and a specific map of Wotje—reflects a culmination of exchange of geographical and navigational information between the scientists of the *Rurik* and navigators of several atolls.

Our only knowledge of the initial conversations of voyaging practices that took place between the European and Marshallese navigators comes from the journals and depictions of Kotzebue, Chamisso, and Choris.[57] Kotzebue published his journal, *Entdeckungs-Reise in die Süd-See und nach der Berings-Strasse* ("A Voyage of Discovery into the South Seas and the Beering's Straits"), in two volumes, to which was appended Chamisso's *Bemerkungen und Ansichten* ("Notes and Opinions") in a third volume. Chamisso then published his own account of the voyage in two volumes by combining his *Bemerkungen und Ansichten* with a *Tagebuch* ("Journal"). Choris also described the voyage and compiled his illustrations in *Voyage pittoresque autour du monde* ("Picturesque Voyage around the World") and *Vues et paysages des rérions équinoxiales recueillis dans un voyage autour du monde* ("Views and Sceneries of Tropical Regions, Collected during a Voyage around the World"). Fortunately, these writings and drawings capture in vivid detail their impressions of encountering the Marshallese. Chamisso was intensely interested in people and their traditions, while Kotzebue was focused on geographical knowledge. Their travelogues provide glimpses of the exchanges of seafaring knowledge, in which navigators from different cultures came to a common, albeit partial and approximate, understanding of each other's concepts.[58]

En route to the polar north, Kotzebue sighted Utrok and Taka in the northern part of the Ratak chain on May 21, 1816. Although he and the crew had a few encounters with the Marshallese from those atolls, the first real exchanges of geographical and navigational knowledge occurred on Kotzebue's return the following year. After an initial brief land sighting of Mejit, Kotzebue entered the protected lagoon of Wotje on January 6, 1817, where he explored the islets and met the local inhabitants. Kotzebue quickly entered into reciprocal exchanges of gifts. Not only did he give the Marshallese food crops, animals, and valuables, but he and his crew offered their services, such as demonstrating how to make a garden, and he invited the Marshallese to visit their ship. In return, the islanders of Wotje prepared food and reciprocated with gifts.

The sailing vessels themselves served as an initial point of common interest for the ambassadors of two seafaring societies. The Marshallese were equally amazed at the size and construction of the *Rurik:*

> These clever mariners, whose skill compels our admiration, naturally devoted the most rapt attention to the gigantic structure of our ship. Everything was observed, investigated, measured. It was an easy thing to scramble up the masts to the flagpole, inspect the yards, the sails, everything up there,

and to rock back and forth joyfully in the breezy net of the rigging. But it was another thing to let oneself down through the narrow hole and to follow the enigmatic stranger from the joyous realm of air into the terror-provoking mysterious depths of his wooden world.[59]

The Marshallese were particularly intrigued by and ready to trade for the ship's metal, as they were apparently already familiar with it from ship-wrecked vessels. The officers and crew of the *Rurik* were equally enthralled at the speed and design of the Marshallese sailing canoes. Choris captured in paint several perspectives of a typical Marshallese sailing canoe, and Kotzebue enticed the people of Wotje to build a large canoe model to aid in his understanding.[60] Kotzebue wrote of his first encounter with Marshallese in May of 1816:

> On the island, at the north of which there is a charming grove of cocoa-trees, we observed people, and a large boat on the beach, which we soon after saw advancing towards us under full sail. I immediately ordered to lay-to, admired the ingenious construction of it; and the surprising skill with which it was managed, increased our curiosity still more, and made us believe that we had to do with a people only half savage.... We admired the rapidity with which their boats sailed close to the wind: it had only one disproportionably large sail, of fine woven mats, which was in the shape of an acute-angled triangle, the acute being the uppermost. The skill and quickness with which they put about their boat in tacking, deserved the admiration of every seaman.[61]

The navigational abilities of the islanders of the Ratak chain astonished Kotzebue, especially when learning that they could locate the lone island of Mejit. In discussing the return trip of a young chief from Mejit who had storm-drifted fifty-six miles westward to Ailuk, Kotzebue reflects in wonder how the Marshallese could sail against the northeast trade winds such a distance with only the use of the stars and describes their navigational abilities as superior to those of Europeans:

> It is astonishing how the savages can make a course of fifty-six miles against the [northeast] monsoon, to a point like Miadi [Mejit], which they can hardly see at six miles' distance. As they only tack, they are two days and a night on the voyage, without any other means to calculate their course than the stars, which they see only with the naked eyes; a skill which the Europeans do not possess.[62]

On Wotje, Kotzebue befriended an elderly Marshallese named Lagediack by presenting him with gifts. Lagediack began to teach Kotzebue the rudiments of the Marshallese language, which importantly allowed the two to communicate in more than gestures. This developing friendship prompted Kotzebue to stay at Wotje. When Kotzebue asked Lagediack whether he knew of the existence of any other atolls, Kotzebue, without waiting for a reply, promptly showed Lagediack his compass. Lagediack was intensely intrigued with the compass but readily comprehended its function, for he aimed the compass at a group of islands to the southwest. He portrayed the islets and navigable channels that constituted Wotje and Erikub, first on a slate tablet and later in the sand by representing islands with coral pebbles. Lagediack indicated that a voyage between the two atolls required sailing from sunrise to sunset to the southwest, or a "day's voyage." In order to learn about the geography of additional atolls, Kotzebue asked what islands were located to the north, south, east, and west of Wotje. Lagediack readily understood and marked in the sand in terms of a "day's voyage" the positions of the northern atolls Ailuk, Utrok, Bikar, and Likiep, and the southern atolls Maloelap, Aur, Majuro, Arno, and Mili. The positioning of the coral pebbles indicated to Kotzebue that each of the named atolls—most of the Ratak chain as well as Kwajalein and Ailinglaplap in the Rālik chain—could be reached in one or two "sailing days."[63] According to Chamisso, Lagediack also assisted Kotzebue by indicating directions to the islands according to Kotzebue's compass bearings. With this new information, Kotzebue determined to chart the rest of Wotje and the nearby atolls through astronomical observations.[64]

Following Lagediack's sailing instructions, Kotzebue sailed to the southeast and sighted Maloelap on February 10, 1817. There he met a chief named Langedju, for whom he drew in the sand his newly acquired knowledge of the eastern Ratak chain. Langedju was quite impressed, but corrected the positions of the atolls and included Mejit and Jemo. Kotzebue also learned that Langedju knew Lagediack and other people from Wotje whom Kotzebue had met. From this he inferred a high frequency of interisland contact.[65]

After charting the position of Aur south of Maloelap, Kotzebue sailed north past Wotje toward Ailuk, which he sighted on March 1, 1817. On "Krusenstern"—the name Kotzebue bestowed on Ailuk in honor of the man he first voyaged with—he met an old chief named Langemui who told Kotzebue of a western Rālik chain of atolls and islands. After expressing his rage at the violent war being fought with the islanders of Rālik, Langemui described, in a similar fashion to Wotje's Lagediack and Maloelap's Langedju, the geographical positions of those western atolls. Langemui placed coral pebbles on a mat to represent the atolls and islands of both chains. He then "sailed" a coral pebble at sunrise from Ailuk toward Jemo and continued in the same direction to arrive at Likiep. Indicating the next morning, Langemui "sailed" west for two days and two nights to reach Kwajalein in the Rālik chain. Langemui then "sailed" to the other eight atolls and three islands within the Rālik chain. Kotzebue noted the course and the number or fraction of sailing days, which he then converted to miles based on his previous knowledge from Lagediack that a sailing day is approximately forty miles.[66]

From the three Ratak chiefs, Lagediack, Langedju, and Langemui, Kotzebue learned about the extent of geographical knowledge and the critical concept that "the distances are reckoned according to a day's voyage,"[67] and he used this information to draw a map of the Marshall Islands (Figure 2.3). Notably, Kotzebue made astronomical sightings of only nine atolls in the Ratak chain to determine their longitude and latitude. He drew from the native testimonies and etchings in the sand to produce a Mercator projection that includes the locations of the remaining atolls in the southern Ratak chain and the entire Rālik chain. Kotzebue also acknowledged in his writings the involvement of Langemui's information in the production of the Marshall Islands chart.[68] Unfortunately, when Kotzebue departed the Marshall Islands in November of 1817, the expedition did not sight any of the Rālik atolls, thus missing the opportunity to verify the information from the Ratak navigators or to expand the map by talking with Rālik navigators.

The widespread interaction within and beyond the "Sunrise" and "Sunset" chains that occurred during the precontact era, evidenced through linguistics and archaeology, seems to have continued to some degree through the early nineteenth century, as documented largely by the *Rurik* expedition. While Kotzebue did not apparently inquire directly into local navigation methods, his map clearly reveals the extensive—and accurate—geographical knowledge of the main Ratak and Rālik chains held by navigators on three different atolls in 1817. Shortly after Kotzebue's visits, voyaging declined dramatically in the middle to late nineteenth century for a variety of reasons, including demonstrations of prestige through the use of Western technology and ideas, social changes during waves of colonial administrations, and the myriad impacts of heavy militarization. But voyaging also persisted in a few isolated regions. The canoe traditions of Ailuk, for instance, have remained largely intact from the time of Kotzebue's 1817 visit through today. While Kotzebue mapped Langemui's geographical knowledge, Choris' sketched vistas of sailing canoes. Their descriptions and imagery of the canoes strongly resonate with my sailing experiences on Ailuk nearly two hundred years later, encapsulated in the opening scene of journeying across the lagoon to Kilon's ancestral land aboard his family's canoe.

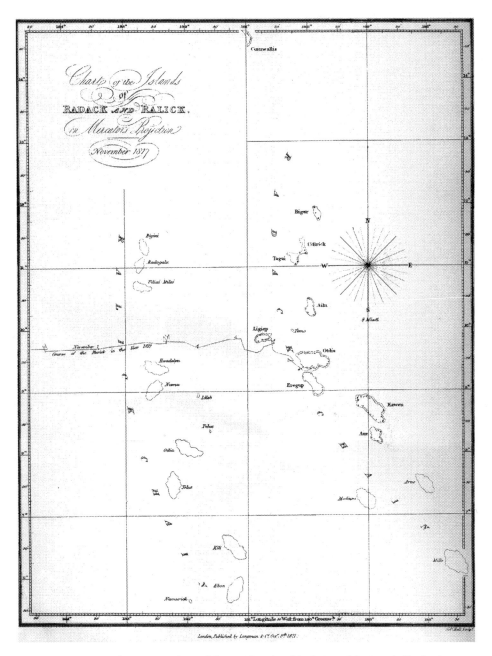

Figure 2.3. Kotzebue's 1817 chart of the Ratak and Rālik chains of the Marshall Islands, based on descriptions from navigators Lagediack of Wotje, Langedju of Maloelap, and Langemui of Ailuk; the solid line shows the route of the *Rurik* departing the Marshall Islands just north of Kwajalein (Kotzebue 1821, vol. 2).

If Kotzebue had voyaged either a slightly more northern or southern route upon departure from the Ratak chain, the *Rurik* expedition might have come across two centers of navigation. I try to imagine what Kotzebue might have encountered if he had sailed slightly more north of Kwajalein and met the inhabitants of Adjokḷā—the atolls of Rongelap, Rongerik, Ailinginae, and Bikini in the northern region of the Rālik chain. It was in this region, with Rongelap at its center, where Captain Korent's ancestors learned navigation at a training center, knowledge that continued in an unbroken line of succession until their homeland became irradiated during the era of U.S. nuclear testing.

Chapter 3

Exodus from a Stronghold of Navigation

To find your way you need the combination of seamarks discovered and remembered in the epic journey of our founding source of knowledge.
   —Bikini navigation apprentice Alson Kelen[1]

My people are lost at sea and they have taken down their sail. They drift and they've given up. They no longer look for their island. Alright, do you understand my story? Some say they are sick from poison [radiation] so they don't live but instead wait to die.
   —Rongelapese navigator Lapedpedin Lakabol[2]

~   ~   ~

Years after my sailing experience racing across the lagoon of Ailuk, a more solemn canoe journey would return my aged Marshallese father Kilon to his beloved ancestral island of Enejelar. As if preceding that event, Captain Korent leads me in silence to a different graveyard in 2005. We walk on a barely visible path from the islet's only house toward the protected side of the lagoon. All that remains of the islet's former settlement are some bare cement foundations of houses. We stop just short of the sandy beach, temporarily relieved of the scorching sun from the shade of several coconut trees. I can barely make out the cement tombstones, as they are nearly overtaken by invading plants. Captain Korent pays his respects silently and then begins to clear away some of the brush. Alson Kelen and I give him the time and space he needs. After a while, he pauses and tells us, "My great-grandparents are buried here, but not my grandfather, Henri. I want to bring his body back here but I cannot. He was buried on another atoll. The bomb forced us into exile and altered our way of life forever." Not sharing anything else at this profound moment, he quietly resumes beautifying the resting place of his ancestors.

We had just flown to Rongelap from Majuro to observe the navigation training reef where Captain Korent had learned as a boy from his grandfather in the early 1960s. He had not been back to Rongelap since he left in 1964, as the community had later imposed self-exile in 1985. The burial site of his ancestors was the first place he wanted to go after we landed. Over the course of the week, I have the chance to discreetly talk to Captain Korent about Rongelap in my stuttering Marshallese and his broken English. We talk about this stronghold of navigation that had nurtured his grandfather Henri and other elders before him. This ancestral knowledge includes not only a suite of *bwebwenato* but also information about sacred places, constructed models and maps, and practical experience gained through the reef simulation and lagoon sailing.

Captain Korent's stories of his childhood are offset with constant reminders of the dark, nightmarish history of Rongelap. The place is surreally quiet, with only a skeleton crew to work on the construction of houses for future resettlement. These workers must take a leave of absence every few months, and we are warned to not eat any of the food from the land due to possible lingering radioactive contamination. Drinking fresh coconuts and eating savory coconut crabs carries a perception among this community of a clear death. Instead we eat imported cartons of biscuits and frozen chicken in the compound's kitchen. The place feels lonely and abandoned. We are on Rongelap but prevented from really experiencing it.

The walk to the navigation training reef from the graveyard is brief. We stand on the northeastern tip of the islet and look directly north at a coral reef barely exposed at high tide. Captain Korent begins to point out the wave patterns and diagrams his ideas in the sand. There should be a canoe or at least a dingy that he could use to demonstrate how his grandfather had taught him. He reminisces on how his grandfather towed him in a small outrigger canoe around the circular section of exposed reef to feel the waves. But the skeleton crew on Rongelap had no such vessel. We had just traveled the breadth of the archipelago to witness the location of this famed navigation center, and we found ourselves excluded from experiencing it the way Captain Korent had in his youth. This is the postnuclear reality that Captain Korent confronts on his return to his ancestral homeland—a tangible link to his traditional maritime past, but a link virtually severed and haunted with disturbing memories.

The material stability, continuity, and sacredness of Marshallese voyaging and navigation waned dramatically in the late nineteenth and early twentieth centuries in the Marshall Islands for a variety of reasons. In this chapter, I describe the forces that shaped the penultimate stronghold of navigation in the Marshall Islands and how voyaging emerged as a site of resistance within a virtual cessation. In addition to traditional chiefly authority that restricted the use of navigational knowledge, various efforts by the colonial administrations of Germany, Japan, and the United States diminished the importance of this form of oceanic knowledge and travel, and the Marshallese themselves began to view their seafaring traditions differently. Amidst massive societal changes wrought by successive waves of missionization, colonization, militarization, and development, the two neighboring regions of Kapinmeto (Ujae, Lae, and Wotho) and Adjokḷā (Rongelap, Rongerik, Ailinginae, and Bikini) retained their specialist navigation and voyaging traditions to some degree. During this time period, the traditional protocols and regulations on the use and transmission of navigational knowledge had largely endured within these regions, as did the sacredness of navigation. It was the Rongelap school of navigation—with spiritual elements of navigation firmly intact—that received the direct radioactive fallout of the world's first thermonuclear weapon-grade detonation in 1954. While the Kapinmeto navigation lay dormant but largely intact in the minds of a few navigators, the Bravo singularity forced the surviving Rongelapese navigators, their children, and unborn grandchildren into a nightmarish existence of radiation exposure, medical experiments, and exile from their homeland that ultimately contributed to a virtual cessation of voyaging. What had formerly been one of the greatest spheres of voyaging in Oceania was fading to become a nearly unsalvageable memory. This was the world of a young Korent Joel.

Restrictions and Disruptions

The sophisticated lateen-rigged outrigger voyaging canoe of the Marshalls—the *walap*—and the wave-based system of navigation enabled widespread communication within and beyond the two main island chains during precontact and early historic times that resulted in the greatest geographical extent of a single linguistic group in Oceania. Interisland voyaging traditionally connected communities, making life on resource-poor atolls possible. As a result, the specialized bodies of knowledge comprising voyaging were especially powerful. Canoe building, weather forecasting, astronomy, and navigation encompassed highly specialized proprietary knowledge and techniques that remained tightly held by members within lineages. Here and throughout much of Oceania, village elders or hereditary navigators controlled the use and transmission of this specialist knowledge.

Historian Paul D'Arcy, in his synthesis of historic-era Pacific Islander connections to the sea, demonstrates that the time period between 1770 and 1880 witnessed the waning of numerous voyaging cultures throughout Oceania. By this time, many of the inhabitants of the high volcanic islands, with access to sufficient resources, had lost the ability to mount long-distance overseas voyaging expeditions, and, in the case of Yap and Chuuk, relied on specialists from surrounding atolls. Even though voyaging on the small, low-lying coral atolls was essential for survival, it still declined. D'Arcy argues that the fragility of seafaring institutions, exacerbated during times of catastrophe, contributed to such demise rather than a gradual erosion of seafaring ability in the wake of Western influence. D'Arcy notes that historically throughout Oceania the dissemination of navigation, astronomy, weather forecasting knowledge, and to a lesser extent that of canoe building, was restricted and tightly controlled. Island societies could draw from a wide pool of sailors to handle the canoes, but there were relatively few trained navigators, astronomers, weather forecasters, and canoe builders. Natural disasters coupled with introduced Western epidemics could annihilate a community's seafaring expertise very quickly.[3]

According to Erdland's observations in the early 1900s, four levels of hierarchy, largely pertaining to land tenure, characterized the precontact social structure of the Marshall Islands. The *kajur*, or commoners, were effectively serfs with rights to some of the resources on a single allotment of land; the *ledikdik* were commoners with elevated advisory status to the chiefs with rights to a single allotment of land inheritable by their descendants in perpetuity; the *buirak* of low chiefly lineage held rights to more than one allotment of land; and the *iroij* of the highest chiefly authority maintained rights to land on the same atoll and occasionally on other atolls. The advisory *ledikdik* also had a class of *atok*—"strong and powerful" individuals with specialist skill, knowledge, and wisdom, including male and female warriors, medicinal healers, sorcerers, and navigators. Their positions became hereditary—the title and associated knowledge were passed on to the eldest skilled child after the death of his or her *atok* parent.[4]

The distinct yet related cultural domains of voyaging—canoe building, weather forecasting, astronomy, and navigation—were tightly controlled within this tiered social and political system. The voyaging specialists of *atok* class worked with their *iroij* in a reciprocal relationship. In return for providing the *iroij* with the means of interisland transportation and communication, the specialists were taken care of by their chiefs. Canoe-building specialists, for instance, received special gifts for their services such as mats, rope, and food, while the regular workers—hundreds in number—simply received food during the construction.[5] Given that interisland voyaging connects distant communities and makes atoll life possible, the knowledge, techniques, and personal fortitude required of navigators were held in the highest respect.

Among the neighboring Carolinian atolls, for instance, skilled and intrepid navigators could attain status greater than that of a chief.[6]

The system of reciprocity between the *atok* voyaging specialists and *iroij,* as documented by Erdland in the early 1900s, resonates with ancient cosmologies. Recorded narratives describe how *iroij* served as living intermediaries between ancient deities and chiefs and commoners. By appealing to their chiefly ancestors, commoners sought productivity of their terrestrial and marine resources in exchange for offering a portion of that abundance to their chiefs.[7] Just as these exchanges were ritualized, the *atok* specialists worked for their *iroij* under strict protocols of knowledge use and transmission.

The *iroij* permitted their navigators and weather forecasters, and to a lesser extent their canoe builders, to impart their knowledge on only a few apprentices, who were usually their children. Only a select number of people in a few lineages (*bwij*) held the titles as specialists of these forms of knowledge. The titles of navigator (*ri-meto*), astronomer (*ri-jedjed iju*), weather forecaster (*ri-lale lañ*), and canoe builder (*ri-jekjek wa*) were not necessarily hereditary. But anthropologist Jack Tobin describes how the knowledge of navigation, as the property of the chief, was selectively passed down to the chief's close male relatives—usually their maternal sons and nephews and sometimes favored nonrelatives and their daughters. The process of selection may have involved the chief appointing an apprentice or the aspiring navigator ritualistically asking the chief for permission. It would be a severe breach of etiquette to ask directly, so a stylistic petition involved presenting the chief with food and fine mats and asking "to seek for light."[8] Bikini navigation apprentice Alson Kelen elaborates this process and describes the sacred quality of this lineage-based knowledge:

> *Bwij* is the family lineage that holds the power on land. Things come down through the *bwij.* The elders will sit around the cooking fire and consider who will be the next in line, even if the parent of the unborn child is still a child himself. They all focus on that unborn child. Once born, he will absorb the stories of the grandparents so the navigational skills from the whole lineage and broader clan will transfer to him. It is a big decision that is only shared among a few people. Sometimes this might involve two or three children. Some may be slotted to learn canoe building and others medicine. Navigation is more sacred than canoe building and weather forecasting. It involves higher training. And you train from the time you are a baby with the motion of the basket floating on the water until you grow up. Canoe building can be learned later, but navigation you learn from the moment you lay down in that basket as a baby. That is a lot of commitment from the *bwij.*

On Ujae, back in 1995, the stories of navigation started to float around, and I looked at the waves with the navigator. But I couldn't say anything because I didn't have the permission from the chiefs. They said it would be okay to learn it but never to talk about it with others. The chiefs own the knowledge. People have been talking about navigation, but very silently because it's passed on from generation to generation and is very sacred.[9]

This restriction in the transfer of voyaging knowledge, especially navigation, reinforced a professional secrecy and rivalry between navigators of different chiefly authority. Not only did this contribute to the chief's power in relation to rival chiefs, but it also led to the development of distinctive lineage-based schools of navigation.[10] Unlike the descriptions of the culturally distinctive, formal schools of navigation among the neighboring Carolinian atolls, however, there has been little ethnographic attention to such differences in the Marshall Islands.

Many of the early studies conducted by German ethnologists in the late nineteenth and early twentieth centuries on voyaging were centered on Jaluit (Figure 3.1). The stick charts acquired during that time largely map the southern Rālik chain, and it would thus not be surprising if a particular school of navigation characterized this "southern ocean" of Rak in Meto. The other locally named regions of the two island chains—En in Meto for the northern part of the western chain, Ratak En for the northern area of the eastern chain, and Ratak Rak for the southern atolls of the eastern chain—may have had their own variations in navigation.[11] Distant Enewetak and Ujelang may have developed their own variations as well, as suggested by the apparent lack of use of the stick chart models. Unfortunately, there is very little information available to reconstruct regional or smaller-scale lineage-based variations in navigation. This paucity of information may reflect the potentially Jaluit-centered early ethnographic research. A lack of formalization of any variations in knowledge could also contribute to the lack of ethnographic information. In contrast, the Carolinian atolls developed distinctive, named schools of navigation. The lack of information may also reflect the state of decline in voyaging at the time of the German research and the limited ability of the ethnographers to engage active navigators. It appears that the Rongelap navigation school in the northern Rālik chain, encompassing a network of atolls with lineages governed by the same chiefly authority, went unnoticed by the early German ethnographers, and this isolation may have served as a buffer against the rapidly introduced societal changes.

Social disruptions linked to the periods of missionization, colonization, and militarization of the Marshallese severely hastened the decline of naviga-

Figure 3.1. "A landing with canoes at Jaluit, Marshall Islands," 1883–1885 (Herman Stolpe, photograph courtesy of Bishop Museum).

tion and voyaging, starting in the southern atolls. In 1857, American Protestant missionaries arrived, who, with the help of converted Native Hawaiians, convinced first the islanders of Ebon and then most of the other Marshallese to readily embrace Christianity. While certain aspects of the traditional religious system continue to permeate spirituality today, much of the more esoteric aspects of navigation, weather forecasting, astronomy, and canoe building were either forgotten or retained in memory with a loss of the deeper spiritual meanings. Most navigation traditions throughout Oceania had chants and rituals connected to the spirit world that facilitated all the realms of voyaging, from obtaining the materials to build a canoe to becoming initiated as a navigator. For instance, the renaissance of voyaging in the central Carolinian atolls in the late twentieth century involved the resurrection of a traditional initiation ceremony for master navigators (*pwo*) that involved further instruction in the more esoteric aspects of navigation. Elder navigators who had received formal initiation just prior to the mid-twentieth-century mass conversion to Christianity led this revitalization, which involved chants calling upon patron spirits and associated rituals.[12] In the Marshall Islands, these kinds of connections to the spirit world were recorded ethnographically in the early 1900s. For instance, navigators and their crew voyaging to the northern atolls of the Rālik chain such as Rongelap and Rongerik were prohibited from using particular words.[13] But this sense of spirituality seems to have largely faded from the last vestiges of voyaging.

Within a few generations, from the late nineteenth century through the early twentieth century, massive changes wrought by successive waves of foreign administrations severely contributed to the demise of the traditional voyaging culture. By the 1870s, German traders and the German navy began large-scale commercial trading operations to acquire and export copra—dried coconut meat from which oil can be extracted. The Marshall Islands were officially established in 1885 as a German protectorate after purchasing from Spain. The German colonial administration altered the traditional hierarchical power of the chiefs in several ways. It prevented warfare, which precluded *iroij* from exerting their influence through military prowess. It also created a tax in the form of copra, and because the officials collected the bundles of dried coconut meat from the *iroij* rather than directly from individuals, they essentially strengthened and formalized the power of a select set of *iroij*. This led to the collapse of the social structure, as recorded by Erdland, into the three levels of *ri-jerbal* (commoners), *aḷap*, (lineage head), and *iroij* (chief). New interactions between the divine-like *iroij* and the German colonial authorities and their secular interests in commerce led to differing relationships between the chiefs and the commoners.[14] The German administration began securing the exclusive use of the harbor at Jaluit and special trading privileges in the Rālik chain. The Germans also elevated the status of some Marshallese navigators to that of a "real captain," so that they could sail throughout the islands to collect copra and other forms of tribute for their chiefs.[15]

The most immediate and direct colonial impacts on seafaring during this time period were prohibitions and bans on the use of voyaging canoes and traditional navigation. The German administration placed clear restrictions on interisland canoe travel. They discouraged voyaging because of its presumed inherent dangers, costs of searching for and retrieving shipwrecked and adrift islanders, and lost revenues with their trading companies.[16] Navigation researcher David Lewis comparatively reported that a canoe captain from Ninigo in the Bismarck Archipelago specifically attributed the loss of traditional navigational knowledge on that atoll to the effect of the regulations imposed by the German administration.[17]

The Marshallese developed a distinctive cultural response to the new forms of knowledge introduced by westerners. In many contexts, scholars have observed that the Marshallese have often rejected or acted ambivalent toward their cultural traditions, while valorizing the "other."[18] This inversion of tradition began in the late nineteenth century when the chiefs expanded their economic power through control of European maritime technologies.[19] They used their wealth to begin purchasing European-designed schooners from German and British trading companies, starting with the few wealthiest *iroij* in 1885 and ending with nearly every *iroij* owning at least one small schooner by 1910.[20]

The newly acquired European schooners had a strong impact on the collapse of the social infrastructure behind canoe voyaging. The increased carrying capacity of the European vessels was immediately apparent to the chiefs. As they tightly regulated the use and transmission of voyaging knowledge within lineages, they monopolized this new maritime technology. The shift from traditional canoes to European schooners was increased with the chiefs' perception of the prestige derived from owning this novel European maritime technology. Marshallese mariners, influenced by their chiefs, readily adopted or adapted Western boat construction and design. The earliest account of this piqued interest in Western ship design comes from Kotzebue, who described how a local ruler measured the dimensions of his brig, as well as the yards and sails, with a piece of string during his visit to the Marshall Islands in the early nineteenth century.[21] Overall, the lack of chiefly motivation and support for the traditional canoe-building skills and knowledge threatened community support for the building, maintenance, and sailing of traditional canoes.

Still, some patterns of interatoll communication continued toward the end of the nineteenth century during the time of the German colonial administration. Anthropologist Dirk Spennemann examines a number of factors to develop a model of communication for the late nineteenth century. In addition to linguistic data, ethnographic information on oral traditions, and historic observations of drift voyages within the Marshall Islands, Spennemann discusses the principles of traditional chiefly ownership and reciprocal obligations. Chiefs maintained rights to land, people, and resources on more than one atoll, and chiefly forged interatoll alliances provided relief from natural calamities. For instance, in 1909 a chief on the southern Ratak atoll of Maloelap exercised his right to collect birds and turtles on the far northern uninhabited atoll of Bokak. Safety networks were also invoked after devastating typhoons in 1857 and 1905, with movements of people from Ebon to Jaluit and from Arno and Majuro to Mili. To further characterize the direction and frequency of interatoll communications, Spennemann also traces the spread of communicable diseases and the origin of vessels owned by Marshallese that arrived at and departed from Jaluit.[22]

From the combined information, Spennemann proposed a model of traditional communication in the late nineteenth century. The majority of the communication links occurred within the two main chains; within each atoll, the wetter, more fertile southern atolls were in more frequent contact with each other than among the drier, less-populated northern atolls. In the Ratak chain, the prime interactions included the triangle of Majuro, Arno, and Mili, with northern Wotje serving as a key link between the northern and southern atolls. The strongest links in the Rālik chain occurred between Jaluit and Ebon and between Jaluit and Ailinglaplap, with Kwajalein serving as a strong link to the northern atolls. Interchain voyaging occurred primarily in the south, with strong ties between Jaluit in the western chain and Majuro and Mili in the eastern chain.[23] By the early twentieth century, traditional sailing in the Marshall Islands was essentially limited to voyages between closely spaced atolls and within the lagoons; however, some seafaring traditions within the archipelago and in the broader region persisted amidst the colonial impositions.[24]

In 1919, after Germany's defeat in World War I, the Marshall Islands became a Japanese mandate under the League of Nations, and Japan's influence on the Marshallese culture in general—and voyaging in particular—was considerable. With an expanding empire, Japan aimed to civilize the Marshallese within their doctrine of assimilation. The Japanese altered the local political structure through the creation of government chiefs, positions that were not legitimized in traditional village-based or community authority. This continued the erosion of traditional chiefly authority. The Japanese introduced the

Marshallese to the practical benefits of formal education and health care as well as new, unaccustomed directives and restraints.[25] This included restrictions on the use of canoes and traditional navigation.

During the Pacific theater of the Second World War, the Japanese war effort had a transformative impact on the Marshall Islanders' lives that was highly variable throughout the archipelago. Some Marshallese faced extreme hardships under an increasingly violent Japanese occupation, conditions that actually encouraged a resurgence of local voyaging practices. They suffered physical danger, exhaustion, ongoing air raids, and shortages of food and shelter as the war continued, especially on those atolls that were bypassed in the opening invasion. With dwindling food supplies, starvation was particularly acute at the heavily garrisoned Japanese bases on Jaluit, Mili, Maloelap, and Wotje. Hungry Marshallese were beaten, hung, and even beheaded for attempting to reclaim their food, and some Marshallese feared Japanese threats of extermination.[26] My Marshallese father Kilon, a young boy during the war, retained vivid impressions of narrowly escaping death from the raining torrent of bombs and the lack of food. Some Marshallese made the daring decision to escape on their canoes by sailing or drifting on the ocean to distant atolls. After invoking traditional kinship ties for nurturance and seeking sacred protection through a combination of traditional and Christian beliefs, they sought refuge via the sea. By doing so, they risked dying at sea, being killed by Japanese forces, facing the unknown treatment of the American soldiers, and leaving behind family members who might be killed for retribution.[27] In another case, the Japanese on Enewetak actually used the canoes to transport their soldiers between islets.[28]

During and after the Pacific War, the Marshallese began to implicitly devalue their traditional practices in favor of powerful ideas of development and progress. The U.S. military and subsequent administration of the region, first under the command of the U.S. Navy and later in 1947 as the U.S. Trust Territory of the Pacific Islands, left strong impressions of American power, wealth, and knowledge on the Marshallese. The Japanese had expected the Marshallese to assimilate into their expanding empire and had treated them inhumanely as the tide of the war shifted in favor of the Americans. Witnessing the defeat of the Japanese through American military might, the Marshallese drew a quick contrast between the power of the Americans, manifested also in their generosity and benevolence, and that of the Japanese. Despite the hardships that the Marshallese continued to endure immediately following the war, they maintained a favorable impression of the United States, refashioning the Americans as chiefs.[29]

The Marshallese began to think of Americans as chiefs by attributing the source of American intelligence and military power to their mythological trickster, Etao. Stories describe how Etao escaped southward from his pursuers in Mili after he tricked their chief into roasting himself alive in an earthen oven, and after escapades in Kiribati and other island groups Etao was finally captured and trapped in a bottle by the Americans. According to the stories, the U.S. military tapped into Etao's primordial powers, evident to the Marshallese in the destructive capabilities of the American bombs during the war.[30] The mythological connection to Etao further contributed to a growing cultural valorization of nontraditional knowledge and practices in the postwar era. In 1946, and for several years afterwards, Marshallese from a few atolls witnessed an unfathomable power that could only make sense in terms of Etao's destructive force—a power that would have far-reaching consequences for one of the last strongholds of navigation.

Rongelap and the Seas of Adjokḷā and Kapinmeto

Maritime history, as articulated by surviving elders today, points to the central western and northern seas of the Rālik chain for the last bastions of navigation amidst a world fractured by the destructive powers of World War II. One stronghold of navigation centers on the atolls of Adjokḷā, or "our northern wind"—Rongelap, Rongerik, Ailinginae, and Bikini. The other core region is "the bottom of the ocean" in the geographically constricted conception of Kapinmeto—Ujae, Lae, and Wotho. The Kapinmeto atolls were connected to the northern Adjokḷā atolls through histories of voyaging.

Captain Korent and his uncle Isao Eknilang shared with me a *bwebwenato,* passed down from their Kapinmeto ancestors, that describes the mythic origin of navigation, the spiritual nature of navigation, and the greatest navigational feats during recorded history. This following *bwebwenato* chronicles how a female ancestor named Litarmelu learned to read the surface of the ocean from two navigators hailing from distant islands to the west; how her son Lainjin sailed throughout the archipelago, detecting spiritual beings in the form of waves, birds, and other environmental phenomena that served as seamarks for the locations of each island; and how his son Ḷotop so impressed the naval officers of the German colonial administration during the early 1900s that they lifted a ban on traditional voyaging:

> Lainjin is a real person. Lainjin's mother is Litarmelu. This is the story of these two people. There were two Yapese men who stayed in Namorik. After they adopted Litarmelu they asked whether she wanted to learn how to really sail, and to this day the Marshallese only navigate this way. Litarmelu's adopted father asked her if she would like to learn their knowledge of

the ocean in order to sail from one island to the next. She answered her father that it would be good to learn such knowledge. The younger of the two
Yapese men asked Litarmelu, who said, "Yes, I should learn those ideas of
the waves." After she learned their ways on the ocean, Litarmelu happily
taught her son Lainjin.

The story that we heard was that Lainjin learned on the ocean side of
Madmad islet on Namorik at a certain rock. He went next to the rock and
asked Litarmelu about the currents to the west and to the east as well as the
surrounding currents, and then he knew the answer to what was there. He
asked questions about what signs are used at sea. He began to know more
about the ocean and started to sail.

There are four important waves that Lainjin followed. The wave flowing westward is called *buñto*. The wave flowing eastward is *kaleptak*. The
wave coming from the north is *buñtokeañ* and the wave *buñtokrōk* comes
from the south.

Litarmelu and her son Lainjin were very real at one time, unlike Jebrọ
and Etao. Litarmelu's clan is Ri-Kwajalein from the western atolls. Lainjin
stayed on Lae, Rongelap, Rongerik, Bikini, Kwajalein, and all the atolls of
the Ri-Kwajalein and Ri-Ut clans within the Rālik chain. When he sailed he
made his song-story. There has not been another song-story in the Marshalls
other than from Lainjin.

One time sailing at sea, Lainjin gained a deeper understanding of navigation. He was less than twelve years old. He rode with two chiefs. As the
story goes, the chiefs wanted to sail to Nauru, Kiribati, Ebon, Mili, and other
islands. As he chanted, Lainjin jumped from the canoe and went swimming.
He chanted for fresh water in the ocean in a region called Kortolok. This is
really fresh water like rain that falls from the sky. The chief asked Litarmelu,
the mother of Lainjin, because she could confirm what her son had said. The
chiefs then listened to what Lainjin had to say. He chanted, "You drink only
at Kortolok, Etao's fresh water." But to prove it he grabbed a scoop, jumped
over with it into the depths of the ocean, and returned to the surface with
fresh water. They say it is Etao's fresh water.

Lainjin had one son, but before his son was born his mother had become lost at sea. This is *wiwijet*. *Wiwijet* happens when people become lost
at sea regardless of their good sailing skills. *Wiwijet* is like getting lost,
really lost, where you don't remember anything. Litarmelu was so lost that
her canoe flew across the ocean upward to the sky and vanished. This is
what we were told about Litarmelu getting lost and flying into the sky. Litarmelu disappeared and has yet to come back.

Lainjin's son Ḷotop reintroduced voyaging to the Marshalls after the

Germans restricted its use. He did not use a compass, sextant, or nautical chart. He simply used waves, choppy seas, and feelings of the how the waves roll back and forth, and how they appear. He sailed throughout the archipelago. Ḷotop opened sailing throughout the atolls from the Germans and the Japanese. He took a test to show that Marshallese could sail with Marshallese navigation. He sailed with the Germans on one of their ships and remained below deck. They purposely sailed an erratic course to confuse him. Each time they questioned him on their location, he confidently pointed toward land. They asked him again to recite the chant that his father Lainjin had made on his earlier trip about Etao's fresh drinking water at the sea called Kortolok. The Germans then told the Marshallese they could sail without the use of a compass or sextant.

Today we work together to comprehend the knowledge of the ocean once held by Litarmelu, her son Lainjin, and her grandson, Lainjin's son Ḷotop.[31]

This narrative encodes several motifs that represent salient aspects of Marshallese culture. Notably, a man, Lainjin, and his son Ḷotop achieve heroic deeds after being granted cosmological power from a woman, Litarmelu. By beginning with the origins of navigational knowledge and ending with a specific voyage in the early 1900s, the *bwebwenato* joins the mythical past with historical events and keeps this continuum of knowledge within the matrilineage and larger clan to which Captain Korent and Isao Eknilang belong.

The voyage of Lainjin, referenced in the narrative, remains the most incredible journey remembered by the Marshallese today. In this epic voyage, Lainjin searches for his mother Litarmelu after she became lost at sea. He recognized and committed to memory various waves, currents, marine life, and other environmental features that served as navigation signs or seamarks (*kōkḷaḷ*), some benevolently indicating to him the locations of specific islands, atolls, and seas (Figure 3.2). In his search, Lainjin sailed from Pohnpei to the northwestern atolls in the Marshall Islands, southward down the Rālik chain, then eastward toward the Ratak chain, sailing as far north as Enen-kio before returning to his home of Rongelap. The resulting *ikid*, a flowing "song-story," is a mnemonic device that chronicles the navigation signs as well as signs for weather forecasting and sailing conditions that Lainjin encountered on his monumental journey. As Alson states in the opening epigraph, Lainjin is the source of the principal navigational knowledge of seamarks.

Isao Eknilang and his younger sister Lijon Eknilang performed two different versions of *ikid eŋ an Lainjin* (Lainjin's Song-Story), which references most of Lainjin's mapped navigation signs. Similar in form to other docu-

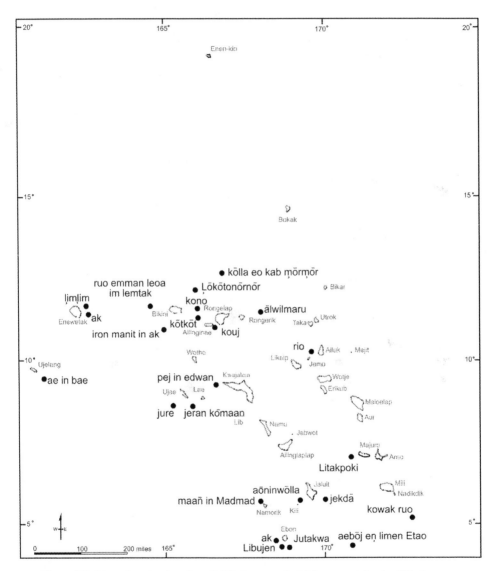

Figure 3.2. Map of navigation signs (*kōkḷaḷ*), most of which are contained within Isao Eknilang's *ikid eṇ an Lainjin* (Lainjin's Song-Story).

mented versions, Isao's rendition of the song-story is chanted in an almost continuous, low monotone, while that of Lijon shifts from singing to speaking to chanting in a series of verses. Traditionally, navigators chanted these song-stories to recall specific nautical information as well as to stay awake during long voyages. The words of the song-story compose an older, esoteric form of wave language known only to the navigators. Isao assisted in the translation of his chanted rendition to clarify the seamarks and celestial objects in relation to specific atolls and seas, but this literal translation does not convey the deeper meaning through the use of metaphor and allusion:

> We go to the east, we see a white seagull, the current of foam (*ae in bae*), is to the east of Ujelang
> The foam of Enewetak (*ļimļim*) passes to the north, we take down the sail, drift and sleep
> The frigate bird (*ak*) is looking for the east, windward of Jinme
> The male ruddy turnstone bird (*kono*) paddles, it takes a long time to bring the canoe there, who can steer a straight course and hit Jokdik directly?
> Make provisions for your canoe with a hollow drifting log, Ļōkōtoñōrnōr, to the north
> Going to the north you see the garbage dump and the foam (*kōlla eo kab ṃōrṃōr*), to the west a white bird asks with a chant the female birds to the north, chants to make a straight course because of two paddles, hit Najiben directly to the southwest
> Start to sail, you know the course and have the light from a torch of dried fronds, the sailing course is clear, you stand firm on the canoe, stick to the course, and have confidence
> You drink only at Kortolok, Etao's fresh water (*aebōj eŋ limen Etao*)
> Draw up water and drifting from Kili, tell Liske and Lejur on the ocean to try for strength, the location of the galaxy (*aōinwōlla lañmaad*), hold onto the wave, don't stray from the course on the wave but make it a straight course, now it's easy
> The bird flies to the north, the bird (*jedkā*) flies to the south, chirping, chirping
> Look at the front of the wave there (*ṃaan ņo*), from the wind of Jabot to Likiep (*tor Juel*) to the circular current of Rongerik (*aleelee*)
> Come to the east directly, don't sail around the island in the day
> We come to the south of Kapen, big waves (*elap ņo*) you stand firm on the canoe, let the boom out
> We go to the east and see the frigate bird, let the sheet out to luff the sail and examine the bird, the kite of Inedel (*liṃaakak eo nejin Inedel*)

> The brown booby flaps his wings and flies to the northern atolls west of
> Majuro, Litakpoki makes it confusing, away then close, makes prints in
> the water, turbulence forms the whirlpool Likapijwewe
> Two whimbrels (*kowak ruo*) fly apart from each other, one speaks Ratak
> language but where is the other whimbrel? A bird from Makin [Kiribati]
> plays a song in the Kiribati language
> Coming from the south is the frigate bird Libujen who is looking for the
> giant eel Jutakwa, looking up towards Ebon
> The pandanus branch is the pandanus from Madmad (*maañ in Madmad*),
> pandanus from Wundik land tract
> A flock of frigate birds (*ak*) is flying to the east with provisions, carrying a
> basket of arrowroot to have a feast after finishing the construction of a
> canoe before launching it to sail straight to Wotho.[32]

Narratively, Lainjin, upon sailing eastward from Pohnpei, encountered particular current streams and concentrated foam near Ujelang (*ae in bae*) and Enewetak (*l̗iml̗im*). A frigate bird (*ak*) also marks the eastern side of Enewetak. Lainjin then sailed eastward toward Bikini, detecting a male ruddy turnstone bird (*kono*) northwest of Rongelap. Venturing farther north beyond the Rālik chain, Lainjin encountered a drifting hollow log named L̗ōkōtoñōrnōr and another foam of currents (*kōlla eo kab m̗ōrm̗ōr*). Heading south down the length of the Rālik chain, Lainjin found the underwater source of fresh drinking water in the Kortolok seas north of Kiribati (*aebōj el̗ limen Etao*). Sailing in the southern Rālik chain, Lainjin's faint sighting of a galaxy in the night sky (*aōinwōlla lañmaad*) marked the sea between Kili and Kwajalein, and a bird named Jekdā indicated to Lainjin the location of Jaluit. Lainjin detected a wave pattern (*m̗aan l̗o*) at Jabot that leads to the eastern side of Likiep (*tor Juel*) and Rongerik (*aleelee*), and he found another distinctive wave (*elap l̗o*) located west of Ailinglaplap. A kite-shaped asterism named Lim̗aakak (*lim̗aakak eo nejin Inedel*) marked for Lainjin the southern atoll of Ebon. Sailing to the southern Ratak chain, Lainjin observed that a brown booby named Litakpoki created a whirlpool named Likapijwewe west of Majuro. Two whimbrels flying in opposite directions northward and southward marked the southern limit of the Ratak chain at Mili (*kowak ruo ko*). Sailing west again, Lainjin noticed south of Ebon that a frigate bird named Libujen was looking for a giant eel named Jutakwa, as well as a flock of frigate birds (*ak*). Finally, a floating pandanus leaf (*maañ in Madmad*) revealed to Lainjin the presence of Namorik.

The *ikid el̗ an Lainjin* performed by Isao and Lijon do not capture the full suite of navigation signs used by navigators but do provide a glimpse into the diverse set of environmental features that navigators can draw upon to find their way. Indeed, the various forms of navigation signs were—and continue to be—a foundation of Marshallese navigation. Some of these signs are meteorological to aid in weather predictions, and others are oceanographic in nature—general swell patterns and zones of currents or local sea conditions. Most of the navigation signs encoded within the *ikid eṇ an Lainjin,* however, are marine and bird life traditionally associated with a hierarchical order of beings called *ekjab.* Variously glossed as "sea life" or "seamarks," these *ekjab* spirits reside in and around an atoll in the sky, the ocean, and natural phenomena such as reef formations, rocks, waves, marine creatures, and birds. Most *ekjab* often benevolently guide a lost or disoriented navigator safely toward land and serve as confirmation that the navigator is on course. Other stories, although rare, suggest that some malevolent *ekjab,* sometimes referred to as *tiṃoṇ* (demons, a loanword from English) may lead a navigator astray to become lost at sea.[33]

In addition to *ekjab* navigation signs, Lainjin's song-story contains oceanographic and astronomical phenomena that are not necessarily laden with spiritual qualities. Lainjin named several location-specific waves that any competent navigator could detect. And the sighting of the kite-shaped asterism named Liṃaakak, also known as the Southern Cross, assisted Lainjin in finding a southern atoll, Ebon. It is possible that the height of this asterism above the southern horizon at the latitude of Ebon may have helped Lainjin to recall some of the atoll's locational information.

Lainjin, whose mother Litarmelu first learned navigation and whose son Ḷotop impressively navigated a German vessel from the confines of a locked windowless cabin, seems to straddle the mythical and historic past. His ancestral world witnessed the development of a distinctive wave-based navigation system, while his descendants maintained, shared, and elaborated it. Several oral traditions assert that navigation originated in the Kapinmeto region in the Rālik chain and that the islanders of the eastern Ratak chain learned the knowledge from their western neighbors.

Some of the descendants of Lainjin grew up on Rongelap, a famed center of navigation surrounded by the seas of Adjokḷā in the northern Rālik chain, according to recollections today. A few Rongelapese elders remember that in their youth in the 1950s and 1960s, their grandparents—the descendants of Lainjin—taught them as a cohort of navigation apprentices. They describe how the particular geography of Rongelap fostered the development of a regional training school.

The atoll of Rongelap is almost circular, with most of the atoll's sixty-one islets spanning its long eastern ring (Figure 3.3). The reef, some thirty

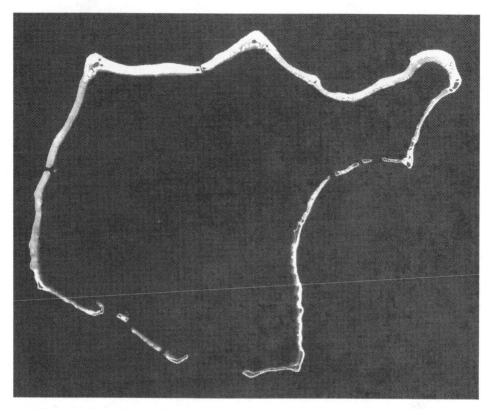

Figure 3.3. Rongelap (Landsat image courtesy of the U.S. Geological Survey).

miles long and twenty miles wide, encloses a lagoon area of approximately 390 square miles, with most of the dry land area, about three square miles, focused on the southeastern main residential islet, also called Rongelap. The relatively large lagoon figures prominently in oral traditions of the origins of the atoll. Rongelap, which translates as "big hole," contrasts with the lagoon of neighboring Rongerik, which, as its translation of "small hole" implies, has a lagoon of merely fifty-five square miles. *Bwebwenato* describe the origins of the atolls from the generative acts of a supernatural being named Lojo-likiep. By creating large and small fire pits for the burning of his trash, Lojo-likiep created the atolls Rongelap and Rongerik.[34]

Because much of the western section of Rongelap is devoid of any islets, swells flowing from the west enter the lagoon through a deep pass and strike the western sides of many of the atoll's islets. At one of these tiny eastern islets, which is so low it becomes submerged at high tide, navigators noticed the intersection between the westerly waves that had traveled across the lagoon and waves that had dissipated from the breaking of the easterly trade wind–driven swell. Here, in few feet of water, this small circular reef perfectly simulates how ocean swells transform in the vicinity of land (Figure 3.4). This natural wave simulation became the focus of what was to develop into a navigation school that attracted apprentice navigators from the northern Rālik chain. They hailed from Bikini, located more than eighty miles to the west, and from Kwajalein, located more than one hundred miles to the south.

The inhabitants of Rongelap and the northern atolls of Adjokḷā had developed some links of regular communication. Oral traditions of genealogies indicate some interatoll marriages between the Rongelap and Bikini communities in the early 1800s, but minor variations in the speech of the Bikinians suggests that overseas voyaging was not frequent.[35] Storied places of the environment speak to connections to other places. During our visit to Rongelap in 2005, after Captain Korent led Alson and me to the graveyard, we walked to the oceanside beach. A large coral rock on the southern, ocean-facing side of Rongelap islet, called Malkwon, served as a landmark for a back-sighting on an outward voyage southward to Kwajalein. Captain Korent's grandfather Henri would locate Malkwon, which conspicuously measures about ten feet in height, while sailing southward to Kwajalein. A legend shared by Isao also names Eneaitok, a small islet to the north, as the final landing place of a brown booby called Litakpoki. This is the spiritual seamark of Majuro that Isao chanted within his rendition of Lainjin's song-story. The story describes how the booby was knocked down by a slung rock as it was fleeing northward in its attempt to carry a man and a woman to safety after they had stolen a canoe in Majuro.

Over the course of a year, from the fall of 2005 through the summer of 2006, Captain Korent, Alson, and I had the opportunity to work with and learn from three elders who had studied at the Rongelap training school. Isao Eknilang, born in 1941 on Rongerik, was a youth of seven years old when he began to learn navigation and weather forecasting from a number of elders, including his father Turlik Eknilang, adopted father Monaean Jokanirik, and grandfather Lapedpedin Lakabol. Lijon Eknilang, Isao's younger sister of five years, learned informally as a child alongside Isao by absorbing their elders' stories. Emboldened by the legend of Litarmelu's instruction of navigation, which her father often told her growing up, Lijon fervently learned navigation as the only female. A cousin, Willie Mwekto, who was born in 1948, learned from his grandfather Mwekto Leaju, Isao's adopted father Monaean Jokanirik, and other elders. They reported to us that the school, in the late 1940s and early 1950s, was comprised of about eight students with about the same num-

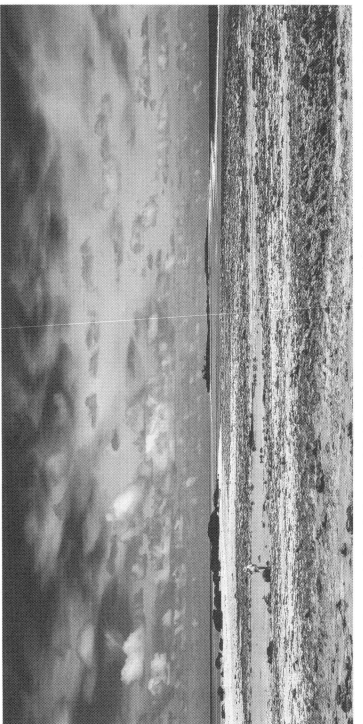

Figure 3.4. Wave simulation reef at low tide, facing north from Rongelap islet, with waves approaching from the ocean (right) and lagoon (left); Captain Korent Joel in foreground, 2005.

ber of instructors. In 2006, Isao, Lijon, and Willie were the last of that group, and now, more than a decade later, only Isao survives.

Captain Korent, born in 1948, also learned some aspects of navigation, but not as part of the formal navigation school. Eleven years later, Hemmerik Lewia informally taught his grandson Korent about the waves at the reef and while sailing across the lagoon to fish. This sharing of knowledge had not been sanctioned by their chief. Traditionally, informal learning would also have taken place at sea when younger sailors could observe navigation in practice. Lapedpedin Lakabol, Isao's grandfather, described to former Peace Corps volunteer Gerald Knight a voyage that he had taken as child with his father, Lakabol, as navigator. While the vessel drifted off course under the command of an inexperienced captain, Lakabol showed the young boy how to look inside of a water-filled bucket to discern the wave patterns. The sloshing motion mirrored the rise and fall of the bow and helped him to visualize the ways that the swells altered the motion of the canoe.[36]

The navigation training at Rongelap that was occurring in the 1950s and early 1960s would have, under normal conditions, followed a progression generally from land-based to sea instruction. This successively included recitation of chants and stories; the coral reef simulation; models and maps of the waves; experiential learning in the lagoon; and, finally, a navigation test at sea. The elders would command the apprentice to sail toward a specific location, and if they deemed the voyage successful, the individual would *ruprup jokur*, or emerge with the wisdom of a navigator as suggested by its literal definition, "breaking the shell." As Alson Kelen describes it, "You are breaking the turtle shell to bring out the meat, or the fresh knowledge, of the new navigator."[37] Other definitions of *ruprup jokur* include "to initiate" and "to begin," meanings that connote a ritualistic process of initiation. Erdland documented in 1914 that at the conclusion of the apprenticeship, the student's trial voyage of *ruprup jokur* would take place.[38] Alson elaborates the process of *ruprup jokur*:

> The literal translation of *ruprup jokur* is "breaking the turtle shell." *Ruprup* is "breaking" and *jokur* is the shell. You are actually breaking a shell. The biggest shell we have is the turtle shell, so all the skills and knowledge are in there. You break the shell and it is like you are coming out of an egg. I was told that *ruprup jokur* is like a test. It is your first task of one thing. Building your first canoe is your *ruprup jokur* and that will tell you how much you know. You are a trainee or apprentice first. It is very spiritual. Canoe building doesn't start now. It started fifty years ago. For my canoe *ruprup jokur*,

my great-grandfather had that in mind. He prepared and planted a breadfruit tree that would survive. He reserved it. The outrigger booms are naturally curved, so he planted trees on the windward side of the island. It is a process that starts before you are born. When you grow up, you learn the process, and in doing so are preparing for your own grandchild. Once you are ready to build the canoe, and the master carver thinks you are ready, then you go and build the canoe. That is your *ruprup jọkur*. For the sailors, you grow up learning to be a navigator. During one course, the teacher will say, "the ocean is yours." In the legend of Lainjin, he tells the others that he can navigate, and that he is giving them the ocean. When you sail with the navigators and they ask you if you are ready, they will say that the ocean is yours. Once you pass the course, you are breaking the shell. You are no longer the apprentice. You are the navigator. This is *ruprup jọkur*. It is an old system, I believe from the creation of time. If you *ruprup jọkur* from Kwajalein to Rongelap, you would see the rock called Malkwon first. You sail from that rock and then back to the same rock. When you take the test, you don't go just to an atoll, you go to that specific rock. You have to arrive at the rock or it would be considered a loss, a failed test.[39]

On Polowat in the neighboring Carolinian atolls of the Federated States of Micronesia, anthropologist Thomas Gladwin documented in 1970 the process of learning navigation and uncovered a different level of significance for the student's first voyage.[40] There, the instructor usually sailed with the student after his initiation, and while symbolic of the new status, it primarily served as a final phase of instruction at sea. In the Marshallese traditions of the northern region of Adjokḷā, this first voyage has a dramatically higher level of significance, serving as the rite of passage to becoming a navigator. For the Rongelapese, the typical test involved sailing several hundreds of miles north from Rongelap before returning home. Alternately, the voyage could head south to Kwajalein and return to the rock called Malkwon on the southern shore of Rongelap islet. Navigators on other atolls would follow other routes for their sea trial. Of those four individuals learning on Rongelap in the mid-twentieth century, only Isao took his *ruprup jọkur* test. The chiefs deemed it a failure. It was a shorter test from Rongelap to Rongerik, and although he made landfall he did not arrive at the correct location. The other Rongelapese students and the young Korent, who was learning as an unsanctioned apprentice, lost their chance to *ruprup jọkur*. Their childhood did not advance with canoes and lore of the sea as it should have—their imperative was now to survive a world that to them had become a nuclear holocaust.

Nuclear Testing and Exile

Between 1946 and 1958, the U.S. government detonated sixty-seven atomic and thermonuclear bombs on the atolls of Bikini and Enewetak as part of its program of nuclear weapons testing after World War II (Figure 3.5). From the research and development project that started in 1942, known as the Manhattan Project, came the first detonation of a nuclear bomb in New Mexico in 1945. After the dropping of nuclear bombs on Hiroshima and Nagasaki that same year, military planners wanted to more accurately ascertain the maximum extent of damage inflicted by nuclear weapons. The Marshall Islands were the ideal location for U.S. nuclear strategists to develop such a long-term testing program, with the rising tensions between America and Russia during the era of the Cold War. From the American perspective, the atolls were distant from the mainland, sustained relatively low populations of people, and were surrounded by vast tracks of ocean. The northwestern atolls of Bikini and Enewetak had the greatest degree of relative geographic isolation from the rest of the archipelago, and the nuclear scientists anticipated that the easterly trade winds would blow any radioactive fallout into the empty western ocean. Overall, the net yield of the nuclear testing in the Marshall Islands was equivalent to dropping 7,200 Hiroshima-sized bombs, or 1.6 Hiroshima bombs every day for twelve years.

Figure 3.5. Underwater nuclear weapons test, Bikini lagoon, 1946 (United States Department of Defense).

The nuclear weapons testing had differential consequences for the Marshallese. The inhabitants of Bikini and Enewetak were relocated prior to the tests. The Bikinians were first moved to Rongerik, where near starvation for two years due to a lack of critical food resources led to their relocation in camps on Kwajalein. They later found some refuge on the solitary, tiny island of Kili, but they remain today in permanent exile from their ancestral homeland, with only a skeleton crew who temporarily reside on Bikini in their service as stewards of their ancestral homeland. The Enewetakese were similarly relocated to Ujelang, and while some have been resettled on Enewetak, they live near a two-mile wide, potentially leaking concrete storage facility for the containment of irradiated soil and debris. Exodus from Bikini and Enewetak has resulted in community fragmentation, a severe social change that the Rongelapese were about to similarly experience.[41]

On May 1, 1954, the U.S. government released the world's largest thermonuclear weapon above Bikini, a fission-detonated fusion bomb code-named Castle Bravo that blasted an unprecedented explosion equivalent to the force of 15 million tons of TNT. This was one thousand times as powerful as the bombs that had been dropped on Hiroshima and Nagasaki in 1945. Coral debris from three vaporized islands and the surrounding seawater formed a giant mushroom cloud twenty-five miles in diameter that released radioactive fallout. Meteorologists noticed a westerly wind shift in the upper atmosphere several hours prior to the detonation, and military personnel on the atolls that lie upwind to the east were evacuated. The Marshallese, however, had not been evacuated. The wind carried the radioactive particles as ash in the direction of Rongelap, one hundred miles away. The 226 residents of Rongelap, Ailinginae, and Utrok were the closest to the ground-zero location of the Bravo shot and received near-lethal doses of radiation.[42] They immediately suffered from acute radiation sickness due to direct exposure to the fallout, internal exposure from ingesting and inhaling radiation, and by living on contaminated islands. The Rongelapese, who had previously been evacuated from Rongelap in 1946 at the start of the nuclear testing era and later returned, were, in 1954, not evacuated until two days *after* the Bravo detonation. Eventually moved to the islet of Ejit on Majuro, the Rongelapese then faced a polio epidemic. They were told by the U.S. government that it was safe to return to the main islet of Rongelap in 1957, where they remained living in a nuclear-contaminated world until their self-exile in 1985. The immediate experiences of the Rongelapese are captured in excerpted statements written by the former mayor of Rongelap, John Anjain:

> Early in the morning of March 1, 1954, sometime around five or six o'clock, American planes dropped a hydrogen bomb on Bikini Atoll. Shortly before

this happened, I had awakened and stepped out of my house. Once outside, I looked around and saw Billiet Edmond making coffee near his house. I walked up and stood next to him. The two of us talked about going fishing later in the morning. After only a few minutes had passed we saw a light to the west of Rongelap Atoll. When this light reached Rongelap we saw many beautiful colors. I expect the reason people didn't go inside their houses right away was because the yellow, green, pink, red, and blue colors which they saw were such a beautiful sight before their eyes.

The second thing that happened involved the gust of wind that came from the explosion. The wind was so hot and strong that some people who were outside staggered, including Billiet and I. Even some windows fell as a result of the wind.

The third thing that happened concerned the smoke-cloud which we saw from the bomb blast. The smoke rose quickly to the clouds and as it reached them we heard a sound louder than thunder. When people heard this deafening clap some of the women and children fled to the woods. Once the sound of the explosion had died out everyone began cooking, some made donuts and others cooked rice.

Later some men went fishing, including myself. Around nine or ten-o'clock I took my throw net and left to go fishing near Jabwon. As I walked along the beach I looked at the sky and saw it was white like smoke; never-theless I kept on going. When I reached Jabwon, or even a little before, I began to feel a fine powder falling all over my body and into my eyes. I felt it but didn't know what it was.

I went ahead with my fishing and caught enough fish with my throw-net to fill a bag. Then I went to the woods to pick some coconuts. I came back to the beach and sat on a rock to drink the coconuts and eat some raw fish. As I was sitting and eating, the powder began to fall harder. I looked out and saw that the coconuts had changed color. By now all the trees were white as well as my entire body. I gazed up at the sky but couldn't see the clouds because it was so misty. I didn't believe this was dangerous. I only knew that powder was falling. I was somewhat afraid nevertheless.

When I returned to Rongelap village I saw people cooking food out-side their cookhouses. They didn't know the powder was very dangerous. The powder fell all day and night long over the entire atoll of Rongelap. During the night people were sick. They were nauseous, they had stomach, head, ear, leg and shoulder aches. People did not sleep that night because they were sick.

The next day, March 2, 1954, people got up in the morning and went down to get water. It had turned a yellowish color. "Oh, Oh" they cried out and said "the powder that fell down yesterday and last night is a harmful thing." They were sick and so Jabwe, the health-aide, walked around in the morning and warned the people not to drink the water. He told them that if they were thirsty to drink coconuts only....

At three o'clock in the afternoon of March 2, 1954 a seaplane from Enewetak Atoll landed in the lagoon of Rongelap and two men came ashore. Billiet and I asked them why they had come to Rongelap and they responded by saying they had come to inspect the damage caused by the bomb. They said they would spend twenty minutes looking at all the wells, cement water catchments, houses and other things. The two men returned quickly to their plane and left without telling anyone that the food, water, and other things were harmful to human beings....

On that day we looked at the water catchments, tubs and other places where there was a great deal of water stored. The water had turned a strong yellow and those who drank it said it tasted bitter.

On March 3, early in the morning, a ship and a seaplane with four propellers appeared on Rongelap. Out of the plane came Mr. Oscar [de-Brum] and Mr. Wiles, the governor of Kwajalein Atoll. As their boat reached the shore, Mr. Oscar cried out to the people to get on board and forget about their personal belongings for whoever thought of staying behind would die. Such were the words by which he spoke them. Therefore, none of the people went back to their houses, but immediately got on the boats and sailed to board the ship that would take them away. Those who were sick and old were evacuated by plane....

At ten o'clock in the morning we left Rongelap for Ailinginae Atoll and arrived there at three in the afternoon. We picked up nineteen people on this atoll and by five o'clock we were on our way to Kwajalein.

From 1959 to 1963 and 1964, after the Rongelapese had returned to Rongelap from Majuro, many women gave birth prematurely to babies which looked somewhat like animals. Women also had miscarriages. During these years many other strange things happened with regard to food, especially to fish in which the fertilized eggs and liver turned a blackish color. In all my forty years I had never seen this happen in fish either on Rongelap or in any of the other places I've been in the Marshall Islands. Also, when people ate fish or [arrowroot] starch produced on Rongelap, they developed a rash in their mouths. This too I had never seen before....

I, John Anjain, was magistrate of Rongelap when all this occurred and I now write this to explain what happened to the Rongelap people at that time.[43]

For the Rongelapese, the consequential damages of the Bravo test undermined their health and subsistence as well as their community integrity, and their psychosocial well-being was further damaged by their treatment as human subjects in biomedical experiments.[44] The Rongelapese affected by the radioactive Bravo fallout were monitored in a massive, long-term scientific experimental study on the effects of human uptake of radioactive isotopes called Project 4.1, "Study of Response of Human Beings Exposed to Significant Beta and Gamma Radiation Due to Fall-Out from High Yield Weapons." This was an elaborate study that documented the radiation effects on the acutely exposed populations from Rongelap and Utrok in comparison to control populations. No medical treatment was provided by the scientists for the burns that sometimes went as deep as the bone, and today the exposed communities continue to feel that they were used unwittingly in an experiment without their consent.

In addition to forced participation in Project 4.1, the women began to experience birth defects. After I had known Lijon Eknilang for a year, I asked of her experiences on Rongelap during and after the Bravo shot. She described to me how the women of Rongelap, like the women of Utrok, suffered from miscarriage pregnancies, stillborn births, and live births of malformed fetuses that were not recognizable as human, referred to as "jellyfish" or "clam" babies. These intergenerational effects continued to happen in the subsequent decades and were a prime reason for imposing self-exile. Beyond the horrific nature of the birth defects was the shame and social stigma experienced by those women, as well as a general fear that the radiation was contagious. Such medical and emotional trauma was also experienced by residents on other atolls irradiated by the Bravo test, but further complicating their consequential damages is the fact that the U.S. government still does not officially recognize their exposure despite declassified documents that confirm the high levels of radiation exposure on atolls such as Ailuk. My host mother on "unexposed" Ailuk, for example, hinted to me about past birth defects on the atoll. Without official recognition linking abnormal births to the radioactive fallout, the Ailuk women and their families internalized their shame and humiliation.[45]

Compounding these overt damages to the Rongelapese and other Marshallese affected by the nuclear tests is a daily bombardment of symbolic violence. Symbolic violence is an unconscious mode of domination subtly embedded in everyday thought, practices, and objects that maintains its power precisely because it is not recognized as violence. The complete erasure of the history, experiences, and legacies of nuclear testing in the Marshall Islands permeates our popular culture. This started even before the first test. The two-piece swim suit, first modeled by Micheline Bernardini in 1946, was designed by French clothing designer Louis Réard just prior to the detonation of the first nuclear test in the Marshall Islands. Comparing the anticipated nuclear armageddon to the societal effects wrought by the new suit, Réard named it "bikini."[46] Such erasure of history happens even younger when children watch SpongeBob SquarePants, the cartoon character whose origin derives from radioactivity in the depths of Bikini lagoon. Beyond Bikini, the radioactive fallout from the Bravo test reached the Japanese fishing vessel *Daigo Fukuryu Maru* (Lucky Dragon No. 5), and the crew's reports of a thrashing "sea monster" inspired Ishiro Honda's 1954 film *Gojira* (Godzilla).

These and other examples of symbolic violence have become normalized even to the Marshallese, but recently Marshallese government representatives immediately condemned an utter misappropriation of their past. In 2012, a haunted house event in Rockville, Maryland, featured a zombie apocalypse that made an explicit connection to the radioactive burns of the Rongelapese documented but not treated under Project 4.1. This Halloween attraction, called "The Warehouse: Project 4.1," imagines how a private company continued to conduct experiments on the nuclear victims of the Bravo test, which resulted in the creation of mutant zombies: "Quarantine rooms, blood-smeared walls and eerie lighting fill a large abandoned warehouse while heaps of zombies lurk around narrow halls and extend decaying hands through rusted cages at those who pass by."[47] Commenting online to newspaper articles, many Marshallese offered scathing criticisms, and government official Tony deBrum instantly condemned the attraction as a "sad example of gross insensitivity."[48] Being connected to the creation of zombies adds another layer of dehumanizing experiences for the Rongelapese and other Marshallese affected by the nuclear testing. This is perhaps the ultimate example of exactly the kind of symbolic violence and emotional suffering that the Marshallese are so fervently trying to overcome as they seek both justice and forging an identity not based on victimhood.

Holly Barker and Barbara Johnston, following in the wake of other applied anthropologists helping the Marshallese seek reparations and other forms of social justice, have comprehensively traced these and other consequential damages of the nuclear testing and responding acts of resistance.[49] Building on their foundational work is the impact of the nuclear era to the voyaging traditions as experienced and expressed by the Rongelapese elders steeped in navigation lore. In an instant, the 1954 Bravo test prevented Isao Eknilang, Lijon Eknilang, Willie Mwekto, and others, then in their early childhood, from continuing their learning of navigation on Rongelap. Captain Korent was only six years old at the time, but he has clear impressions of the blast that he witnessed from Kwajalein some 120 miles to the south.

Now there's something different in the story of our growing up and living on Bikini, Rongelap, Rongerik, and Ailinginae because when my ancestors lived and grew up on these atolls they had their customs. Their culture was very strong. They didn't need to look for food. They got their food from coconuts and pandanus on the islands. They ate fish from the ocean. But after the time of the bomb they moved from the places where pandanus grew.

After the bomb, when I was six years old in 1954, I stayed on Kwajalein. After three years, the two of us, my grandfather Henri (short for Hemmerik) and I, returned to Rongelap. When I was eleven, in 1959, I started to learn how to sail the canoe with him. The two of us sailed and he began to tell me about the many waves. He took me to the school at the reef where he had learned. Every day we sailed to Ane Aitok, straight north from Rongelap islet. There was no food on Rongelap so we sailed to Ane Aitok and brought back food every day. He showed me the waves when we went sailing. On the way home we would stop at the training reef during low tide. We learned at the reef about ten times during those five years.

When I saw the bomb's light, I stood up in the house on Kwajalein and looked down, as it was very bright. I didn't know what it was but I thought it was a very big moon. Wow, everything was very bright. I could see some smoke, but I was thinking at that time it was a cloud—a very big cloud. It's only 120 miles from Kwajalein to Bikini. So I can see the cloud and it's really a big cloud. My mother stayed on Ebeye but all the children of my mother's younger sister got burned. Even my grandmother and grandfather all got burned—everybody there.

Two young men were fishing. One still lives. When the radiation fell on the two of them, they said "snow." Early in the morning one young man said to the other, "Ah, it's snowing in the Marshalls." He said snow fell on everything.

All the elder navigation teachers were from Rongelap. Some of them died and some stayed—Lapedpedin stayed; Antak also stayed there; Monean stayed on Kwajalein; Iturtak stayed there; Jiblik stayed there; and Joob lived and stayed there. Of all the elders, half died. They were old, very old. There were some that were sixty years old, some seventy years old. I saw those guys. They bathed in water that was contaminated.

The Rongelap people have stopped going to the place at the reef to learn navigation because there are no more people there. I would have learned many things if I had stayed on the island, such as making canoes. I probably would have made my canoe and its measurements. If I had stayed on the island I would now know canoe-building. But due to the bomb I haven't returned to study. I repeat, if I had stayed on the atoll I would know these skills. My knowledge has not yet grown like that of my ancestors. I haven't learned yet how to build canoes or how to sail. I don't know how to build canoes now.

The bomb stopped everything. If the bomb didn't happen, Henri would have taught the school or asked the chiefs if he could teach.

There are no teachers now. If we were to return there, all the old teachers are gone. There is Isao. He can teach but he cannot go out sailing. They said it's okay if you drink coconuts, and they ate coconut crabs and other foods. My grandfather Henri went to small islets and caught coconut crabs and ate them secretly. But he knew it was bad food. Nevertheless, he wanted to eat. Even though he knew he was already sick with poison [radiation] he never changed his lifestyle. Every day he went fishing, climbed coconut trees, and moved around. I saw him in Hawai'i at Queen's Hospital when I came to Honolulu. I didn't see his death. He was buried on Kwajalein on a small islet alongside his wife.

But what can I do? There is nothing we can do. He told me to go ahead and enjoy my life. My grandfather comes from Bikini and the Bikini people allowed the bomb to be dropped. He used to travel back and forth all the time, but no more after the bomb. Those people didn't know what the bomb meant. There was no understanding.

They tested the bomb and studied how to end the war. And that means that when the Americans asked they said it was good. If another war comes you will drop the bomb to end it. You will drop the bomb and end all wars. That means that they didn't understand the bomb, right?

Nothing is left. The history of the Marshall Islands ended. There was no food. The chiefs didn't stay on Bikini or Rongelap. They moved to Ebon, Namorik, Kili, Jaluit, and Kwajalein. Sometimes people say they are fortunate or blessed because they receive money from America. But I tell them otherwise. The bomb forced us into exile—we don't have any land of our own, and we can't return to our islands.[50]

In 1959, two years after the Rongelap community's resettlement on their home island, the young Korent began quietly learning at the age of eleven from his ailing grandfather, Hemmerik Lewia, first at the simulation reef and then during lagoon fishing trips. His grandfather took him to the training reef about ten times, and they sailed to one of the small islets on Rongelap almost every day. Hemmerik would talk to Korent and simply call out "Navigation sign!" each time an ocean-based navigational signal could be felt within the deep lagoon waters. They also sailed to Ailinginae and Rongerik several times. Korent studied navigation for five years, but by then his grandfather suffered from severe radiation sickness. By this time, the community was convinced their homeland was still radioactive despite the response from the U.S. government that it was safe for human habitation and subsistence. This state of fear drove the family to decide that Korent, now sixteen, should leave. Later, completely distrustful of scientific reports claiming the land was suitable for life, the community resettled on distant islands, where they remain today, including the previously uninhabited islet of Mejatto on Kwajalein. Living in near-permanent exile with great uncertainty about the possibility of returning to their ancestral island, Captain Korent and his Rongelapese family effectively became nuclear refugees (*jipǫkwe*). When talking about Rongelap, Captain Korent reminisces about catching coconut crabs, fishing, and hunting for lobsters, but those memories often shift to a sad longing, with his ending of the story issuing a final statement about living in exile.

Captain Korent's story highlights the missed opportunity for him and others to become navigators from Rongelap. Not only did he and the others lose their teachers to the effects of radiation exposure, but they also lost the requisite community infrastructure to build and sail voyaging canoes once they became displaced and relocated to distant islands, first on Ejit islet on Majuro in 1954 and then on Mejatto on Kwajalein in 1985. Even if their elders had desired to continue their teachings on those islands, verbal instruction alone would have been insufficient for amassing the required embodied knowledge that rests primarily on feeling the waves indirectly through the motion of a canoe. Without that experience, they could not attempt their *ruprup jǫkur* sailing tests, and without such a trial at sea they could not obtain the title of navigator. Yet through these devastating social changes, the traditional protocols of chiefly authority in controlling who would take and pass their *ruprup jǫkur* test seem to have stayed strongly intact.

The teenage Korent left the Marshall Islands in 1968 for Hawai'i, where he finished high school and attended a maritime academy in Honolulu. He returned to the Marshall Islands to captain government cargo and transportation ships and later guided search and rescue vessels.

> I moved to Honolulu in 1968 after starting high school on Majuro. I fell in love and we left for Honolulu, where I finished the eleventh grade at McKinley High School. I met a man named Captain Albertson after reading about him in the newspaper. I did not have any money, but he let me stay with him, and he paid my tuition. I studied at the maritime academy for two years, and he taught me how to navigate by taking sights with a compass. I graduated with a certificate for firefighting and damage control. I was the first Marshallese to graduate from that maritime academy. One time he asked me, "Why

don't you tell us how you navigate in your islands?" I didn't really think about it at the time because I really liked using the sextant. I never mentioned anything about what I knew. I just stayed calm.

In 1970 I returned to Majuro but then found work in Canada working on an oil rig. My parents and the high commissioner wrote a letter to the Division of Transportation in the Marshall Islands to let me work on our government boats. I started as third officer, then second officer, and finally became the captain. I later transferred to a company operating out of Saipan with a four thousand tonnage license. After three years I came back and worked as a captain on the *Ralik Ratak* transporting cargo. Sometimes the radar of the *Ralik Ratak* wouldn't work, but that ship never ran aground. Before you would reach the island, you would feel the current—it would wake you up!

After four years I was transferred to the sea patrol. I captained the patrol boat *Lomoor* over the entire 200 [miles of] exclusive economic zones for the entire archipelago. I worked with the sea patrol for twelve years doing search and rescue. One time I rescued an American who fell from a plane and disappeared between Mejit and Johnston Atoll. The hydraulic control of the airplane failed. I found him ninety miles northeast of Mejit. I got an award from the American ambassador. I was involved in many kinds of these rescues, especially rescuing young Marshallese men who ran out of fuel. Sometimes I brought back people who were sick before they built the airport in 1982. Before that, all the rescues were done with *Lomoor*.[51]

Captain Korent made his own observations of the waves while working on the government vessels and discreetly discussed his ideas with one of his former Rongelapese elders, Reban Okjenlan. Working on the vessel *Ralik Ratak*, named after the two island chains, Reban secretly gave Captain Korent his navigation test, and despite the fact that his grandmother's brother had tried to trick him, Captain Korent knew his correct position. Although he had learned sextant-based celestial navigation at the maritime academy in Honolulu, he knew his position from the slight wave-induced movements of this four thousand-ton ship. Shame would have come to Captain Korent's grandfather if the chief would have learned of the unsanctioned teaching, so Reban decided to remain quiet:

Reban Okjenlan was my mother's uncle. He was the chief officer on *Ralik Ratak*. He also graduated from the Rongelap navigation school and had sailed with me. I was the captain and he was the chief officer. Because I came from Honolulu I used the sextant, but he knows local navigation. We went all over the Marshall Islands on the *Ralik Ratak*. Sometimes he would try to fool me. One time we were heading to Namorik and he steered in a westerly direction, the wrong way. We were supposed to see land about four o'clock. I knew. I came up to the deck and told him. He laughed. I caught him two times. Maybe I passed my test. I think he could not tell me because he knew I could use the sextant. He didn't tell the chief. If you don't pass the test, the chief cannot use you. If the chief says, "Take me to another island," then you know you have passed. A Marshallese proverb is "Only the chief knows." I am scared. *Jipǫkwe* is an old word for exile. My elders told me, "If you fail the test move away from Rongelap and don't ever come back." So I only told them that I know how to navigate with a sextant. I have never been able to tell anyone what I know because my grandfather decided himself to teach me. He did not want me to get lost when I sailed from Rongelap to Kwajalein. But the chief didn't know. People saw me and Reban together and they think he taught me. Many people ask me to teach them, but I do not want to tell them. I just tell them that I don't know.[52]

Captain Korent sailed with Reban on the *Ralik Ratak* but could not share with anyone what he had learned or proven to his uncle unless he wanted to risk living in exile (*jipǫkwe*). Captain Korent uses the term *jipǫkwe* to also characterize his disconnection to Rongelap. Some two decades later, one of Captain Korent's teachers, Lapedpedin, shared similar sentiments, as emphasized in the second epigraph. He continues, with a tinge of optimism in the possibility of returning to his voyaging and navigation roots: "My people have all lost happiness to sail. And no one to say, 'Alright! Enough of this drifting westward. Let us tack back and see what we find.'"[53]

The nuclear testing severely contributed to the demise of the stronghold of navigation in the northern atolls of Adjokḷā, with a virtual cessation of voyaging throughout the archipelago characterizing the rest of the twentieth century. The voyaging-related impacts of the nuclear testing extended beyond Captain Korent's generation. A younger extended family member, Alson Kelen, spent several years of his childhood on Bikini in the 1970s when the community had temporarily resettled. Alson, who until Captain Korent's recent passing was serving as his navigation apprentice, reflects on this time on Bikini:

I was born on the island of Ebeye on Kwajalein in 1968. My biological mother, Army Jakio, is from Bikini in the northern part of the western chain of atolls, and my biological father, Bear Lanje, is from Ailinglaplap to the south in the central part of the western chain. When I was two weeks old, I was adopted by my maternal grandfather's sister, Lirok Joash, and my granduncle, Kelen Joash. In our culture, if a member of your family does not bear any children, other members of the extended family with children are obligated to give a child to him or her to become their caretaker. My adopted parents are from Bikini in the northern Marshall Islands. During the testing years, the people from Bikini, including my adopted parents, were relocated to other islands in the Marshall Islands. In 1968, the U.S. declared the island was safe to resettle. My maternal grandfather, Andrew Jakio, settled Bikini along with all his brothers and sisters.

My adopted family and I stayed on Ebeye until 1974 when we relocated to Bikini. We moved there so that my adopted mother could take care of her mother, who was very old. I can still remember going fishing on Bikini. It is surrounded by long white beaches, which did not really exist on Ebeye. I would spend most of my days enjoying the beautiful beaches and fishing. We did not have any television, but every day my dad would use his arm as a pillow and he would ask me to close my eyes, and he would tell me all kinds of stories about canoes and sailing, about sailing between Rongelap and Kwajalein. He had sailed all around the northern atolls. He sailed along with his father and others. They all used traditional navigation. They mainly sailed for bringing things to and from Bikini and Rongelap.

If we would have stayed longer on Bikini, the canoes and navigation would have been a part of my upbringing. We did have a canoe, and there was one boat on the island. Before coming to Bikini, on Ebeye, I had never seen a canoe. My mother's father was a canoe builder, and he made a canoe and gave it to my adopted parents. I watched him make it, but at the time it was not really my interest. But when the canoe was finished I would skip school to go on it. We never had anything like that on Ebeye. My dad would try to not tell me he was going fishing, since he knew I would skip school. Fishing and sailing became the biggest source of fulfillment in my life. I would listen intently when my dad would talk at night about his experiences on the canoe. Sometimes even the teachers would take us fishing, and that would be part of the day's lesson. Everyone was very happy.

In 1978, I saw three ships come to Bikini. They were the high commissioners of the Trust Territory to talk with my grandfather. They wanted to move the Bikinians from there. We packed up our clothing and our pet pig, our canoe, and other valuable things. Then we moved to the tiny island of Kili where my biological grandfather and his brothers, still on the ship, declared that they would not get off the ship. They told all the women to stay on Kili until they could find somewhere else to live. We had our canoe on Kili, but the swells were too big and it rotted away, along with our traditional skills. My biological grandfather knew this ahead of time, and didn't want to struggle. They wanted to live. We stayed on Kili for a few months until my adopted father broke his jaw on a boat because the waves were so big. That was the end of Kili for us. We came to Ejit on Majuro in 1979. My grandfather came ahead to make those arrangements. At that time Ejit was a place for plantations to be grown on Majuro. So now we had a lagoon but no canoes.[54]

Decline and Resistance

With the termination of the navigation training on Rongelap and the forced exile of the Adjokḷā communities, traditional voyaging in this stronghold came to a complete stop; only in the Kapinmeto atolls of Ujae, Lae, and Wotho did the traditions remain somewhat intact. Compounding this loss of the use of traditional skills were pronounced societal changes in the postnuclear era introduced by the administration of the U.S. Trust Territory of the Pacific. The "motor-boat revolution"[55] that swept across the region in the 1960s introduced convenient, fast transportation through imported fiberglass and metal motorboats. With a growing cash economy and relatively inexpensive fuel costs, the Marshallese deemed these new vessels more profitable for fishing than the wind-dependent canoes, and they also connoted prestige, modernity, and success in an increasingly monetized world.[56] These vessels were fast, reliable, and could be launched anytime regardless of the wind conditions. In less than a generation, many of the atoll communities throughout the archipelago had shifted entirely to these new modes of sea transportation.

The shifting visibility of oceangoing canoes was a tangible indication of this state of decline of traditional voyaging and the rise of the outboard motorboats. Carucci observed during his early fieldwork on Ujelang in 1976 and 1977 that the last of the seaworthy canoes on the atoll were being constructed. Of the four built canoes, only one, a thirty-foot vessel, was still being sailed on Enewetak in 1983. This canoe quickly fell into disrepair due to a combination of the owner's advanced age and lack of canoe-building materials on Enewetak. Although the Enewetakese had been partly repatriated from Ujelang after their forced exodus during the nuclear testing, the atoll had just been recently replanted, so no materials were available for the canoe's maintenance.[57]

Significant shifts in social organization have paralleled the decline of canoes. The communal nature of the construction, sailing, and maintenance of canoes changed during the influx of the cash economy and an emphasis on individual possessiveness. Central to the fabric of Marshallese culture was the weaving of the pandanus sails by the women, the plaiting of sennit and sharing of stories by the older men, the constant maintenance of the canoe by the men, and the rushing of boys from shore to help beach the canoe in exchange for part of one's catch. Carucci noted on Ujelang and Enewetak, for instance, that these solidarity-building reciprocal activities among the community had faded almost entirely.[58]

Some mariners applied their navigational knowledge on the newly purchased outboard motorboats. Stories linger today of a few navigators who regularly motored their small fishing vessels between atolls. Lewis, whose pan-Pacific survey of navigation techniques in the late 1960s and early 1970s involved talking and sailing with surviving navigators, seemed to have missed a chance to voyage with one of the last master navigators of the Marshall Islands. Lewis visited Majuro in 1976 and met with Captain Leonard deBrum. Leonard was the son of Raymond deBrum and grandson of Joachim deBrum, whose Portuguese father José deBrum had moved to the Marshall Islands during the German colonial administration. In the early 1960s, Raymond co-wrote two articles on navigation that have provided a distinctive insider voice on the salient features of the wave navigation system. And Raymond's father Joachim had previously provided some navigation information to Captain Winkler of the German navy in 1898 and preserved in writing his knowledge of weather forecasting. Lewis discussed with Leonard his understandings of the navigational information written by his father Raymond and by Winkler on the knowledge of Leonard's grandfather Joachim. Leonard apparently offered to immediately demonstrate to Lewis his navigation techniques at sea, but Lewis reluctantly declined because he had to catch a plane to Hawai'i![59]

This encounter speaks to continuity of navigational knowledge within the deBrum family, centered on Likiep in the Ratak chain. Although Lewis does not provide information on what type of vessel Leonard would have taken to sea, the meeting of these two navigators suggests the likelihood of the continuing practices of some interisland voyaging in outboard motorboats. The present-day maritime community shares stories that describe several instances in more recent times of short voyages undertaken with outboard motors without the aid of navigation instruments. Such voyages typically occur between closely spaced atolls that are intervisible, such as the ten-mile crossing between Majuro and Arno, or close enough that a large target area is deemed not navigationally difficult. For instance, Alton Albious regularly made the thirty-mile crossing north from Namu to Kwajalein, a target almost impossible to miss considering the ninety-mile breadth of the atoll.

Only one person remembered among the maritime community today stands out as having voyaged longer distances in recent times. Toshiro Jokon regularly traveled by motorboat between Maloelap and Majuro, a distance of eighty miles. Captain Korent used to work for the government's search and rescue operations, and one time he was called to find Toshiro. In the mid-1990s, Toshiro had been motoring around Maloelap when he ran out of fuel. Although he was within sight of land, Toshiro began to drift. Two days later, Captain Korent found him based on estimates of current drift. Toshiro, who passed away in 2003, apparently suffered a decline in his physical and mental abilities to voyage after his drifting at sea. Whispered stories of Toshiro's panicked state of *wiwijt* are a tragic reminder of the cultural ramifications of a navigator becoming lost at sea.

Leonard deBrum of Likiep, Alton Albious of Namu, and Toshiro Jokon of Maloelap represent some of the few remembered mariners who applied their navigational skills on outboard motorboats in the postnuclear world of the latter half of the nineteenth century. Undoubtedly there were other such navigators who continued to navigate short distances. Meanwhile, the Ronge-lapese and Bikinians watched silently as their navigational skills became re-tained only in memory. Although mariners such as Leonard, Alton, and Toshiro hailed from different regions of the archipelago and likely held differ-ent interpretations of the waves, they shared one thing in common: they were still highly constrained by the rigid protocols of the use and sharing of navi-gational knowledge. Even after Captain Korent saved Toshiro at sea, he could not share with anyone that he knew how to navigate. And after Toshiro's death, Captain Korent could still not claim expertise even though he had be-come one of the last reputed navigators.

While the navigational skills of the people of Bikini and Rongelap di-minished to mere memory, in the 1980s their exiled community and neighbor-ing residents on Kwajalein used their preserved knowledge of canoe sailing as an act of resistance. In 1960, two years after the last nuclear test in the Marshall Islands, the U.S. military expanded its installation on Kwajalein. More than four thousand residents from two-thirds of the atoll were relocated to the islet of Ebeye to allow the use of Kwajalein as a bulls-eye target for the testing of intercontinental ballistic missiles (ICBMs). Dissatisfied with the emerging agreement to lease the land, which formed the heart of the unfold-ing Compact of Free Association between the United States and the newly sovereign Marshall Islands, the landowners peacefully protested their reloca-tion and appalling living conditions on Ebeye, their disagreement over eco-nomic compensation, the length of the lease of their land, the possibility of making their nation an exclusive U.S. military preserve, and their overall ill treatment. Their way of protesting involved launching a series of canoe "sail-ins" between 1977 and 1982. By sailing canoes to several islets that were re-stricted in the testing range, the residents of Kwajalein succeeded in disrupting several ballistic missile tests. These protests climaxed with a four-month long "sail-in" coined "Operation Homecoming" that eventually expanded to more than one thousand Marshallese demonstrating on restricted islands enabled by canoe travel. These acts of resistance forced the United States to re-negotiate the developing Compact of Free Association, which economically and militarily linked the two nations with its enactment in 1986.[60]

The voyages of resistance at Kwajalein were effective in part due to the clear symbolism of canoes with traditional culture, but after the inaugural canoe protests the Marshallese developed other ways to express their dissatisfaction with the limited scope of reparations.[61] As part of the negotiations of the Compact of Free Association under Section 177, the United States agreed to provide monetary compensation to members of only four island communities officially recognized as exposed to nuclear radiation: Enewetak, Rongelap, Utrok, and Bikini. This legislation also established the Nuclear Claims Tribunal to review and award nuclear-related personal injury and property damage. The funds, however, were vastly insufficient and the compensation could not extend to individuals beyond the four atolls such as my family on Ailuk. Asking the U.S. Congress for additional compensation would require acceptance of a Changed Circumstances Petition, which to date has been denied despite the new information that has surfaced. In the late 1990s, Johnston and Barker chronicled the damages to the Rongelapese from their perspective in their own voices, sifted through the newly declassified documents, and submitted their report to the Nuclear Claims Tribunal in 2001. In 2007 the Nuclear Claims Tribunal awarded over $1 billion for remediation and restoration of Rongelap and Rongerik and damages to a loss of way of life, as well as personal injuries from living in a radioactive environment and from human radiation experimentation. However, securing the funds to actually pay for the award to the nuclear survivors would take legislative approval from the U.S. Congress.[62]

Against these structural barriers to their rehabilitation and as a culturally appropriate way to resist the U.S. government's representations of their history and lived experiences, the Marshallese compose and perform lyrical songs and poetry in their efforts to heal. Sung in Marshallese and in a humorous style to ease the pain, "Mr. Urine" tells of the dehumanizing examinations of Rongelapese male and female patients enrolled in Project 4.1 who had to urinate in front of each other. The letters of the song "ERUB"—also the Marshallese term *erub* (to explode)—stand for the four officially recognized contaminated atolls and remind people within the Marshallese community how the nuclear testing program impacted other atoll populations. The "177 Song," in reference to section 177 of the Agreement of the Compact of Free Association, speaks of emotional trauma and longing for a peaceful existence.[63] Contemporary Marshallese poets—the children and grandchildren of survivors—continue to compose pieces about the legacies of nuclear testing to raise awareness beyond the Marshall Islands. For instance, Kathy Jetnil-Kijiner's poem, "History Project," describes the pain and anger she feels in trying to share the experiences of her people to an audience of insensitive non-Marshallese judges in a high school history fair. Her poem refuses to let the violence of nuclear testing be forgotten or easily explained away:

> God will thank you, they told us
> Yeah, as if God himself ordained those powdered flakes to drift onto our
>   skin, our hair, our eyes, to seep into our bones
> We mistook radioactive fallout for snow
> God will thank you, they told us
> As if God has just been waiting for my people to vomit, vomit, vomit all of
>   humanity's sins onto impeccable white shores gleaming like the cross
>   burned into our open scarred palms
> At one point in my research I stumble along a photograph of goats tied to
>   American ships bored and munching on tubs of grass
> At the bottom the caption read
> "Goats and pigs were left on naval ships as test subjects"
> "Thousands of letters flew in from America protesting animal abuse"
> At fifteen I want megatons of TNT, radioactive energy, and a fancy degree
> Anything and everything I could ever need to send ripples of death through
>   a people who puts goats before human beings
> So their skin can shrivel beneath the glare of hospital room lights
> Three generations later as they watch their grandmother, their mother, their
>   cousin's life drip across that same black screen
> Knots of knuckles tied to steel beds cold and absent of any breath
> But I'm only fifteen[64]

"History Project" is grounded in survivors' stories and testimonies about their lived experiences with radiation and living in exile. Some of these stories were voiced in the late 1990s by the Rongelapese in their overt attempt to seek social justice for the myriad social, biological, and environmental damages from the nuclear testing and its program of biomedical experimentation.[65]

It was not until a chorus of Rongelapese voices called for improvements to their community's social and cultural health that chiefly permission for elders to instruct their youth in navigation began to be openly discussed. This idea ultimately took form when, as described in this chapter's opening vignette, Captain Korent journeyed to Rongelap to begin to share his knowledge of navigation as he had learned it in his youth, but not before visiting the resting place of his ancestors. With the Rongelapese navigation lingering only in the minds of its last guardians, Captain Korent became the unsung champion to resurrect the old navigation skills. This time at the dawn of the millennium was characterized by a colossal shift in the protocols and regulations of navigational knowledge. For the first time in the Rongelap community, the chiefs were about to open the knowledge beyond family lines of inheritance, but that very act would paradoxically weaken the traditional context that gave it meaning in the first place. Sentiments of losing their identity as a navigator were so strong that some elders preferred, against the directive of their chief, not to share their knowledge and even take it, literally in written format, to their graves. Alson Kelen and I walked into this tense atmosphere as we began our own navigation of how to possibly revive this nearly lost art of still-guarded wave navigation.

Chapter 4

Navigating the Cultural Revival of Voyaging

In the old days, the chief hid the secrets of navigation and could kill people or throw them off of the land if they revealed the secret knowledge. Even today, one must obtain permission from one's chief before revealing this knowledge to anyone.

—Anthropologist Jack Tobin[1]

We must *jitdaṃ kapeel in meto* (seek knowledge of the ocean).

—Bikini navigation apprentice Alson Kelen[2]

~　　~　　~

eaving Captain Korent behind, Alson Kelen and I step off the small twin-turboprop plane with trepidation into the scorching sun of the shadeless, cleared strip of coral that serves as the atoll's runway. Although I had flown several times to other atolls, I am still amazed at how the pilot lands the plane, with its deflated tires to avoid puncture on the crushed coral rocks that make up the seemingly short length of the runway. We exhale a small sigh of relief as we come to a stop on the main islet on the atoll of Namu in the central portion of the Rālik chain. We look for our main contact, an aged navigator named Alton Albious. Neither Alson nor I have family connections to this community, and Captain Korent could not leave his work to accompany us. Without established relationships, we know we will have to tread very carefully when introducing our project to work with Alton. Armed with a high sensitivity to broaching the topic of navigation, I am animated to meet a navigator who has apparently completed his *ruprup jọkur* voyage. My excitement is instantly put in check.

As Alson and I walk down the stairway, looking, as always, for recognizable faces, we both feel an immediate, palpable undercurrent of hostility. One individual speaks quietly to his friends as he approaches us, "These men are going to learn our knowledge of navigation and go back." As our first day unfolds, people often approach us to ask, "When are you going to leave?" This question was often posed when I had visited other atoll communities and might arise out of a frank inquisitives of the duration of the stay, but now Alson and I both detect an underlying harshness to the question. We follow the progression of men toward Alton's house, and no one speaks a word. We learn shortly that Alton did not personally meet us at the airport because he was effectively immobile—his legs had been amputated as a result of complications with adult-onset diabetes.

As Alson and I discover on Namu over the course of the next three weeks living with Alton, the process of metaphorically navigating the revival of voyaging is like clinging to the deck of a canoe during a violent storm. The old protocols surrounding navigation are still in effect and pull us toward a mode of silence and secrecy. The survival of a few aged navigators gives us the opposite imperative to almost force the sharing of knowledge before it is lost forever with their passing. Pulled in different directions, Alson and I, as the cofacilitators of the voyaging revival, constantly feel like our figurative vessel is about to capsize. In this chapter, I reflect on our collective experiences of navigating the revitalization of voyaging in the Marshall Islands.

The precarious nature of twenty-first-century cultural revitalization in the Marshall Islands follows in the wake of previous attempts to restore the sailing canoes. An influx of development that swept through the region in the postnuclear era hastened the decline of voyaging, and it was only the efforts in the late 1980s of an American boat builder, inspired by the feats of *Hōkūle'a*, that helped bring the canoes back. What started out as a salvage documentation project of canoe designs and the construction process on a few atolls shifted to a training program for youth to build their own canoes. These efforts of canoe revitalization spurred a democratization of canoe building and sailing, where the knowledge has essentially escaped the strict chiefly regulations of lineage-based traditions and is now open to everyone. This resurgence inspired Captain Korent to share his knowledge—knowledge that, unlike canoe building, has retained to a high degree its traditional chiefly authority, power, and prestige. An increased potency of a virtually unpracticed knowledge made the revival project challenging for myself as an outside academic researcher, for Alson as a Marshallese researcher and navigation apprentice, and for Captain Korent, who was not yet a titled navigator. Sharing the knowledge might allow for the preservation of the old ways of navigating, but it would also ensure the loss of power and prestige of its owner! It was this tension that Alson and I faced on Namu when, upon our landing, we were prematurely charged with stealing the community's knowledge.

Salvage Documentation

Near the close of the twentieth century, the social infrastructure of voyaging had declined to such an extent that only a few atolls continued to build and sail canoes for regular transportation, and among these communities travel was limited to lagoon sailing or sailing immediately offshore. The persistent use of traditional canoes in these few atoll communities caught the attention of American boat-builder Dennis Alessio. In 1988, Dennis had sailed to the Marshall Islands on *Tole Mour*, a schooner that facilitated medical attention for inhabitants on the outer atolls. He was shocked to discover that most of the vessels were made of plywood or aluminum and powered with outboard motors. Inspired by the experimental voyages of *Hōkūleʻa*, Dennis pledged to preserve and facilitate the revival of the building and sailing of the long and graceful canoes that had first captured the attention of Kotzebue in the early nineteenth century.

Through the government's cultural Alele Museum, Dennis developed a project in 1989 called Waan Aelōñ Kein (Canoes of These Islands) to work with the surviving canoe builders to document their designs and construction techniques of the various classes of outrigger sailing canoes. A kind of salvage ethnography, Dennis documented regional variations in the canoes by enlisting the help of carvers from Jaluit, Likiep, Namorik, Ailuk, Enewetak, and then on Ujae with the collaboration of his new Marshallese counterpart Alson Kelen.[3] Dennis was particularly impressed with Alson's ancestral and emotional connections to the canoes and his willingness to learn ethnographic documentation methods.

During the documentation projects, Dennis observed the construction process of the canoes by apprenticing himself to master canoe builders. At this time in the late 1980s and early 1990s, the transfer of canoe-building knowledge was still highly regulated by each carver's governing chief, despite the clear decline in the use of canoes. As Dennis was a cultural outsider to the Marshallese communities, the canoe builders, guided by their chiefs, usually adopted Dennis into their families. This way, the knowledge would, in a sense, stay tightly linked to their lineage of canoe specialists. As a ship builder himself, Dennis also had an immediate connection to help build rapport with the builders.

In preparation for the 1992 Pacific Arts Festival on Rarotonga in the southern Cook Islands, Dennis shifted the focus of Waan Aelōñ Kein to the documentation of the building of a large oceangoing canoe (*walap*) and the facilitation of a long-distance voyage. He organized a project with canoe builders of Enewetak. Carucci had previously observed the last construction of smaller, seaworthy Enewetak canoes on Ujelang in the late 1970s but knew that a few elders retained the ability to construct the larger forms. Images from Enewetak during the nuclear era show *walap* of sixty-five feet in length. The extraordinary size of these canoes, very sleek in design with a narrow hull, made them well suited to the turbulent waters surrounding Enewetak.

Enewetak canoe builders constructed the *walap* on Majuro for the Waan Aelōñ Kein project, directed by the Alele Museum. Dennis recruited Lombwe Mark, a master canoe builder at seventy-one years of age, and his slightly younger assistant, Hertes John, to build the canoe. With eight trainees, they carved drift logs that had washed up on the shores of Enewetak and lashed the resulting interlocking sections of a knife-edged hull, which measured a little over fifty feet in length but less than two feet across at its widest point.[4]

The building of the *walap* evoked strong atoll identities. According to Carucci, the rest of the Marshallese felt that the geographically isolated Enewetakese were less sophisticated, while the Enewetakese believed that their canoe-building skills made them superior. The building and sailing of the 1992 *walap* became a contested site of these perspectives. Other Marshallese believed the Enewetak canoe was too narrow and would collapse when encountering strong ocean waves, and the lack of naming the vessel contributed to sentiments of inferiority. But trial sails in and around Majuro demonstrated its seaworthiness and fast speed, confirming for the Enewetakese the strength of their building skills.[5]

Within the context of the newly emergent, sovereign Republic of the Marshall Islands, there was an expectation that the canoe would represent the entire nation at the 1992 pan-Pacific canoe race in the Cook Islands. The identity of the canoe as either an Enewetak canoe or a Marshallese canoe was hotly debated. The Enewetak officials threatened to withdraw the canoe from the voyage until it was accepted that the captain and sailing crew would be Enewetakese. However, Enewetak lacked a navigator and thus required an expert from beyond their atoll. Toshiro Jokon of Maloelap, the most renowned navigator at the time, was enlisted to serve as navigator.

After the *walap* was shipped to Aitutaki in the Cook Islands, the canoe builders reassembled it while Toshiro Jokon prepared to guide it with traditional navigation techniques to Rarotonga, a distance of 160 miles. In the light winds that characterized the voyage, the *walap* quickly outdistanced the heavier double canoe *Hōkūleʻa* as well as her own escort vessel, *Tole Mour.* The Marshallese had to occasionally heave-to and wait for their escort to catch up. During the night, strong waves struck the canoe and shattered the mast near its base. The crew tried to rejoin the two sections but eventually jury-rigged a shortened mast with a reefed sail to reach Rarotonga. The winning of the outrigger class race confirmed for the Enewetakese their canoe-building and sailing prowess and began to shift the attitudes of other Marshallese about the Enewetakese. But following the race, the canoe was shipped to a museum in New Zealand, where it has remained, and this marked a new sense of ambiguity for the Enewetakese.[6]

According to Dennis Alessio, Maloelap navigator Toshiro Jokon started the voyage heading south from Aitutaki to Rarotonga by detecting a dominant southeast swell. During the night, prior to the dismasting event, Toshiro began to feel how the island of Rarotonga was deflecting this southeast swell. Based on the angle and size of the swell, Toshiro sensed that the *walap* was close to land and sighted the island about the same time as the navigator aboard *Hōkūle'a*.[7] This landfall was one of the last demonstrations of traditional Marshallese wave navigation on an outrigger voyaging canoe.

After the documentation and voyage of the Enewetak *walap*, Dennis, and now his Marshallese collaborator Alson Kelen, chronicled Thomas Bokin's construction of a canoe from Ujae and experienced its maiden voyage of about 350 miles to Majuro via Kwajalein. Alson developed an apprenticed relationship to Thomas, who would later reveal that he was a titled Kapinmeto navigator. In 1996, after eighteen months of directing the canoe-building process, Thomas guided this large thirty-foot *tipñōl*, named *Laninmantol*, or "flight of the shearwater," across the sea of Lolelaplap from the Rālik to the Ratak chain. The navigational aspects of this substantial water crossing were off limits to Alson and Dennis. While they had secured the chiefly permission to document Thomas' canoe-building expertise, they were forbidden to ask questions pertaining to his navigational knowledge.

Since the salvage documentation of the canoe designs and methods of construction through Waan Aelōñ Kein, the regular building and sailing of canoes on most of the atolls has virtually disappeared. Of the five atoll communities surveyed by Dennis and Alson, only Namorik and Ailuk have continued the building and sailing of outrigger canoes for local subsistence fishing and regular intra-atoll transportation. Whereas canoe building and sailing on the urban centers of Majuro and Ebeye are strongly linked to the symbolism of traditional culture and maritime identity, activities on Namorik and Ailuk center on daily subsistence practices and gathering of materials for export. While most of the other Marshallese use motorboats for local transport of copra, the people of Namorik and Ailuk use canoes to haul the dried coconut meat from their family-owned islets to the cargo ships moored at the main villages. This is partly economical—income generation from handicraft and copra production is usually too little to pay for prohibitively expensive fuel, which in 2006 reached $4 per gallon and by 2015 spiked to $10.[8] By retaining their ability to sail, the residents of Namorik and Ailuk can offset their hunger during times when the cargo ships are delayed by lagoon and offshore fishing.[9]

Canoe building, like navigation, identifies a person within their lineage and broader atoll community in terms of their knowledge and technical ability, and this prestige contributes to the persistence of canoe building on Ailuk and Namorik. Often, the status and respect afforded a canoe builder and his family of sailors become visible to the community during races. In 2006, I witnessed the impromptu racing of two *tipñōl* on Ailuk. I watched from the beach as the two sailing canoes, having returned from a fishing expedition, came close together on converging courses. Although too distant to hear each captain's commands, it was clear to everyone onshore that the two canoes adjusted their courses to sail parallel with each other toward a distant islet. As they pulled in their sheets to harness the strong trade wind on an ideal beam reach, a crew member from each canoe moved out slightly onto the outrigger platform to keep the outrigger down. Occasionally, the bow of one of the canoes plummeted into a big wave, sending forth a massive wall of water. Having slowed down, the other canoe would race ahead. As this was happening, a crowd built around me, at first whispering and then shouting out in a cacophony of voices as one of the canoes emerged victorious. It was this still-thriving competitive spirit of racing that spurred a resurgence of canoe building and sailing in the Marshall Islands toward the close of the twentieth century.

Resurgence

Dennis Alessio and Alson Kelen had observed such impromptu lagoon races on several atolls during their Alele Museum–directed Waan Aelōñ Kein canoe documentation projects in the late 1980s and early 1990s, and they harnessed this energy toward revitalization. These efforts coincided with a shift in the vision shared by Dennis and Alson to move beyond preservation to more active engagement in revitalization. This involved an institutional shift and a name change. During the 1992 Pacific Arts Festival in Rarotonga, Dennis and Alson became acutely aware of the fact that the Marshallese understood the name of their project, Waan Aelōñ Kein, as "Canoes of These Islands" but that other Pacific Islanders could not identify the island group! As Dennis and Alson shifted from a government-funded program to a nonprofit organization in 1996, they renamed their program Waan Aelōñ in Majol, or "Canoes of the Marshall Islands." The emphasis shifted from documentation of canoe design and construction methods to training and outreach.

When Dennis and Alson saw sailing races similar to the one I observed on Ailuk, they initiated and promoted canoe festivals and races to tap into this competitive spirit and the larger community's deep cultural connections to

canoes. The canoe races developed largely through the combined efforts of
Mary Lou Foley at the Marshall Islands Outrigger Hotel, Waan Aelōñ in Majol, and other organizations and individuals to promote the Marshallese sailing culture. Local races on various atolls with small prize incentives eventually developed into national races held annually and for special events.
Despite the fact that the races were developed only in the mid-1990s, they are
today the most celebrated cultural events in the Marshall Islands.

Annual sailing races today include the widely celebrated Coconut Cup
and President's Cup, as well as smaller races held on Culture Day. The Coconut Cup is a unique multiclass lagoon regatta with one-man *kōrkōr* and two-
man *tipñōl*, modern sailboats, dinghies, and windsurfers that is held every
spring on Majuro. The President's Cup celebrates Independence Day by racing one-man *kōrkōr* and two-man *tipñōl* on Majuro. In preparation for the
President's Cup, each atoll that wishes to enter must first hold a local competition. The winning sailing crew then represents the entire atoll at the national
race. Weeks before the 2006 President's Cup, I witnessed the local race between the two canoes on Ailuk. Onlookers wildly cheered this impromptu
race across the lagoon, but the outcome seriously decided who would represent the atoll at the national race. As is customary, however, the individual
winners humbly refrain from boasting, so that their actions would seem to be
part of the larger atoll community.

Honorary sailing races punctuate the annual events, spurring the canoe
builders and sailors to even higher levels of competition. In 2003, a mayor's
conference created an honorary sailing race in Ailinglaplap to celebrate their
liberation from the Japanese in 1944. Iroij (Chief) Mike Kabua centered the
festivities for the Liberation Day on the reenactment of the popular legend
about how the woman named Lōktañūr introduced the sail to the outrigger
paddling canoe. Just like the twelve brothers who raced across the lagoon,
twelve atolls entered their best canoes in the race. Rather than paddling, according to a strict interpretation of the legend, the canoes followed Jebrọ's
lead by sailing. Since Ailinglaplap had a limited number of seaworthy canoes,
Iroij Mike Kabua and representatives from the other atolls devised a plan to
rebuild the canoe culture of the atoll. The mayors from each participating
atoll agreed that if their canoe did not finish ahead of the Ailinglaplap canoe,
they would forfeit their canoe to the Ailinglaplap community. The Ailinglaplap canoe indeed won the race, so the other sailing teams had to leave behind their canoes. By invoking the popularity of the legend of Jebrọ, the
Ailinglaplap Liberation Day race united many atolls and strengthened a collective cultural identity.[10]

During these and other competitions and festivals, the named canoes and the family of canoe builders and sailors shine in the national spotlight. Like the Ailuk race but scaled up, on Majuro several hundreds of spectators flock to the shores to watch the events. Meanwhile, outer-island residents listen intently to live radio broadcasts. A sense of family pride from winning these events drives the competition. This is highlighted by my conversations with Ailuk sailors about an attempted voyage to Majuro. In 2000, a fleet of several *tipñōl* began to sail from Ailuk toward Majuro, a distance of over two hundred miles, to participate in the annual national sailing race. They wanted to sail their canoes rather than have them transported on a cargo ship, as had become standard procedure for outer islanders to participate in the annual events. The Ailuk skippers did not have a deep understanding of navigation techniques but were confident they would arrive in Majuro with the aid of a compass. Unfortunately, a dismasted vessel forced the fleet to prematurely return to Ailuk. Atoll pride was the greatest reason for attempting the trip. They simply wanted to prove to the other Marshallese that they, as people of Ailuk, were the best sailors and that Ailuk alone has retained its canoe-building and sailing knowledge.

Through the pioneering organization of the canoe races, Dennis and Alson tapped into the community's deep cultural connection to the canoe. The canoe remains at the core of Marshallese culture in the face of its overwhelming decline. It is in fact this loss in practical utility that paradoxically gives the canoe its elevated meaning today. For most Marshallese, the canoe is today primarily a symbol of prestige and identity. Yet largely under the influence of Waan Aelōñ in Majol, the traditional chiefly regulations governing the select use and transmission of canoe-building knowledge have undergone a process of democratization, where the knowledge has essentially become unrestricted and open to everyone.[11] Dennis and Alson initially required chiefly permission to share their knowledge with others, but as more and more students learned from them how to build canoes, the restrictive chiefly protocols began to loosen.

In addition to the shift from documentation toward facilitating canoe races, Dennis and Alson initiated and strengthened a program of intensive training for youth within Waan Aelōñ in Majol that is centered on the core cultural values of the canoe, and this has contributed to the relaxing of the chiefly protocols on the transmission of canoe knowledge. At-risk youth who have dropped out of school due to problems associated with alcohol, drugs, or other factors learn about their culture while gaining marketable job skills by learning how to build traditional outrigger canoes. The use of power tools complements traditional carving skills and provides expanded vocational skills such as modern boat building, fiberglass technology, carpentry, and woodworking. The central element in this Waan Aelōñ in Majol program is the canoe, the vitality of which stems from its democratization. And it is this slackening of the protocols that made possible an unprecedented shift in the use of navigational knowledge.

Without Precedent

The country's resurgence in traditional canoe building and sailing, largely facilitated by the founding efforts of Dennis Alessio and Alson Kelen, first through Waan Aelōñ Kein and then through Waan Aelōñ in Majol, allowed for the possibility to consider documenting and revitalizing the more powerful, hidden realms of weather forecasting and navigation. However, these related domains of voyaging knowledge had decidedly not been subjected to the widespread canoe democratization process. Whereas the canoe knowledge had become open, navigation remained unquestionably closed. Previously, during their documentation of canoe building on Ujae in the early 1990s, Dennis and Alson wanted to inquire about such extant navigational knowledge from Thomas Bokin but lacked the chiefly permission. For their governing chiefs, it was premature to proceed with documenting Kapinmeto navigation.

A shift in the potential sharing of navigational knowledge began with the Rongelap community in the late 1990s. Anthropologists Holly Barker and Barbara Johnston collected testimonies by Rongelapese survivors to ascertain the extent of damages from their experiences with the nuclear testing. The resulting report informed the Nuclear Claims Tribunal on their decision to award more than $1 billion for remediation and restoration of Rongelap and Rongerik for damages to a loss of way of life, as well as for personal injuries from living in a radioactive environment and from human radiation experimentation (although funding is sorely inadequate to pay for the award). One of the ideas voiced by the Rongelapese to begin to restore the social and cultural health of their community was the construction of a Rongelap community center. This structure would serve as a central meeting place where elders could instruct the younger generation about their customs and history, land rights, and traditional knowledge. Rongelapese knowledge and skills of canoe building and navigation were featured in these discussions.[12]

The death of Maloelap navigator Toshiro Jokon in 2003 elevated the status of Captain Korent, with his reputed depth of navigational knowledge, to that of the "last navigator" within the Rongelapese community and the broader Marshallese community. Captain Korent had followed the inspirational stories of how *Hōkūle'a* was reawakening the voyaging spirit of so many Pacific Island cultures, and he realized that the fate of Marshallese

canoe voyaging now rested with him. The Kapinmeto navigation still resided in memory with Thomas Bokin, but there did not appear to be any
active teaching of his knowledge, and Thomas, a generation older, had reportedly diminished in his mental health. Captain Korent was also driven by
a keen curiosity—he wanted Western science to validate his knowledge and
explain its lingering mysteries. Given the imperative for Dennis and Alson
to begin working with Captain Korent in earnest after Toshiro's death, the
process of tapping into his knowledge was thoroughly complicated by several factors.

Captain Korent's unsanctioned learning on Rongelap and forced exodus
as a result of the nuclear testing precluded him from attaining the formal title
of navigator (*ri-meto*), or "person of the ocean," in his youth. He had not been
able share his knowledge with anyone and only held a few secretive conversations with his teacher Reban aboard the *Ralik-Ratak* vessel during his four
decades of captaining government transport ships. Still, he made his own observations at sea, and the maritime community suspected but could not openly
articulate their belief in his navigational prowess. In line with Marshallese
directives on how to inquire about another's knowledge, no one could directly
ask Captain Korent if he knew how to navigate. This could only come through
hints, guesses, and whispers by those closest to him.

As the last presumed navigator accepting the responsibility of resurrect-
ing the nearly lost art of wave navigation, Captain Korent faced a paradox in
the use of his knowledge.[13] Any attempt to document and revitalize navigation ran the risk of recontextualizing his traditional knowledge and eroding its
relationship to chiefly authority, and it is precisely such chiefly regulation that
continues to give navigation its particular cultural significance. This had already happened to a degree with the canoe-building knowledge as a result of
the open documentation and resurgence in canoe sailing led by Waan Aelōñ in
Majol. Anyone with sufficient resources can learn how to build an outrigger
sailing canoe, and this openness is precisely why the deeper cultural meanings and sacredness of the canoes have basically disappeared. Without such
chiefly sanctioned knowledge about the canoe, it is just a vehicle. Captain
Korent felt that navigation could not just become a technical way to get from
one island to the next.

While ancient chiefly potency had been undergoing considerable change
over the past 150 years,[14] the tight link between navigation and chiefly power
that constrained Captain Korent's ability to share his knowledge in 2005
seems to have been in place at least half a century earlier when he began
learning navigation on Rongelap. He felt an obligation to maintain the navigational knowledge within his family in deference to his *iroij*. Echoing To-

bin's remarks in the opening epigraph, Captain Korent would not risk damaging his relationship to his *iroij* by violating the chiefly protocols.

A solution to Captain Korent's dilemma emerged from the traditional chiefly authority of his *iroij*. Iroij Mike Kabua and Iroijlaplap (Paramount Chief) Imata Kabua gave Captain Korent and others from Rongelap permission to share their navigational knowledge with an extended family member from Bikini—Alson Kelen—who was by then an integral member of Waan Aelōn̄ in Majol. This was without precedent.[15] For the first time, the sharing of Rongelapese navigational knowledge extended beyond direct family lines of inheritance. But at least the knowledge would initially stay within the extended family by Alson serving as Captain Korent's apprentice. However, the *iroij* also gave Captain Korent and Alson permission to enlist outside academic help, a decision that knowingly would result in the widespread distribution of the knowledge through publications, community outreach, and the development of educational materials. By this time, the rippling effects of the Hawaiian renaissance of voyaging had reached the Marshall Islands, and Dennis and Alson invited anthropologist Ben Finney to assist in their navigation revival project. After I enrolled as a graduate student in anthropology at the University of Hawai'i–Mānoa, Ben introduced me to this emerging project.

Foreign canoe builders, sailors, and academics have figured prominently as catalysts in the revival of voyaging traditions throughout Oceania. The resurgence of long-distance voyaging between the central Carolinian atolls and Saipan during the last three decades started with a challenge issued by David Lewis to the Polowatese navigator Hipour. From three generations of transmitted knowledge, Hipour accepted the challenge and successfully completed the voyage in Lewis' yacht in 1969.[16] This set in motion other collaborations to revive long-distance voyaging. Influenced by Lewis, journalist Jim Sears worked with Kiribati mariners to build and sail a large voyaging canoe 1,500 miles from Kiribati to Fiji. In Hawai'i, Finney was instrumental in reviving Polynesian voyaging by cofacilitating the construction and sailing of *Hōkūle'a* to Tahiti in 1976, while Lewis recruited Satawalese navigator Mau Piailug to guide *Hōkūle'a*.

The politics of academic research have been highly visible in Oceania, especially in regard to the Hawaiian renaissance of voyaging. Many Hawaiians viewed the participation of Finney and Lewis negatively leading up to and during the maiden Tahiti voyage, yet the outcome has been a synergy of research and cultural revival. During that tumultuous time, no one dared dream that future generations of Hawaiian navigators would be leading *Hōkūle'a* on a three-year voyage around the world (2014–2017). This has contributed to an awareness that anthropologists and other researchers in

Oceania must now consider the collapsing distinction between cultural insider and outsider and their multiple and shifting obligations, responsibilities, and audiences, where indigenous communities are increasingly asking critical questions about research. Drawing from Finney's pioneering work and sensitive to the politics of academic research, he and I worked with the leaders of Waan Aelōñ in Majol and Captain Korent to develop a collaborative and interdisciplinary project that aimed to synergistically combine navigation research with cultural revival.

The collaborative nature of the project was soon tested. Captain Korent had been able to reconcile his previously unsanctioned learning with his *iroij* and gain permission to share his knowledge with Alson, his extended family member. As an outsider with only loose "family" connections to my adopted family on Ailuk, I presented a new dilemma to the protocols of knowledge transmission. In addition, Captain Korent's reputation as the "last navigator" had led Dennis and Alson to believe that he was already a sanctioned, experienced traditional navigator.

I met Captain Korent for the first time in the fall of 2005 at the Majuro dock for the government's search and rescue vessel that he captained, and we walked with Alson to a nearby restaurant for lunch. He was soft-spoken and humble about his knowledge of navigation but was also very forthcoming in directing the revival project. He candidly revealed to us that he did not know the system of navigation in its entirety and was not yet a qualified navigator. The moment Alson and I sat down for lunch, Captain Korent shared his concerns and anxieties with us:

> I want to know how the waves work. I learned from my grandfather on Rongelap, but I don't really know why those waves come. I never took my test. My chief didn't know I was learning from my grandfather! But I think the scientists will come and they will make the waves appear on their computer. Then we will know. We do this now, you and me. This will be the last opportunity. This is why we have to do more scientific studies to work it out. We must do it the right way and everything that we can for it. Then you can put it in the computer and everybody can use it. We might just accomplish this. The chief of Rongelap already approved us to go ahead and document the navigational knowledge. But I am not sure whether I can go back to Rongelap and teach again. There is no one else.[17]

He was not a navigator! Alson and I reeled from Captain Korent's revelation, desperately trying to reconsider the scope of the quickly faltering revival project. The plan had been for Alson to learn directly from Captain Korent as his apprentice. Not knowing if we would have another meeting with him, I asked Captain Korent how Alson and I could assist him. In response to our query about how to proceed, Captain Korent conceptualized the project as a way for him to more fully learn the science of the waves with the aid of a computer model, which would allow him to finish his training. This would enable him to then undertake and complete a voyage using the wave knowledge and finally become recognized as a navigator through the process of *ruprup jọkur*. Captain Korent simultaneously envisioned that an explanation of the waves grounded in Western science would prove that Marshallese navigation was a legitimate knowledge system. He also articulated our shared understanding that for this project to be truly meaningful, the knowledge would need to be passed on to others.

Captain Korent suggested we first travel to Rongelap to see and experience the wave simulation reef of his youthful training. According to traditional protocols of instruction, experiences at this training reef came before the onshore stick chart teachings, so Alson, who would be learning as Captain Korent's apprentice navigator, should start with this primary experiential knowledge. Once this was complete, we would work with oceanographers to develop the computer model. We already had an oceanographic field study in place to investigate the wave patterns, but we had to reorient our focus. While Captain Korent would share his knowledge of the waves, he would also be learning from us. To continue his traditional training, he began to invite several elder family members, primarily from Rongelap, to discuss their navigation and weather forecasting knowledge with him. Captain Korent's role continuously shifted; he was our consultant, teacher, and colearner. An example of the latter role comes from the relationship between Captain Korent and navigator Thomas Bokin. We journeyed to Ujae, where Thomas Bokin constructed a wave model in his home to share his ideas with Captain Korent (Figure 4.1).

Alson's multiple roles and capabilities were crucial in the design, development, and implementation of the project. In addition to his family ties to Captain Korent and the Rongelapese community, Alson brought a local research perspective to the project from years of experience with Waan Aelōñ Kein and conducted interviews based on previous collaborations with ethnographically trained archaeologists with the Historic Preservation Office. Alson facilitated my Marshallese language acquisition and the translation and transcription of interviews. He served as my cultural intermediary with the community and *iroij*. With the appropriate family relationship and community ties, knowledge of canoes, and experience in anthropological research,

Figure 4.1. Author Joseph Genz (left) documenting Thomas Bokin's (center) instruction
of a stick chart wave model to Captain Korent Joel (right) on Ujae, 2006.

Alson was more than just a researcher. He apprenticed himself to Captain
Korent with the aim of becoming the next navigator.

In anticipation of learning under Captain Korent, Alson had coordinated
the building of a thirty-five-foot voyaging canoe—a small *walap*—that he
had christened *Jitdaṃ Kapeel*. Many definitions are attached to the terms
jitdaṃ ("seek knowledge, look for the true pedigree, study one's genealogy,
inquire of an authority") and *kapeel* ("skillful, clever, craft, knack, wise, astute").[18] As a common proverb, *jitdaṃ kapeel* proverbially means "seeking
knowledge guarantees wisdom."[19] With these meanings in mind, Alson designed the canoe to be an experiential learning platform for Captain Korent
and himself—a place to seek knowledge. The canoe was also a training project for the program's canoe builders. The first attempts to conduct sea trials of
the canoe revealed some dramatic effects of slight design miscalculations.
The asymmetrical shape of the hull along its long axis was not shaped to the
proper curvature, and this resulted in severe weather helm. When steering,
one person should have sufficed to raise and lower the steering paddle. But

the weather helm—the boat wanting to turn into the direction of the wind—meant that two sailors had to continuously strain to hold the canoe on course. With this difficulty in sailing, *Jitdaṃ Kapeel* remained beached for long periods of time, and poor maintenance resulted in trapped water in the hull. A complete overhaul of the design and construction, with a coat of fiberglass over its wooden hull, would eventually make the canoe seaworthy. But at the time of Captain Korent's initiation of the project, the canoe remained on shore. In a sense, this lost opportunity to voyage on a canoe was symbolic of the challenges that Alson and I were soon to face.

Drawing from the name of the canoe, Alson similarly named the revival project Kapeel in Meto, which can be glossed as "knowledge of the ocean," and this centered on a particularly resonant local concept of research. Several native communication patterns figure prominently among the navigation experts. Well versed in this suite of stories, legends, chants, songs, song-stories, and ancient language, the navigation elders had also become familiar with a newer, contemporary form of knowledge sharing. Previous historic preservation projects under the auspices of the Alele Museum, including Waan Aelōñ Kein, used written documentation to record elders' knowledge. As we introduced the navigation project to Captain Korent and the other experts, Alson and I requested that they share their knowledge with us so that we could document it. We took special care to explain to them and the larger community that my role as the outside academic was *not* to learn navigation. As Alson states in the second epigraph, my task was to assist him, through written documentation, to *jitdaṃ kapeel in meto,* or "seek knowledge of the ocean." In addition to sharing their many stories, legends, chants, and songs, the elders redirected the research to reflect their interests, especially the elicitation of lists of specialized vocabulary and uncovering the older meanings of those terms. Despite these efforts to employ a Marshallese approach to the recovery of traditional knowledge, Alson and I encountered formidable obstacles in our attempts to document the surviving knowledge of navigation and the related domain of weather forecasting.

The biggest challenge Alson and I faced was the enduring value placed on such esoteric bodies of knowledge as navigation and weather forecasting.[20] The virtual cessation of long-distance canoe travel in the Marshalls has not automatically fostered the impetus to share the surviving knowledge. The knowledge has remained highly secretive, carefully hidden, and strategically linked to the power of the *iroij.* The nearly complete lack of interisland voyaging has worked to maintain the prestige of navigation and weather forecasting knowledge from earlier times precisely because it is so rarely used today. The prestige of navigation may even be elevated today. This is different from the family or atoll pride of canoe building and sailing exhibited during the many types of canoe races. The honor of being one of the last navigators or being a supportive family member to that navigator is so high that sharing the knowledge is almost unthinkable.

Iroij Mike Kabua and Iroijlaplap Imata Kabua gave permission for Captain Korent and other elders under their sphere of chiefly influence to share their knowledge of navigation and weather forecasting, but chiefly permission did not equate with willing participation. For instance, one family member held in his possession a locally written book that detailed the techniques of wave navigation. According to Captain Korent, the book is a compilation of descriptions and images from several deceased Rongelapese navigators of their entire repertoire of navigation concepts. The individual who possessed the document, however, refused to share it with us. In fact, he stated to Captain Korent that he plans to "take the book to the grave" with him when he passes away. Captain Korent believed his relative did not want to lose the status that came with the possession of the book, even in the event of his death. In this case, an imperative to safeguard navigational knowledge by protecting one's reputation overrode the chiefly request to share such highly valued knowledge.

Reluctance to share navigational knowledge also spread to an entire atoll community, as introduced in the opening vignette upon our landing on Namu. When Alson and I eventually met Alton Albious at his home, we were greeted with caution. Following the appropriate protocols, we asked respectfully for his permission to allow us to work with him to document his knowledge. Once he realized that Captain Korent was really directing the project, he agreed to talk with us. Like Captain Korent and Kilon Takiah before him, Alton insisted that he adopt us into his family in order to transfer his knowledge according to traditional etiquette. We accepted his request with the assumption that our integration into his family would relieve some of the anxiety, tension, and hostility we had felt upon arrival.

Starting with our departure from the airplane after it had landed on the coral runway, Alson and I felt an undercurrent of suspicion from the community, and this continued despite our incorporation into the family. Walking along the main village path, nearly everyone asked us in passing whether it was going to rain. People repeatedly asked us this question, and I began to think that perhaps they were testing our supposed newly acquired knowledge of weather forecasting. Alson and I finally came to understand that the questions were neither idle conversation nor a test of our ability to predict the weather. Weather forecasting likely held a slightly lower status than navigation, so it was probably more culturally appropriate for them to ask about weather even if they were more interested in the extent of our learning about their navigational knowledge. The seeming restrictions on even talking about navigation highlight the continuing secrecy that surrounds it on this particular atoll. This is reinforced by the fact that on Namu there is no word or title to recognize an individual as a navigator, as no one other than the *iroij* is supposed to know who has the knowledge.

In addition to the cases of individual and atoll-wide reluctance to share navigational knowledge, the elders participating in the revival project also hesitated to talk about navigation among themselves. Alson and I, and to some degree Captain Korent, worked with this group of elders individually and in small groups over the course of a year. They tended to openly share their knowledge with us only when they were alone. In fact, our most useful discussions have occurred while on a canoe, yacht, or ship at sea with only one of the elders present. Despite the fact that all of them are willing to transfer their knowledge to Alson and ultimately share it with the wider community, a certain caution and sense of secrecy remains among each other. This concealment of personal knowledge may have deep roots in traditional protocols of knowledge use.[21] Such reluctance to share knowledge may also work as a sort of impression management. They might impress others—both fellow navigators and researchers—through their silence in order to be recognized as the finest navigator. Concealing knowledge may be a virtuous quality; a reluctance to share knowledge could reveal their personal values of modesty and humility so as not to appear to be flaunting their expertise.[22] Alternately, a reluctance to share might also reflect that a limit had been reached. For the elders, we may have collectively arrived at a point from which going farther would compromise the culturally appropriate ways that the knowledge can be represented.[23]

The concealment of navigational knowledge, as introduced in the opening vignette and sketched in the preceding examples, suggests that families continue to guard their proprietary esoteric knowledge for a variety of personal, familial, community, and cultural reasons, despite the chiefly guidance to openly share. By retaining the knowledge, people assert the traditional aspects of their identities, notably the prestige of elite navigator status for one's lineage, class, and atoll community. The offset of this, of course, is that the knowledge is clearly at risk of being lost forever with the passing of its last custodians. In fact, in 2005, at the start of the project, Alson, Captain Korent, and I had begun to work with eight elders; since then, three of these elders have sadly passed away. Captain Korent's recent death in 2017 adds a profound gravity to the few surviving stewards of the knowledge.

The sharing of navigational knowledge, on the other hand, seems to have several dramatic repercussions. Unlike those who have concealed their knowledge, those elders who have shared their knowledge have enhanced their prestige within the wider Marshallese community but diminished their status among themselves and their elite navigation-centered families. Thus, paradoxically, the efforts to safeguard their specialized knowledge have started to erode their identity and status as navigators.

In addition, the navigation revitalization project may be altering the chiefly authority of navigational knowledge, and the future outcomes of this dramatic shift in power are unknown. The *iroij* gave Captain Korent and the other elders permission to share their knowledge under a new set of chiefly protocols: the navigational knowledge could be disseminated within and beyond their families only through the loose adoption of myself as the outside academic researcher. This has now become the new way to preserve the special relationship between navigators and their *iroij*. By *not* sharing their knowledge now under these innovative directives, they could risk damaging their relationship with their *iroij*. Yet if they do share, the widespread flow of knowledge may ultimately undermine the chiefly authority and power.

The paradoxical dilemma of the revitalization project is not unique; throughout Oceania, the revival of a sacred or esoteric practice risks recontextualizing it and eroding its relationship to chiefly authority, which is what gave the practice its particular cultural significance in the first place. For example, a recent project to revitalize sacred *machi* textiles on Fais in the western Carolinian atolls reveals a continuing link between sacred objects and traditional chieftainship. *Machi* weavings, a unique cultural product of the women of Fais, were formerly obligatory items of chiefly tribute within the *sawei* voyaging sphere that connected distant eastern outer islands to Yap. The *machi* textiles are still very much associated with chiefly authority and status; however, the traditional context of the *machi* has been eroded in the twentieth century with the cessation of interisland chiefly tribute voyages to Yap. With only a few women retaining this knowledge at the dawn of the twenty-first century, a project was developed to prevent the loss of their unique knowledge. The disconnect to chiefly power, however, has lessened the cultural salience of the *machi*.[24]

The politics of navigation in the Marshall Islands, like the Fais *machi*, deeply penetrate Marshallese culture. A tension exists between respecting chiefly restrictions on who can or cannot share navigational knowledge with whom and the diminishing or elevating of status and prestige. Alson and I worked with Captain Korent, who desperately wanted the social identity of a titled navigator and who, after forty years of waiting, finally received chiefly permission to try. Yet the participating Rongelapese elders showed various degrees of reluctance to share, and others disliked their chiefly mandates to share or simply decided to leave this world with their knowledge firmly in their sole possession. Amidst this somewhat tense atmosphere, Captain Korent continued his belated learning over the course of a year. He sought to finalize his understanding of the apex of the voyaging skills. Ultimately his learning of the various maps, models, and simulations of the ocean led to a voyage at sea that served as his *ruprup jǫkur* trial in his quest to become a navigator.

Chapter 5

Maps, Models, and Simulations

The *rebbelith* and *meddo* surely embody the most important mapping concepts, that is, the creation of analogical spaces that make visually explicit relationships not visible from within the original space. But as expressions of mathematical ideas, it is the *mattang* that we consider even more significant, for they serve to model the conceptual framework underlying the wave piloting system of the Marshall Island navigators.

—Ethnomathemetician Marcia Ascher[1]

It is a knowledge not of a formal, authorised kind, transmissible in contexts outside those of its practical application. On the contrary, it is based in feeling, consisting in the skills, sensitivities and orientations that have developed through long experiences of conducting one's life in a particular environment.

—Anthropologist Tim Ingold[2]

~ ~ ~

Suddenly the boat pitches forward, riding down the crest of an ocean swell. This is a new movement for me. I look to Captain Korent, who is standing at the bow. "There is the *kāāj!*" he exclaims with conviction, referring to a wave named after the curved shape of a fishhook. Now the entire crew is alert and focused on the waves. Another five minutes pass. This time we all feel the sudden downward lurching motion as the hull surfs a swell. "There it is," evenly states the captain as he tells the helmsman to adjust his course slightly. I look to the University of Hawai'i graduate student of oceanography, who has a quizzical look about him. Whatever this particular wave phenomenon was, it does not quite make sense to him. We stop for an hour to deploy a small untethered, free-floating wave buoy. Satellite tracking of its movements in three-dimensional space will hopefully provide the data for us to characterize the wave patterns and understand how this "fishhook" wave is forming.

An hour later I reach over the side of the rocking fishing vessel with a pole to snatch the rope handle of the small circular wave buoy. I had just re-checked the radio receiver to confirm it had been picking up satellite signals. As I haul in the wave buoy and set it safely in an old car tire nestled at the stern of the boat, I signal to the boat captain to continue with the course. He looks to Captain Korent, who silently motions our intended course with his hand out-stretched. He plans to follow a progression of these *kāāj* waves for fifteen miles until we see the atoll's coconut trees piercing through the distant hori-zon. Although Captain Korent is not articulating compass directions, we motor in a northeasterly direction toward an atoll that still lies too far away to see.

The boat pitches forward again, surfing down the crest of an ocean swell. "There it is again," Captain Korent says, as he looks at me with a smile. "Do you feel it? The fishhook wave."

Captain Korent again gestures with his hands how a southerly swell and an easterly swell superimpose upon each other, and at the same time a re-flected wave bouncing back from the atoll toward us heaps up this wave even further. Suddenly the boat pitches downward, riding the deepening angle of a swell. There it is again! We scan the ocean with several more of these "fish-hook" waves, and straight ahead we just barely make out the dark green tops of coconut trees penetrating the flat blue horizon.

Captain Korent had just taken a much-needed rest below the deck of a fishing vessel as we skirted around the irregularly shaped atoll of Arno in the southeastern portion of the archipelago over the course of two days. We had been motoring within a few miles of the reef, but while he slept, I had directed the helmsman to sail twenty-five miles off the southeast point of Arno to con-duct a short navigational exercise, just near the described boundary of how far the waves can be detected. Captain Korent awoke knowing that something had changed; he acutely felt the loss of a particular wave signature within the rhythmic motion of the seas. He fell back to his training from a traditional wave model made from the lashing of thinly sliced sections of the aerial roots of the pandanus tree, to orient according to the dominant easterly trade wind–driven swell. The reflected energy of this swell as it bounced off the atoll would heap up an incoming swell through constructive interference. As we had just passed the farthest radiating extension of the energy of the reflected *kāāj* wave from the atoll, it did not take long for Captain Korent to recognize the surfing motion it induced on the fishing vessel. This, in turn, indicated to him an immediate sense of direction and distance toward land.

Captain Korent, upon orienting himself on the ocean and following the series of *kāāj* waves, essentially retraced a route back to the atoll that had been forged by some intrepid sailor in the distant past who had captured such a voyage in the physical cartographic representation of the stick charts. While that individual remains lost to time, his legacy formed the basis of both a mental mapping of the wave patterns and the embodied sensation of those wave movements. Such a degree of the reliance on waves to find one's way through the ocean is unparalleled in navigational systems throughout Oceania. With the extent of this wayfinding knowledge and experience in mind, the oceanographer and I were mystified when we later analyzed the wave buoy data and discovered that no distinct wave pattern could be discerned from the regularly flowing swell. What had we just experienced?

At Captain Korent's invitation, I had cofacilitated this oceanographic study to understand the scientific basis of the wave patterns. With the extreme decline in knowledge and virtual cessation of voyaging in the mid-twentieth century, it is not surprising that there is ambiguity today about the various maps, models, and simulations of wave piloting. The process by which Captain Korent learned and remembered some of the knowledge from his elders highlights both the severely fragmented nature of navigation and Captain Korent's vision and perseverance to restore it. The fundamentals of wave piloting come from a combination of previous ethnohistoric documentation and navigational knowledge held by elders from Rongelap in the northern region of Adjokḷā and Ujae in the Kapinmeto sector. In this chapter, I explain the process of understanding the maps, models, and simulations of wave navigation in terms of Western science and Marshallese theories of the ocean. Captain Korent's interest in using oceanography to understand the waves complements his elders' traditional comprehension, but it remains incomplete. Yet it was the complementarity of these approaches that ultimately gave Captain Korent the confidence in his understanding to undertake a voyage of searching for the waves.

Wave Piloting

Navigation within the seas of Aelōñ Kein Ad developed over the course of two thousand years since original settlement into a system of pilotage. Remotely sensing land through the effects of waves on the movement of a canoe is common throughout Oceania, as researcher David Lewis documented in his pan-Pacific survey of traditional navigation techniques in the late 1960s, but nowhere did it become as elaborated as in the Marshall Islands.[3] Lewis and Gladwin had divided wayfinding into the processes of orientation and course setting, estimating position at sea, and honing in on an island and making landfall. They described how swells are commonly used throughout Oceania for orientation during the daytime when calibrated with the evening stars for orientation and how reflected wave energy and wave shadow effects are often used to indicate the close proximity to land. However, Marshallese wave piloting is uniquely focused among Oceanic wayfinding systems—guiding a canoe by exclusively following a progression of seamarks generated by the ways in which islands disrupt and transform the various swell and gyre streams.

The geography of the Marshall Islands posed acute navigational challenges to the first settlers some two thousand years ago but also afforded a distinctive solution that likely accounts for the development of a wave-based system of wayfinding. The main twenty-nine coral atolls and five coral islands extend in twin parallel chains (Ratak and Rālik) over five hundred miles just north of the equator along a southeast-northwest axis, with the outer atolls Enewetak and Ujelang located some two hundred miles to the west and the atoll Enen-kio (Wake Island) residing five hundred miles to the north.[4] This vast archipelago straddles the seasonally fluctuating boundaries of opposing gyre currents. Two currents flow from east to west—the north equatorial current flows past the northern atolls, and the south equatorial current flows past the southern atolls. Between these two west-flowing current streams is the east-flowing equatorial countercurrent.[5] These looping currents, caused by the Coriolis effect, pose a particular challenge. They are fast-flowing yet variable streams, sometimes reaching three knots, and the atolls may deflect and accelerate their flows. As the tops of the coconut trees on the low-lying atolls can be sighted only about ten miles offshore, an undetected current could easily displace a canoe laterally to the east or west on a northern or southern voyage. Even though interisland distances are relatively short—most crossings are less than one hundred miles and could be made within a day—an inattentive navigator could easily sail past the targeted atoll. During a longer voyage along the length of the Ratak chain or the Rālik chain, intrepid navigators may have had to sail through both of these opposing current streams.

The Marshallese turned to the ocean as the key to staying on course. The northeast trade wind swell, which has been traveling unobstructed for thousands of miles, directly hits the atolls along the Ratak chain and then continues westward to the Rālik chain. This regularly flowing, easily recognizable trade wind–driven swell strikes and flows past these atolls and the current streams, transforming in distinctive ways. The resulting wave action provides information about land locations and thus affords navigational guidance. The Marshallese developed this into a comprehensive piloting system. The closest parallel system of navigation comes from the waters of Indonesia, where Bugis navigators take advantage of localized currents, tides, shoals, reefs, and wave patterns to pilot their way among islands that are close but not quite intervisible.[6] While the two cultures are too remote geographically and in terms of their ancestral origins to expect any direct borrowing of ideas, the concept of "wave piloting" neatly encapsulates the essence of Marshallese navigation. The difference, of course, is that Marshallese piloting extends to long-distance voyages and that waves, which are always in motion, constitute the main environmental feature as seamarks or navigation signs.

Nearly all of the other Oceanic systems of navigation draw from numerous environmental phenomena, with stars and other celestial referents as a key source of information. In 1910, Erdland recorded sixty-six star names that Marshallese navigators used as guides toward neighboring islands,[7] but celestial bodies did not become elaborated into a conceptual compass to demarcate the horizon, as occurred to the west among the central Carolinian atolls. Since Erdland's documentation, the number of relevant, recognizable stars has greatly diminished. Now, Captain Korent recognizes only a few stars of importance to help with orientation but largely dismisses their relevance while at sea. "While the stars move through the night sky, the waves stay put," he asserts, meaning that their regular patterning can be detected.

Oceanography offers mathematical models of how waves change in the presence of islands through processes of reflection, diffraction, and refraction. When a swell approaches shore and moves across shallow water, defined as water that has a depth less than half the wave length, the swell reacts in distinctive ways. As the swell moves into shallower water, the friction of the underwater topography causes the swell to slow down, and this process of shoaling results in an increase in wave height in addition to the reduction in speed. As the swell approaches the shore, different segments of the swell travel in different depths of water. This causes the crests to bend, or refract, and the wave direction continuously changes to be roughly parallel to the underwater bathymetric contours. Wave refraction may result in a swell wrapping itself around a circular island in such a way that the refracted swell components interfere with each other to produce a distinctive crosshatch sea state. When a swell passes an island, some of the energy propagates laterally, or diffracts, as the wave crest extends itself into the wave shadow or the calm leeward area sheltered by the island. When a swell encounters a nearly vertical wall, such as a cliff rising from deep water, a portion of the wave energy is transmitted backwards, or reflected, with a reversed angle of incidence. In addition, islands located in the path of swift equatorial streams are known to perturb the current flows, creating distinctive wake patterns that are observed a considerable distance downstream. Lateral variations in this current field, called current shears, can refract the swell as it passes through, resulting in current-induced wave refraction.[8]

Understanding the particular manifestations of wind-driven and current-induced wave reflection, diffraction, and refraction in the Marshall Islands and how these and other wave and current formations articulate with the seamarks used in Marshallese navigation were of critical importance to Captain Korent as he prepared for his first noninstrumental voyage in 2006. This problem—understanding local wave concepts in relation to an oceanographic explanation—has been posed numerous times since foreigners in the late nineteenth century discovered, collected, and eventually began intense ethnographic investigations to interpret the enigmatic stick charts—the Marshallese cartographic representations of navigational knowledge.

Stick Charts

It is intriguing that Kotzebue's 1817 visit to the Ratak chain produced an incredibly accurate cartographic record of the archipelago based on navigators' descriptions but apparently missed the wave navigation techniques and the physical representations of that knowledge, which would not surface for another four decades. In 1862, the Hawaiian missionary Hezekia Ae'a first wrote in a Hawaiian language manuscript about Marshallese who navigated by the swells. That same year, the American missionary Luther Gulick first recorded that Marshallese navigators constructed navigational aids, and a year later the German geographer Carl E. Meinicke interpreted these devices as *Stabkarten*, translated and now commonly known in English as "stick charts."[9] These astute observers noted that long, thin sections of the aerial roots of the pandanus tree and sometimes the midribs of coconut fronds were bent and lashed with coconut sennit to form a latticework of straight lines and curves. In some cases, navigators lashed cowry shells to the framework to represent atolls. In others, the lashed intersections sufficed to indicate the position of islands. While the general materials and techniques of construction have continued until today, the first written accounts provided by Gulick, Meinicke, and others incorrectly indicated that these devices were either nautical charts or navigational instruments used at sea to somehow map the positions of islands as well as the sailing courses in relation to waves and currents. The devices were, however, never designed to be carried on a canoe, and the types of information conveyed through the charts remained speculative at best.

For the next several decades, published reports of the stick charts increased, as did museum collections. In 1884, the German ethnographer Albert Schück first examined the budding literature associated with the stick charts and their routes to various museum collections, which he compiled in a larger work in 1902. He noted that the first stick charts went to museum repositories in about 1879 or 1880 along the following routes: a Jaluit stick chart obtained by Franz Hernsheim, the head of the Jaluit branch of a German trading company, was brought to Germany; an Ailinglaplap chart was sent to the National Museum of Ethnology in Leiden, Netherlands; and five stick charts reached the Godeffroy family museum of Hamburg, Germany.[10] From then until the early 1900s, at least fifty stick charts, most with provenance information, were collected and held by numerous institutions.[11] Many of the charts depict the region of the southern atolls of the Rālik chain. The relative paucity of stick charts from the Ratak chain may reflect the concentrated efforts of the early German ethnographers, who were based on Jaluit. Despite Schück's systematic treatment of the stick charts, the scarcity of associated navigational knowledge prompted others to search for firsthand explanations.

Captain Winkler, a commander of the SMS *Bussard* of the German navy, conducted the first in-depth study of the *Stabkarten* during two brief visits in 1896 and 1897.[12] Winkler derived explanations and translations from Marshallese navigators, chiefs, and other knowledgeable people on Jaluit through Joachim deBrum, whose father had come from Portugal and married a Marshallese and whose grandson Leonard deBrum talked much later with David Lewis. Winkler importantly learned that the stick charts were land-based teaching devices that depicted the direction of the predominant swell, the transformations of the swell in proximity to land, and the resultant sea conditions that served as seamarks to show the distance and direction toward islands. Drawing from the published literature and museum collections, Winkler documented three distinct categories of stick charts. Winkler's general but critical insights were strengthened by subsequent ethnographic studies in the mid-twentieth century, and his ideas and depictions of the stick charts resonate highly with the two elders, Isao Eknilang and Thomas Bokin, who wove and lashed similar devices in 2006.[13]

Continuity between the present guardians of the wave knowledge and those who were first consulted in the 1860s exists but is also constrained. Regional variation between and within the two main island chains would be expected based on regular voyaging networks. This is coupled with both generational loss and innovation through time, with the changes in tradition exacerbated by the forces of rapid waves of colonialism. Ethnomathematician Marcia Ascher has begun to make sense of these spatial and temporal differences by discussing how the misnamed charts actually convey processes of mapping and modeling for the purposes of onshore instruction.[14] Drawing from Winkler and others, Ascher describes one class of stick charts that maps the real positions of atolls and islands in relation to actual swell and current patterns. These analogical planar representations of the islands and the wave- and current-based paths that lead from one island to the next may depict a particular region or larger portions of the archipelago. Using a Jaluit-centered terminology, Winkler assigned the names *meddo* and *rebbelib* for these maps. The *meddo* represents the ocean environment of a few atolls within one island chain, while the *rebbelib* depicts most of an entire chain or both chains.

Illustrative of Ascher's notion of mapping is a photograph of a *meddo* (Figure 5.1) from Winkler's pioneering investigations and an illustration of its drawn features (Figure 5.2). This particular *meddo* maps the relative—not true—geographical positions of the southern region of the archipelago, spanning both Ratak and Rālik chains. It, like other collected *meddo*, is a regional representation of important oceanographic information. In particular, navigators described a current-free region south of Ailinglaplap to zoological researcher Max Walker de Laubenfels in 1940. Navigators spoke of Eon Woerr, an anomalous shallow sea, translated as "over coral," extending between Namorik and Jaluit that acted like a lagoon—rising tides flow inward and falling tides rush outward of this region. The channel of these apparent open-ocean tidal movements is marked by the angled chevrons between Namorik and Kili.[15] The mapping process in this *meddo* also includes representations of common oceanographic phenomena but in specific geographical locations. The curves represent eastern and western swells; the V-shaped chevrons (aside from the sea Eon Woerr) indicate the crossing of swells; and the horizontal lines represent specific named distances at which islands can be detected.

Scaling up the nautical information represented in the *meddo*, a particular *rebbelib* documented by Winkler indicates wave patterns that extend between atolls called *okar* (root) as well as a larger geographic region. A photograph of this *rebbelib* (Figure 5.3) and an illustration of its drawn features (Figure 5.4) reveal Winkler's interpretations of how it maps the islands of the Rālik chain from Ebon in the south to Bikini in the north. Winkler describes how the angled chevrons indicate the heaped-up wave nodes from the crossing of the eastern and western swells between Namu and Kwajalein, Kwajalein and Rongerik, Rongerik and Rongelap, and Ailinglaplap and Jaluit. These nodes of intersection along the *okar* path are called *booj* (knots). The chevrons between Namu and Ujae and between Jaluit and Namorik indicate the "knots" along the *okar* from the crossing of the northern and southern swells.

The other class of stick charts described by Ascher models the conceptual framework underlying Marshallese navigation, as in the opening epigraph, by isolating and idealizing the most fundamental components of the navigational system. Winkler recorded the Jaluit-centered term *mattang* in

Figure 5.1. A *meddo* collected by Captain Winkler in 1898 (Catalogue No. E206188-0, photograph courtesy of the Department of Anthropology, Smithsonian Institution).

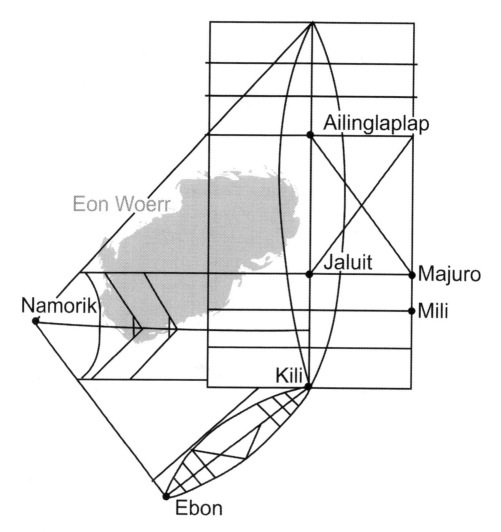

Figure 5.2. Drawing of mapped locations of islands of the *meddo*.

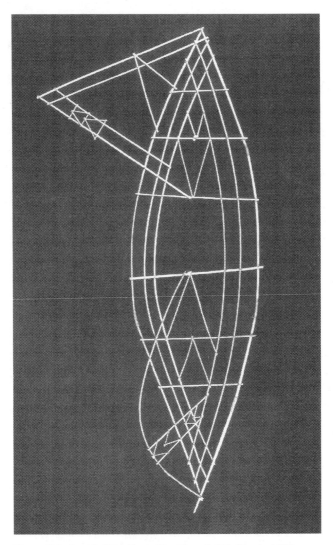

Figure 5.3. A *rebbelib* collected by Captain Winkler in 1898
(Catalogue No. VI 15283, photograph courtesy of the Ethnolo-
gisches Museum der Staatlichen Museen zu Berlin–Preußischer
Kulturebesitz).

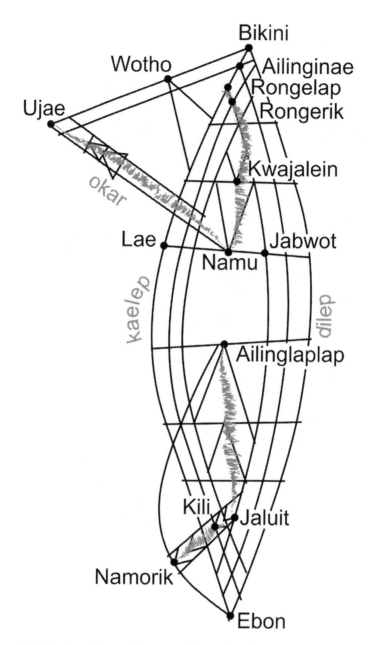

Figure 5.4. Drawing of mapped locations of islands of the *rebbelib*.

1898, while Isao Eknilang uses the term *wapepe* today. The visual patterning of the *mattang* and *wapepe* are strikingly similar. Illustrated here by a photograph of a contemporary *wapepe* (Figure 5.5) and the drawn features of a nearly identical *mattang* (Figure 5.6), Winkler uncovered the fact that the geometry of the curved and straight lines and their intersections models the swell and its transformations in relation to wind direction and land. In this abstract representation, the island or islands of interest become idealized to a point of intersection, and the important locations and shapes of the most foundational seamarks are idealized and frozen in space and time. The thinly

Figure 5.5. *Wapepe*, constructed by Isao Eknilang.

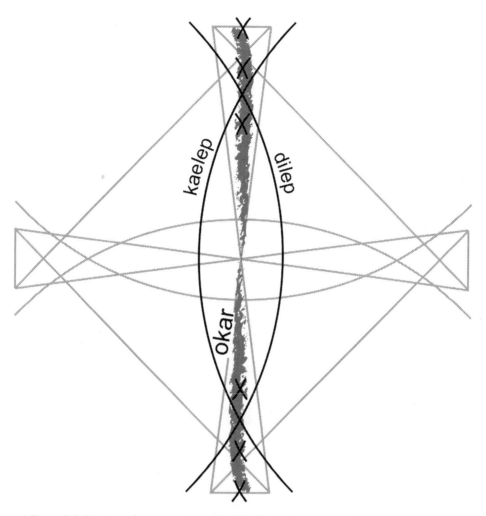

Figure 5.6. Drawing of a *mattang* (virtually identical to the *wapepe*) documented by Winkler in 1898, showing *okar* leading to an atoll at the center of the latticework.

shaven sections of pandanus root indicate the wave crests of those salient swell patterns from a bird's-eye perspective, and particular sticks may also show the locations—but generally not the physical characteristics of—current patterns.

The most striking feature of the *mattang* documented by Winkler in 1898 is that four curved sections of pandanus roots are lashed in such a way as to encircle the central point of intersection of the latticework. That central point idealizes an island, and the curves model the bending, or refracting, of swells as approaching land. As swells from opposite directions bend around the island, their bent wave crests intersect to form the heaped-up *booj*, with a series of such wave interference patterns forming an *okar*, or a line like a "tree root," to the island. According to Winkler, the east swell (*dilep*) and west swell (*kaelep*) intersect north and south of an atoll to form an *okar* path leading the navigator toward land. Winkler understood from Joachim deBrum that staying on this series of wave intersections was the navigator's highest art: "As the root, if you follow it, leads to the palm tree, so does this lead to the island."[16]

The model makers Isao Eknilang and Thomas Bokin, in their instruction to Captain Korent, concur with the central significance of following a series of *booj* to find land, but their progression of waves, called *dilep*, meaning "backbone," is fundamentally different. Like the supportive backbone in our human body, this foundational line of waves extends between islands. When Captain Korent first explained to me the prime significance of *dilep* as the foundation of his navigational system and offered an explanation to account for its formation, I was skeptical. Even watching him demonstrate the *dilep* waves with hand movements while looking at the training reef on Rongelap, I remained doubtful. Only one previously published account of Marshallese navigation mentioned *dilep* as a "sailing route," and other accounts that referred to Winkler's offshore *okar* did so in terms of swells refracting as they approach an atoll.[17] And Winkler's *dilep* referred to the dominant east swell rather than a path of waves.

Then Isao constructed a Rongelap-centered model, and Thomas made a Kapinmeto-centered model similar in design to Winkler's *mattang*. Their explanations involved multiple, sometimes contradictory perspectives, but they were centered on the *dilep* wave. In their explanations, swells flowing from opposite directions do not refract but instead intersect to form a path of waves that connects a navigator's home island to every distant island within the archipelago. Based on their diagrams and drawings in the sand, I visualize the home island to be like the center of a spider's web, so that all the strands of silk (waves) radiate outward, connecting to distant points (the unseen islands). Sharing this idea with oceanographers at the University of Hawai'i left me with serious misgivings about the existence of a *dilep* wave. How could swells flowing through the open ocean intersect in ways that could provide "roadmaps" to every possible destination island? Baffled, I turned to the teachings of Isao and Thomas through their models to better understand the *dilep* and the other wave patterns.[18]

Isao, at his current home on Majuro, wove together and lashed thinly

shaven aerial pandanus roots to form two slightly different *mattang*-like lat-
ticeworks, while Thomas, on Ujae, interlaced coconut palm midribs through
the interwoven strips of pandanus leaves of a sleeping mat to produce an immediate but ephemeral *mattang*-like device. The ideas embedded within these
models represent the last surviving cartographic knowledge of navigation today; Isao explained his Adjoklā ideas to Captain Korent, Alson, and me in the
maritime academic classroom on Majuro, while Thomas demonstrated his
Kapinmeto ideas on the floor of his home, illuminated by the light of a lantern. Each device similarly models three different perspectives. From a bird's-
eye view, the latticework of each model can show the following: the swells, or
the wave field, as experienced by a navigator sailing on a canoe at sea or
standing upon the shore of an island; the wave and current patterns extending
between a home island and the targeted island destination (i.e., the *dilep*); and
wave patterns in closer proximity to the destination island that serve as land-
finding seamarks. While the models converge on showing these three different perspectives, Isao and Thomas offer somewhat different interpretations.

Isao's most representational model is the *wapepe* (see Figure 5.5).[19]
Like Winkler's *mattang*, the octagonal frame of Isao's *wapepe* frames a series
of lashed pandanus sticks, some of which intersect each other through the
center of the latticework, while others are bent to form a pair of lenticular
shapes that encircle the central point. Unlike Winkler's *mattang*, the *wapepe*
can be interpreted in three different ways (Figure 5.7). The term *wapepe*
means "floating canoe," and from one perspective, Isao envisions that the
central point of the device is a canoe at sea, or alternately an island. Whether
on land or at sea, the navigator envisions how the swell flows toward him.
This wave field is very important to the navigator, as it provides a general
sense of orientation. Four swells are conceptualized as flowing from the cardinal directions east, west, north, and south, named according to either the
direction they flow or the direction from which they emanate. The dominant
easterly trade wind swell is called *buñto,* or "swell flowing to the west." In the
opening vignette, Captain Korent immediately recognized this east swell
upon waking from his sleep below deck, out of sight of land. Because the
exact direction of this swell is wind dependent, the swell may flow from due
east, south of east, or north of east. The various directions of this swell are
encompassed within the convex portion of the vertical lenticular stick that is
located to the right of the center of the latticework. The western swell, *buñtak,*
or "swell flowing to the east" (also *kaeleptak*), is similarly represented as
flowing from a range of directions, as is the northern and southern swell,
buñtokeañ, or "swell coming from the north," and *buñtokrōk,* or "swell coming from the south," respectively. Upon leaving the home island and exiting

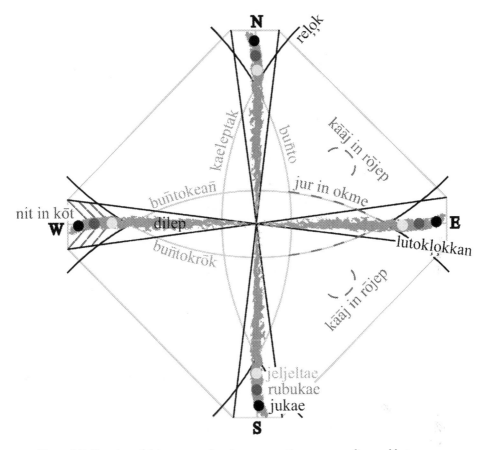

Figure 5.7. Drawing of the *wapepe*, showing wave patterns surrounding and between islands.

the protected lee waters or wave shadows of the atoll, the navigator would ascertain the directions and strength of these swells compared to the cardinal directions and adjust his mental orientation accordingly. For example, upon leaving the pass of Majuro and heading north toward Aur, Captain Korent can quickly determine if the trade wind swell is flowing from due east or is slightly north or south of east, and he would calibrate the angle of the swell to the known direction of Aur (due north) and build this into his mental imagery of the *wapepe* model.

These four swells flowing across the sea assist with directionality, but they do not contribute substantially to spatial orientation at sea once out of sight of land. Navigators do not articulate the sailing course and heading of the canoe in terms of swell. The navigator would not say, for example, "Steer toward, or at a certain angle to, the direction of the east swell." Rather than a direct course heading, directions are related to the relative configuration of the outrigger sailing canoe to the wind. The main directives are to sail more upwind (*bwābwe*) or downwind (*kabbe*). A largely proprioceptive way of knowing—passive perception governed by "proprioceptors" in the navigator's sitting body in relation to the movement of a canoe—prompts the navigator to direct the helmsman to make subtle shifts in direction. This is especially salient once out of sight of land, where the only guides to position come from the sea itself.[20]

As the navigator journeys away from land and orients himself in relation to the flow of the various swells, he begins to pilot the canoe toward the destination island. From a second perspective, the *wapepe* models the sea conditions between islands that a navigator would follow to guide his canoe toward land. The four shorter ends of the octagon represent islands, and the latticework shows oceanic phenomena between eastern (right) and western islands (left) and between northern (up) and southern islands (down). Of course, not all islands are situated in such ideal quadrants, but the navigator adjusts the wave concepts depending on the actual sailing route. My sketched wavy vertical line models the *dilep* wave extending between northern and southern islands, and the similarly shaped horizontal line models the *dilep* between eastern and western islands. Isao, along with other consultants from Rongelap, describe the *dilep* as an extension of reflected swell energy radiating seaward from the targeted destination island.

The notches in the straight vertical and horizontal lines represent three zones of currents (*ae*) called *jukae, rubukae,* and *jeljeltae.* While the *dilep* wave is the result of swell transformations, these *jukae, rubukae,* and *jeljeltae* are current-induced wave patterns, glossed as "first zone of currents," "second zone of currents," and "third zone of currents," respectively. With the ending of *ae* (current) on each term, *jukae* stems from *juk* (going into or crossing into), *rubukae* derives from *rubuk* (crossing), and *jeljeltae* comes from *jeljelat* (loosening or unraveling). According to Isao, these current streams form regions of choppy waves in an otherwise normal sea state. The sequential ordering of these regions of currents provides the navigator with distance estimates toward land. Isao envisions that *jukae, rubukae,* and *jeljeltae* radiate outward from each island in concentric bands, and these can be detected about ten, fifteen, and twenty miles offshore, respectively.

In the event that the navigator strays from the path of the *dilep* or misgauges the distance afforded by the successive zones of *jukae, rubukae,* and *jeljeltae* currents, wave-based navigational signs, or seamarks (*kōkḷaḷ*), re motely indicate the presence of land. A third perspective of the *wapepe* models the wave transformations of the easterly trade wind swell in the vicinity of an island. Now, the center of the latticework singularly represents an atoll. As modeled by Isao and also drawn in the sand by Captain Korent, four distinct wave patterns extend seaward from every atoll and island in specific quadrants up to twenty-five miles away. The visual patterning of each wave and, more importantly, how its motion affects the movement of the canoe indicate to the navigator the direction toward land, and the wave's relative strength suggests the distance toward land.

With the predominant wind from the east, superposition of the incoming swell and its reflected wave energy produces wave patterns to the east, or windward, of an atoll. The farthest extent of this reflected wave energy is called *jur in okme.* This term refers to the curved shape of the end of a pole used to harvest breadfruit and is represented in the *wapepe* by portions of two intersecting curves represented as dotted lines. The northeast and southeast limits of *jur in okme* are delineated by a series of waves called *kāāj in rōjep,* which refers to the curve of a hook to catch flying fish, also represented as dotted lines. Of note is that the *kāāj in rōjep* patterns are not actually modeled in the *wapepe.* If a navigator correctly identifies these windward navigational signs, he would discern that he is upwind, or to the east, of an atoll. In the opening story, Captain Korent, in his excitement to announce that he had detected a seamark, shortened *kāāj in rōjep* to simply *kāāj.* In that case, the reflected wave energy of a southeasterly swell likely superimposed with the incoming swell to produce a heightened wave. This induced the vessel into a downward surfing motion, effectively steering it toward the direction of Arno. Captain Korent gestured the motion of this wave with his hand, outstretched into a horizontal C-shape. This is the curve shape embedded within the term *kāāj in rōjep.*

As the easterly trade wind swell passes by the atoll, it wraps around it so that the wave crests cross in the protected wave shadow. This creates a confused sea state called *nit in kōt* to the leeward, or west, of an atoll. Literally meaning "a pit for bird fighting," *nit in kōt* evokes the image of a cage. In the *wapepe,* the navigator must indicate the position and shape of *nit in kōt,* represented graphically by a series of short, angled chevrons to the left of the central point. These lines represent the crossing of the southern and northern components of the easterly swell. This crosshatch pattern affords the navigator critical information that he is downwind, or to the west, of an atoll.

In the unlikely circumstance that the navigator misses the target island, the *wapepe* offers correcting mechanisms. Going back to the second, regional perspective, the straight vertical and horizontal lines of the *dilep* waves are flanked by angled lines. These misleading wave patterns, called *lutoklọkkan*, or literally "pouring out, away from you," can lead the unobservant navigator astray as he continues to sail past the atoll. The portion of each curve in the *wapepe* that extends beyond the *lutoklọkkan* represents another wave pattern indicative of being lost, called *relọk*, which literally translates as "plunge into the sea." If a navigator can recognize his navigational errors by reading such waves, he could shunt his canoe and search for land in the direction from which he came.

Armed with, but not entirely confident in, the explanations provided by Isao about the modeling of the *wapepe*, Captain Korent sought the expertise of Kapinmeto navigator Thomas Bokin, who had previously built a voyaging canoe and navigated some 350 miles from Ujae to Majuro.[21] As Captain Korent, Alson, and I discussed with Thomas his experiences as a canoe builder and navigator, he stepped outside of his home, cut two coconut fronds with a machete, and stripped the leaves to reveal only the midribs. He picked up a few coral pebbles from the ground and proceeded to rapidly construct his teaching device. As he spoke, he interwove the coconut midribs with the sleeping mat to resemble the curves in Isao's *wapepe* and Winkler's *mattang*. But rather than notched sticks or lashings, Thomas symmetrically incorporated the coral rocks in the design to represent islands and currents.

The teachings of Thomas created for Captain Korent three conceptual differences from what he had remembered from his youth and relearned from Isao. For Thomas, the three zones of currents did not serve as merely nearshore seamarks for an atoll. They instead served as gauges of distance along the *dilep* path between islands. In this view, the first zone of currents is located near the home island and the third zone of currents is located near the destination island, but the second zone of currents is located at the halfway point in the voyage. The second difference is that the seamarks used to hone in on an island are not due to reflected wave energy or the bending of waves in the protected lee. Thomas maintains that the wave patterns are the result of either the intersections of swells or the blocking effects of islands to create wave shadow effects. But most striking was Thomas' idea that the *dilep* does not emanate from reflected wave energy but instead originates from a crossing of swells flowing in opposite directions, much like the "knots" formed along Winkler's *okar*.[22]

Memorization of the wave information mapped and modeled in the stick charts is but one form of knowledge about swell-pattern navigation, and Captain Korent's progression of learning expanded to these other representations of navigational knowledge as he sought to fully comprehend the nuanced differences laid out by Isao and Thomas. Reflecting the complementarity of Marshallese and Western science, these additional ways of knowing center on the experiential wave simulation on Rongelap of Captain Korent's youth and the development of computer-based wave models.

Traditional Wave Simulation

Captain Korent learned about the core wave concepts in his youth by directly experiencing the ocean through a wave simulation. As anthropologist Tim Ingold remarks in the second epigraph, this is a kind of knowledge based in feeling, generated through longtime engagement with the environment. While the *wapepe* and all the other stick charts statically model and freeze in time the flowing of the swells and their transformations in the vicinity of land, a particular coral reef actually simulates the feel of these wave dynamics. This is quite unique. Lewis, during his pan-Pacific survey of navigational techniques in the late 1960s, documented a few other instructional devices, such as a concentric pattern of stones in Kiribati that model wave patterns in relation to an island or canoe at sea similar to the stick charts.[23] In the same archipelago forty years earlier, the resident commissioner and pioneering ethnographer Arthur Grimble also documented how the beams and rafters of certain houses modeled the divisions of the night sky.[24] But there is no documentation from Kiribati or anywhere in Oceania other than the Marshall Islands that refers to experiential simulations of navigational knowledge.

There are a few Marshallese stories of coral reef simulations that were used for teaching. In Jelibor Jam's *bwebwenato* on the origins of Marshallese navigation, he narrated to anthropologist Jack Tobin in 1975 how navigators from distant islands to the west towed Litarmelu in a canoe by hand around a coral rock on Jaluit at low tide. This rock, called Barijur, is located on the western side of the atoll, so its eastern side faces the lagoon and its western side faces the ocean. With Litarmelu's eyes closed, the two foreign navigators towed her around this coral rock and asked her whether she could ascertain her sense of direction in reference to the rock. She did not answer correctly each time, but she ultimately understood that she was supposed to feel the waves coming from either the ocean or across the lagoon. They towed her to the north, west, south, and east of the rock, and let her feel the presence or absence of the waves. In one instance, they towed her to the north of Barijur and had to correct her understandings, underscoring the idea of coral rocks (or islands) blocking waves (or ocean swells):

> They began from the east of Barijur and towed her to the north. Now the man asked, "Where are we now?"
>
> Litarmelu answered, "To the east of Barijur." The man said, "No. To

the north. Wake up and look!" Litarmelu said, "O, I am mistaken! I thought it was to the east of Barijut." Now the man said, "Well, I will explain it again now." Now the man said, "Do you see the wave that is going into the lagoon from the ocean?"

Litarmelu answered, "Yes." The man said, "Do you see the wave that is coming into the ocean from the lagoon?" Litarmelu answered, "Yes." The man asked again, "Is it clear that your body feels the wave is coming into the ocean from the lagoon?" Litarmelu said, "Yes."

Now the man explained, "Do not say to the east of Barijur, for it is clear that these waves strike together. If it were to the east, one of those waves would be absent."

Litarmelu replied. She said, "What wave is absent?" The man answered, "Waves coming in from the west are absent and there are waves coming in from the east only. The reason the waves coming in from the west are absent is because they are blocked off by Barijur. And here we are at the north. And your body is feeling all these waves."[25]

The particular coral reef that Hemmerik used in 1959 to teach his grandson, a young Korent of eleven years, is located just north of the main islet of Rongelap, at the extreme southeastern end of the atoll (see Figure 3.4). At high tide, the entire reef is submerged, but low tide reveals a nearly perfect circular coral reef. Rongelap islet lies several hundred feet to the south, while the next islet lies a few hundred feet to the north. To the east lie several hundred feet of shallow water above the reef before hitting the ocean, and the lagoon lies to the west past a similar section of shallow-water reef. A northeast trade wind–driven swell directly approaches this area of the atoll, and once it breaks on the reef smaller wavelets ripple across the shallow water toward the circular coral rock. The far western side of the atoll contains few islets, so that the western swell flows relatively unchanged through the lagoon, and once it breaks on the reef it similarly flows as smaller wavelets toward the training area. It is the flow of these waves and their resultant intersections near the exposed coral "island" that simulate the transformed wave patterns near islands on the open sea.

Traditional instruction involved a student lying blindfolded in an outrigger canoe while the master navigator would tow him to various positions around the exposed islet. In just a few feet of water, the apprentice would learn to determine his location around this circular reef based on how the transformations of the incoming wavelets from the oceanside and lagoonside reefs affected the motion of his canoe. The reef models a coral island or atoll, which thanks to the blindfold is nonvisible, and the waves simulate the flow of swells from the east (oceanside waves) and the west (lagoonside waves). Watching Captain Korent point out the resultant wave patterns from shore, I was struck by the mental and proprioceptive scaling processes that would be required when sailing at sea. The magnitude of the sensations of wave movements near the coral reef are miniscule (wave heights of a few inches) compared to large, uninterrupted ocean swells. Yet somehow the navigator would be able to physically and mentally internalize these tiny canoe movements and recognize similar movements on the open ocean.

The Rongelap training reef simulates the movements of most of the wave patterns modeled in Isao's *wapepe*. When a canoe would be towed to either side of the reef, the student would detect two major waves of the overall wave field. As the north-south alignment between Rongelap islet and the training reef effectively prevents the generation of southern or northern waves, only the eastern and western waves are present, thus simulating the flow of the east and west swells. When "sailing" between Rongelap islet and the reef, the crossing of the oceanside and lagoonside wavelets simulates the *dilep* between these two "islands." When on this path, the student would feel an equal rocking from side to side. This fits with the stick chart–derived explanation provided by Thomas but contrasts to Isao's idea of reflected waves. When off to either side of the *dilep*, the student can detect the core seamarks. The eastern *jur in okme* is the farthest reflection of the oceanside wavelets, and the western *nit in kōt* is the crossing of those wavelets; both concepts articulate through Isao's *wapepe*. The southeastern and northeastern pair of *kāāj in rōjep* seamarks are the curved wave patterns. But rather than invoke Isao's idea of reflected wave energy, Captain Korent suggests that the crossing of the oceanside and lagoonside wavelets create a crosshatch pattern that flows in a curved shape toward the reef.

The aftermath of the 1954 thermonuclear Bravo detonation effectively cut short what would have otherwise been a vigorous training regime at the wave simulation reef on Rongelap for the young Korent and other children. The family's decision to relocate Korent prior to the community's eventual voluntary exodus in 1985 made sense, but his survival also meant the loss of the last formal teaching of the wave knowledge. He carried in his mind the cartographic modeling and mapping in the *wapepe*, which Isao was able to reconstruct from memory fifty years later, and he also carried embodied knowledge of those wave-induced canoe movements from the simulation reef. Yet because he had not been allowed to undertake a traditional voyage at sea, his chief had not conferred upon him the title of navigator under the traditional protocols at the time of his exodus. For the next forty years, he continued to learn and think about the waves in solitude as a government ship captain, but unanswered questions still remained. He turned to Western science, equipped with a positivist epistemology to validate his comprehension of the waves.

Oceanographic Modeling

A systematic oceanographic investigation ensued as an integral part of the revitalization project. Anthropologists had previously attempted to explain the wave patterns according to the physics of waves, but these had not been based on any physical data.[26] Captain Korent desired an oceanographic accounting of the wave patterns. Such a Western scientific understanding would, he reasoned, answer his lingering questions and validate the traditional knowledge of the sea. To date, Captain Korent's twin desires for clearer understanding and authentication have been partially satiated.[27]

A suite of oceanographic data collection techniques and computer wave models and simulations has led to a robust yet incomplete understanding of the traditional wave concepts. Collaborating initially with University of Hawai'i oceanographers, the efforts at oceanographic modeling traced the progression of concepts invoked by Captain Korent and his elderly consultants: sailing toward an island, demonstrating the way to the island through the lashed intersections of the stick charts, and describing his internalized proprioceptive knowledge remembered from his youthful training at the wave simulation reef on Rongelap. These processes involve sensing the four swells for orientation, following the *dilep* wave path in lieu of any explicit dead reckoning procedures, and remotely honing in on the island through seamarks located in particular quadrants surrounding the island.

The presence of four regularly flowing swells in the seas of the Marshallese archipelago from the cardinal directions east, west, north, and south is fundamental to a navigator's orientation when setting a course, but this is only partially corroborated through oceanography. Based on a global-modeled wave data set, the university oceanographers constructed a computer model that shows the swell climatology, or the annual variations in the directional flows of the swells. The dominant swell flows from the east, driven by the seasonal variations of the easterly trade winds. Cyclically, this trade wind swell arrives from the northeast in the winter months, from nearly due east during the spring, and from the southeast during the summertime, followed by a northern shift back to arriving from the east in the fall. The seasonal shifts in the directions from which this swell flows perfectly match the convex shape of the right, vertical lenticular pandanus root of the *wapepe*, which Isao similarly explains as the shifting directions of the northeast trade wind swell. Such a symmetry between oceanographic modeling and traditional wave concepts is completely missing for the other three swells. The oceano-graphic model simply does not indicate the presence of any regularly flowing swell from those directions. Intermittent, storm-driven swells from the south-west tend to characterize the fall and early winter months, but the associated winds would be too strong for safe voyaging, and the resultant wave patterns would be too irregular for navigation.

It seemed evident to me that the swell climatology model may be too general and that swells really did pass through the islands from the four cardinal directions. I just could not seriously accept that Captain Korent, his elders, and several generations before him envisioned four swells and built an entire navigational system on nonexistent phenomena. To obtain ground truth about the model, we deployed a small portable wave buoy at numerous locations, guided by Captain Korent. Floating untethered and gathering data through satellite tracking of its three-dimensional displacement, this buoy measured and recorded wave height, wavelength, and the wave period over the course of an hour at each location. One series of wave buoy deployments occurred on the northward *dilep* wave path between Majuro and Arno, a distance of sixty miles. Directed by Captain Korent, we positioned the buoy on the *dilep* and several miles off the eastern and western sides of the *dilep* in a transect to ascertain the normal, uninterrupted sea state. Thus, we should have been able to characterize the various swells and how they changed in the formation of the *dilep*. The results were startling. Despite Captain Korent's descriptions of feeling a balanced rocking motion from side to side from the opposing west-ern and eastern swells on this northern voyage, the wave buoy detected an eastern swell but provided no wave signature for a swell emanating from the west. The entire transect of wave buoy deployments on and off the *dilep* gave the same lack of information regarding a western swell.

Now, the apparent incompatibility between these two knowledge sys-tems warranted serious inquiry. The prime wave pattern, something that had not yet been documented, was called into question. It did not help that I and the other crew aboard the sailing vessel could not detect it ourselves. Was it a con-ceptual device rather than an oceanographic phenomenon? Following other navigational traditions in Oceania, one of the main methods of steering is to calibrate the direction of the initial course heading to the angle of the dominant swell and steering by that swell for several days. While Captain Korent does steer this way, he adamantly asserts that the *dilep* is distinct from steering by the relative angle of the swell. I also began to wonder if Captain Korent him-self thought he was feeling the *dilep* because it was supposed to be there. Yet Thomas, who had previously sailed 350 miles from Ujae to Majuro, reportedly guided his canoe in reference to a similar *dilep*. Thomas also demonstrated for

Alson and me the *dilep* heading north from Majuro to Aur while sailing just offshore. Sailing in the calm waters at the northern pass of Majuro and gazing northward toward the unseen islands of Aur, we felt and saw a crossing of eastern and western swells. It is quite possible that Captain Korent—and navigators generally—can detect swells that are too weak to be measured by a wave buoy or modeled. Even if swells arrive from opposite directions, however, their refracted wave crests would likely intersect very close to land, as the underwater bathymetry drops off so quickly. If this occurred within sighting distance of about ten miles, the *dilep* wave would clearly not be navigationally useful.

Such incommensurability may reflect local terminology and perspectives on the passage of time and movement through space. While navigators name the four main swells, a four-point orientation framework can generally be used only for direction. A "swell flowing to the west" could be equally coming from the east, northeast, and southeast. Likewise, a "swell coming from the north" could be flowing from the north, northeast, and northwest. With these two examples, a northeast swell could be referred to as either an east swell or a north swell. More importantly, the terminology may reflect the immediate sea conditions rather than tracking wave movements backwards through time and space. The refracted component of an east swell as it flows past an island would be referred to as a northward or southward flowing swell, rather than a "refracted east swell." Thus, a referenced "west" swell (or "north" and "south" swells) may actually be the refracted component of the dominant eastern swell. Still, detection of this type of wave signature is completely lacking from the wave buoy.

A clue to this enigma comes from the older Rongelapese custodians of this knowledge. They place the origins of the *dilep* wave on reflected waves from the destination island. This is similar to a piloting technique in the Santa Cruz Islands in the southeastern Solomon Islands, as documented recently by anthropologist Marianne George. Navigator Koloso Kaveia indicated and described a sailing course to George based on a combination of refracted and reflected swells that is strikingly similar to Captain Korent's descriptions of *dilep* and the visual patterning of the *wapepe*. Matching her description to the *wapepe* (see Figure 5.5), the easterly swell encountering an island in the east (E) and the westerly swell approaching an island in the west (W) each refract. The bending wave crests in the lee of each island continue to propagate until they strike the next island and reflect backwards. These wave transformations produce a lenticular shape demarcated (in the *wapepe*) by the convex arcs *buñtokeañ* and *buñtokrōk*. Kaveia explained to George how a "standing swell" on this boundary will cause a vessel to roll dramatically if it crosses it, while the reflected swells form a direct line between the islands. The navigator would feel the direct collisions of the steep reflected swells while on the direct route and would experience a rolling of the vessel if he veered from the direct route and encountered the standing swell.[28]

Harvard University physicist John Huth recently developed a computer simulation for the Marshall Islands that centers on wave reflection.[29] The programming sent a virtual swell from the east into the archipelago and modeled the resultant reflected wave energy over long periods of time (Figure 5.8). Visually, the darker areas have higher wave energy and the lighter areas have less. The wave shadow effects are clearly visible, but what stands out are concentrations of wave energy, or filamentary structures, that often link pairs of islands. Rather than a direct line, these filaments tend to bend between islands. Breaking of the swell on the coral reefs actually results in a substantial

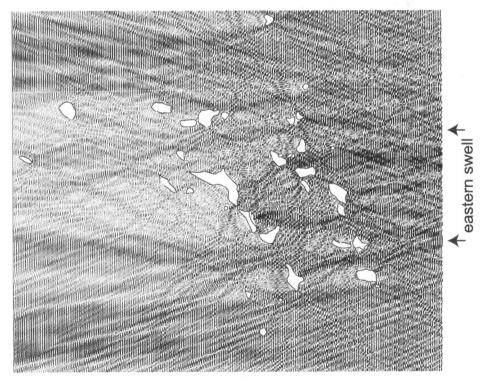

Figure 5.8. Computer simulation of wave reflections in the Marshall Islands (atoll lagoons and single islands in white); darker shading represents more wave energy, often concentrated between pairs of islands (base image by John Huth, with modified version of Paul Falstad's 2016 ripple tank applet).

loss of wave energy, but Huth suggests that weak but regionally distinctive wave patterns could likely be discerned and used as wave paths. And underwater shoals may emit a signature to the surface swell through depth-induced refraction. Although more refined simulations are needed, darkened lines of concentrated reflected wave energy appear to converge on an underwater seamount to the northeast of Rongelap called Ḷāwūn-Pikaar.[30]

Reflected wave energy, in accordance with the explanations provided by Rongelapese custodians and simulated by Huth, may constitute the paths of *dilep* and the windward seamarks *jur in okme* and *kāāj in rōjep*. As the introductory passage to this chapter reveals, Captain Korent detected and followed a progression of reflected *kāāj in rōjep* toward Arno, and I, the oceanographer, and the rest of the crew clearly felt the surge forward as the vessel pitched down a wave. However, the wave buoy did not indicate reflected waves during this trip and subsequent wave buoy deployments. The extremely weak or intermittent reflected wave signals may reside below the sensitivity threshold of the buoy.

Against such discrepancies, there is clear articulation of the leeward seamark *nit in kōt* from traditional Marshallese and Western scientific explanations. Remote detection of the wave patterns afforded by satellite images clearly indicates how an east swell bifurcates northward and southward as it passes by an island, resulting in a zone of intersecting wave crests in the island lee. Informed by satellite imagery and computer modeling, this wave transformation process is due primarily to wave refraction over the sloping bathymetric sides of the island, with minimal wave diffraction. The blocking effect of the island produces a wave shadow with refracted wave crests that extend several tens of kilometers downstream. A composite simulation taking into account the transformations of an easterly swell through reflection and refraction shows how the sea states correspond with the seamarks (Figure 5.9).

Armed with this knowledge, Captain Korent guided a small fishing boat around Majuro to measure wave refraction and empirically validate *nit in kōt*. Fifteen-knot winds from the east accompanied a five-foot-high swell with a period of ten seconds—typical for an average trade wind day. We started our series of wave buoy deployments to the southeast of Arno during the short navigational exercise when Captain Korent slept below deck in order to get data of an uninterrupted sea state, as there are no islands to the east of Arno. With a strong signal of the east swell, we followed its flow west to the channel between Arno and Majuro and finally reaching the western end of Majuro. As we entered the calmer waters of the protected western wave shadow, the data from the buoy strongly indicated that the eastern swell had changed direction with more southern and northern components. As ten-second swell (the re-

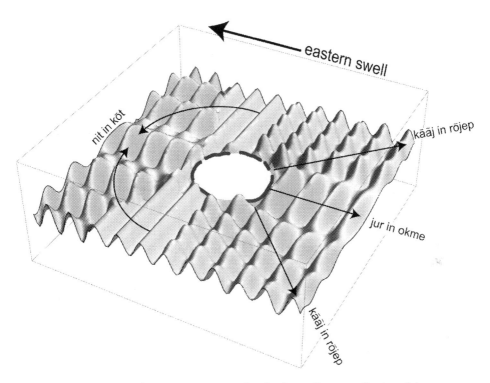

Figure 5.9. Wave interference patterns around a circular atoll: wave reflection of the eastern swell forms *jur in okme* and *kāāj in rōjep,* and wave refraction of the eastern swell as it flows past the atoll and forms *nit in kōt* in the lee wave shadow (base image by John Huth).

fracted components of the eastern swell) arrived from the north-northeast and the south-southeast, I clearly felt the boat rock from side to side with equal force. I actually had to hold onto the railings for fear of being catapulted overboard, such was the violent rocking of these two opposing waves. This was an unambiguous lee-wave crossing pattern. Finally, with a content smile on his face, Captain Korent declared, *"nit in kōt!"*

Captain Korent's satisfaction in Western science validating his knowledge while floating off the western shore of Majuro in the "trapped" waves of the lee crossing pattern *nit in kōt* marked a pivotal moment in his journey toward becoming a navigator. The previous wave buoy deployments that had failed to confirm Captain Korent's ideas of the waves or rectify his doubts were deflating his confidence. He was, after all, the last guardian of this knowledge whose health permitted him to voyage at sea and whose chiefs had given permission to share his knowledge. When I shared with him the visual data output from the wave buoy deployments along the *dilep* between Majuro and Aur and noted there was no signature for a western swell, his sense of failure was palpable. When another series of deployments returned with no signature of the reflected wave energy offshore of Arno that indicated the direction of land, he could just not understand why the buoy was not working! And another two-day excursion was, frankly, just plain depressing when we returned home to find the wave buoy's batteries had failed and had not collected any data.

That moment on the fishing vessel, rocking back and forth in the convergence of *nit in kōt* waves with the atoll awash in brilliant colors from the sun dipping below the horizon at our backs, was a convergence of knowledge systems that restored Captain Korent's determination to elucidate and authenticate the other wave processes in the Marshallese navigational system. At this point, in 2005, Captain Korent had not yet met Kapinmeto navigator Thomas Bokin, living on distant Ujae, whose navigational concepts were similar to those of Captain Korent but with clear differences. Thomas, a full generation older than Captain Korent, was the only known titled navigator in the Marshall Islands. Because the oceanographic models and simulations, wave measurements, and satellite imagery had largely helped Captain Korent only in questioning himself, he sought out Thomas to help clarify these ideas. Yet he still had enough conviction to sail, rather than fly, to Ujae. This voyage had many potential repercussions for the revival project. It was the first chance for Alson and me to obtain firsthand information on wave piloting in action. It would also serve as Captain Korent's much-belated navigation test. The most dramatic, diametrically opposed possibilities of such a voyage would be either finding land, an event that would elevate Captain Korent to the status of navigator and launch his fellow Rongelapese on their journey to reclaiming their ancestral heritage, or becoming disoriented and lost, which would forever cut off the customary route to becoming a navigator and could lead to a fatal deterioration of his mind.

Chapter 6

"Breaking the Shell"

Although the role of navigator brings rich rewards of virtuosity and membership in a distinguished elite, the many who for whatever reason are not so accomplished are never publicly criticized. This is true whether they tried and failed to learn or never cared to try.

    —Anthropologist Thomas Gladwin[1]

Wiwijet: "lose the direction of; panic."
    —*Marshallese-English Dictionary*[2]

~　　~　　~

We have been sailing—but mostly motoring—on a sloop-rigged yacht west against high storm-driven winds and seas for thirty-six hours without sighting a single star amidst a completely overcast sky when Captain Korent shows the first signs of uncertainty. He had strategized prior to departure that feeling a reflected wave pattern would lead us toward land. He scans the rolling swell to the starboard (right) side of the vessel, hoping to sight the wave patterns that should be there but that he could neither feel nor see. The intensity of his countenance does not convey his simple statement, "Probably, it is there. Just a little more time." As time passes, it becomes clear to him that either the navigation sign is not present or its wave signature is masked by the dominant storm-driven waves. Now unsure of our location, he is ready to direct the helmsman to tack through the wind and head on a different course in search of land.

This is the most intense moment of my fieldwork! I know, since I am discretely tracking the vessel with a handheld GPS unit, that if we hold our current course and speed, we could actually sight a tiny atoll that lies about twenty miles distant from our targeted landfall. This would surely give Captain Korent a renewed sense of location. Alternately, if we tack and head in the direction of the new course, we could quite possibly sail out of Marshallese waters without sighting any of the outlying islands. That part of the northern equatorial Pacific Ocean is blue water, void of islands. As we are sailing on a yacht laden with food supplies and U.S. Coast Guard–inspected safety equipment, I am not worried about the physical hardships of becoming lost at sea. But the cultural ramifications of becoming lost are potentially profound. If Captain Korent becomes disorientated to the degree that his *iroij* deems the trip a failure, the route to becoming a navigator—and possibly the entire revitalization of voyaging—would be closed. Even more damaging would be the possibility of entering a state of *wiwijet,* in which, according to *bwebwenato* shared by Captain Korent's relatives, a navigator loses his way, becomes confused, and continues to sail onward toward his death.

The destiny of the voyaging revival and the sanity of Captain Korent hinges upon the next few moments, as we strain our concentrated search for the waves. So many things depend upon what happens next. This journey is serving as Captain Korent's practical application of his navigational knowledge and demonstration of his learning from Isao and the other elders. The trip affords Alson and me our first opportunity to witness and chronicle Captain Korent's navigation and to experience the feeling of the waves ourselves. We had also designed the voyage to make landfall on Ujae, home to navigator Thomas Bokin, in the region of Kapinmeto, where navigation traditions had also remained strong in the minds of its last custodians. Captain Korent would have the ability to discuss his ideas with Thomas, who, a generation older, had previously built and navigated a canoe 350 miles from Ujae to Majuro. We all look forward to this fellowship of the waves with Thomas, of communing with the "distinguished elite," as described by anthropologist Thomas Gladwin in the opening epigraph. Most significantly, the voyage is serving as Captain Korent's *ruprup jọkur* test to become a sanctioned *ri-meto.* As we wait for Captain Korent to redirect the vessel, I wonder whether he will read something in the fluid motion of the waves to reestablish his ancestral intimacy with the sea and find land. In this chapter, I describe Captain Korent's much-awaited voyage of rediscovery in his attempt to "break the shell" and reclaim his Rongelapese identity as a "person of the sea."

Voyage of Rediscovery to the "Bottom of the Sea"

In the afternoon of September 2, 2006, the sloop-rigged, thirty-five-foot yacht *Mali* motored across the narrow southern apex of Kwajalein lagoon and out the southwestern pass and set course due west. This was the beginning of an unprecedented journey for Captain Korent, as well as everyone else onboard. The immediate goal was to reach Ujae, 140 miles distant, using traditional wave piloting techniques. The voyage would serve as Captain Korent's belated navigation test, which, under still-observed strict protocols of knowledge transmission, would allow his chiefs to socially sanction him as a navigator. The trip would allow him the opportunity to verify his rediscovered knowledge and subsequently question and learn from Kapinmeto navigator Thomas Bokin in order to refine his understanding of the wave concepts. The long-distance voyage would also provide Alson and me a much-needed opportunity to feel and begin to internalize the rhythmic motions of the sea.[3]

As we loaded food and water into the cabin and made our final preparations to depart Kwajalein, the differences between the planned and actual flow of this journey were becoming quickly apparent. We had strategized to take this voyage during the summer voyaging season, characterized by light winds and smooth seas, rather than the constant northeast trade winds and large waves of the windier winter season. While more difficult to sail with the light, variable winds, the undulating surface of the sea is more easily sensed. However, frequent summer storms interrupt this otherwise pleasant sailing season, and we were now experiencing the last fragment of such a storm system. About a week earlier, the strongest hurricane ever recorded in the central Pacific, a Category 5 storm referred to as Super Typhoon Ioke, traversed parallel to the Ratak chain, passing 350 miles north of Utrok and then near Enenkio with winds blowing at 155 miles per hour that generated forty-foot waves. Afterwards this typhoon diminished as it continued to travel northward. Over the next few days leading up to our departure, the remnants of Ioke produced shifting and variable winds. Then, on the morning of our departure, the sky was completely overcast and the ocean entirely becalmed of wind. Looking out across the glassy lagoon but mindful of the chaotic wind patterns over the past few days, we were uncertain whether to attempt the trip now or cancel it altogether—a decision complicated by several constraining factors.

Because the voyaging canoe *Jitdaṃ Kapeel* remained in dry dock for maintenance, we had enlisted the help of the local yachting community. At this point in my fieldwork I had become acquainted with most of this maritime group, as the nontransient sailors stayed for extended periods of time, sometimes years, and we shared mutual interests in seafaring. Captain Korent's fame had already spread throughout this community, largely due to his directing of a sixty-foot trimaran that had served as a platform to deploy the wave buoy on a series of transects between Majuro and Aur. It was not until the spring of 2006 that I met two young Kwajalein-based sailors, Eric Nystrom and Priam Kanealii, who jumped at the opportunity to let a Marshallese mariner guide their vessel. We had all just raced in the annual Coconut Cup, a unique regatta that features a variety of vessel classes including yachts, small sailboats, Marshallese canoes, and windsurfers. I had entered the windsurfer division, while Eric and Priam, new co-owners of the yacht *Mali,* had just made their first ocean crossing by sailing from Kwajalein to Majuro to enter the race. Their unbridled enthusiasm to assist Captain Korent in his quest created a concrete target for us: to sail from Kwajalein to Ujae. Because Eric and Priam worked at the U.S. military base on Kwajalein, we were required to have special security clearance to be on the base for a limited and specified period of time, which took several months to obtain. Thus, we had set the departure date for early September to take advantage of the pleasant winds typical of the summer months. Without the traditional foresight of ancestral weather knowledge that might have predicted such a colossal storm, we were now faced with sailing into uncertain weather conditions without any other viable options for rescheduling the voyage.

We discussed the potential impact of the remnant storm system on our plans on Majuro and then on Kwajalein after our short interisland flight, and I could not help but reflect on the tragic capsizing of *Hōkūle'a* in 1978 as a result of an ill-prepared crew sailing in terrible wind and sea conditions. After the Satawalese navigator Mau Piailug successfully guided *Hōkūle'a* 2,400 miles to Tahiti in 1976, a group of dedicated Hawaiians attempted a second crossing two years later. The unforeseen consequences of the decisions and circumstances of that fateful day resulted in the loss of life of legendary surfer Eddie Aikau after the starboard hull of *Hōkūle'a* filled with water, leading to a capsize in the channel between O'ahu and Moloka'i. The loss of Eddie and feelings among the crew and the wider community of guilt, remorse, incompetence, and blame nearly extinguished the spark of the emergent Hawaiian voyaging renaissance. Fortunately, Nainoa Thompson, who had sailed on the return voyage to Hawai'i in 1976, was motivated to turn this tragedy into triumph by sailing *Hōkūle'a* to Tahiti again. Not only did this happen, but Eddie's death catalyzed Nainoa to learn to navigate with the help of Mau Piailug. The subsequent resurgence of Hawaiian voyaging sent waves of inspiration throughout the island communities of Oceania, but the 1978 tragedy awoke the Hawaiian community to the always-present, possibly catastrophic and fatal dangers of voyaging.[4]

As we exited the southern pass of Kwajalein at three o'clock in the afternoon, the fact that we were sailing on a modern yacht with the full suite of standard safety equipment provided us with some reassurance. We had covered the vessel's compass with duct tape and stowed all other modern navigational equipment so as to best mimic a traditional voyage. Eric and I kept track of the voyage on independent handheld GPS units that we stowed when not in use, and this added a sense of comfort. In addition to providing a track of our journey and the ability to mark positions with salient wave patterns, our dual GPS would independently trigger alarms if we unknowingly came dangerously too close to land at night. We each set our GPS to sound an alarm if we came within five miles of land. As Captain Korent had been guiding nonsailing vessels for thirty years, he was also quite comfortable with the idea, if required, of heading straight for Ujae by lowering the sails and motoring, under diesel power, straight into the westerly winds. Because Captain Korent would still rely on traditional navigation, he felt comfortable motoring as an alternative to sailing with a series of upwind tacks. As it turned out, this is exactly what we did.

Light southeast winds met us as we motored out of the southern pass of Kwajalein, but once we cleared the islets and gazed out to the western horizon to envision our distant targets of Lae and Ujae, the winds increased to twenty knots from the northwest and rain severely reduced our visibility. About ten miles out, the westerly winds reduced again to about five knots and the rain dissipated, allowing us a final glimpse of land. With this back-sighting at five o'clock an hour before sunset, Captain Korent directed *Mali* due west.

The simple mechanics of staying on Captain Korent's intended course proved quite difficult. As darkness descended upon us—a rather quick event in the near equatorial latitudes of the Marshall Islands—the completely overcast sky and heavy rain precluded any star sightings. Even though celestial references do not contribute substantially to the Marshallese concepts of orientation, the crew had basic knowledge that one could maintain a course by keeping a certain star "fixed" on the celestial dome in relation to the alignment of the yacht for a certain period of time. Without any visible stars, we were left to our sensory perceptions of the oncoming wind and waves. Even this was challenging. Under sail, it is relatively easy to maintain a course with a constant wind. Turning upwind will cause the sail to luff, and turning downwind will change the pressure on the sails. The vessel's angle in relation to the wind is also felt as differential pressure on the tiller-controlled rudder. With the benefit of engine propulsion, Captain Korent directed us to point the bow directly into the oncoming waves and wind. We simply steered into the direction of the wind, trying to keep the rhythmic pitching motion of the yacht fairly constant; if we fell to either side of the direction of the wind, the yacht would ride up and then down each swell at an angle, with a combination of pitch and roll.

Collectively, our relative inexperience sailing in such conditions made it hard for us to consistently maintain Captain Korent's heading. Assuming that we—like his professional crew aboard the government transport ships—would easily keep the vessel on track, Captain Korent would often head below deck to rest, only to reappear an hour or so later needing to make course corrections. He often looked to me and gestured, sometimes articulating in Marshallese, that we needed to head either more upwind or downwind, and I would accommodate accordingly or relay these slight directional changes to the crew member at the helm. This process of constantly modifying our meandering course, in combination with the incessant pitching of the yacht, battering from the waves that swept over the deck, and unrelenting rain, made for a physically uncomfortable and emotionally draining first leg of the voyage that continued for about thirty-six hours.

While the crew and I faced the elements and struggled to keep *Mali* on course, Captain Korent confronted the much bigger problem of navigation. He had strategized ahead of time on the planned course and associated wave patterns. Diagraming on paper, Captain Korent envisioned sailing on the *dilep* from the southern Kwajalein pass to slightly north of the single, small atoll of Lae and then onward toward the southern tip of Ujae, as the only pass to gain entrance into the protected lagoon lies on the western edge of the atoll. Invoking Isao's teachings, Captain Korent envisioned how a series of current streams (*jukae, rubukae,* and *jeljeltae*) should radiate outward from Kwajalein, Lae, and Ujae, the transitions of which would mark the distance traveled on the *dilep* path. The windward reflected seamarks of Lae and Ujae would provide additional ways to remotely hone in on land. At present, the storm-driven waves dominated the sea, masking all of these more subtle wave patterns.

My first indication that Captain Korent was having difficulty in detecting any salient land-indicating wave patterns occurred the first evening after he retired below deck to rest about nine o'clock. His final directions to me and the rest of the crew were to continue to sail west into the direction of the wind and waves. Because I was actively recording our position every hour on my handheld GPS, I alone was aware of the fact that the westerly wind had just shifted to blowing from the west-northwest. Without any external environmental referents, Eric was maintaining this new direction, thinking that we were still sailing due west. Without my GPS, I would likely not have noticed the wind shift, and I worked hard to not affect the emotional state of the others as we deviated from Captain Korent's intended due-west course. At one o'clock in the early morning of September 3, the winds shifted again to the northwest, but true to Captain Korent's stated directions, Priam, who was at the helm, followed Captain Korent's stated command and inadvertently followed a more northwestern course. At the start of Alson's turn at the tiller at three o'clock in the morning, I saw a light to our starboard and woke up Captain Korent, as it was hard for me to tell what the light signaled and how far away it was in the still rainy conditions. And crew members of a traditional sailing voyage would certainly have awoken their navigator when something new appeared on the horizon. Captain Korent identified this as a light emanating from a Kwajalein islet, which indicated to him that we had clearly tracked too far to the northwest. He desired to head more to the west, but once again he directed us to sail into the direction of the oncoming wind, which now had shifted back to west-northwest and continued from that direction for the rest of the night until the break of dawn.

The Kwajalein light and other fortuitous land sightings helped strengthen Captain Korent's sense of confidence on September 3 as he struggled to maintain a sense of direction based solely on the shifting wind-driven swell, an orientation confounded by the crew's collective struggle in maintaining a straight course. With completely overcast conditions, it remained impossible to determine even the general direction of the rising sun. At the beginning of my shift at the helm at seven o'clock in the morning, I spotted in the diffuse lighting the faint outline of an island to our starboard. Captain Korent, upon waking, believed this was the extreme northwestern Kwajalein islet, called Mejatto. Because we could see the dark outline of the tops of the coconut trees while we were standing up but not sitting down, we estimated that we were at the very edge of visual sighting of land, which, for the low-lying atolls of the Marshalls, is about ten to twelve miles away. Piecing together the possible wind shifts and inconsistencies in maintaining a heading, Captain Korent, with this new fix of his position, radically altered course to the southwest in search of the small atoll of Lae (Figure 6.1). We raised sails and enjoyed a breezy but refreshing close-hauled sail for a few hours. Based on his geographical knowledge of the locations of Mejatto and Lae, however, Captain Korent knew that we needed to head more upwind. Limited by the aerodynamics of the sails and not wanting to embark on a series of upwind tacks against the now twenty-five-knot westerly winds, at noon he ordered the lowering of the sails and decided to motor straight into the wind once again.

After several hours of motoring into the westerly wind and oncoming swell, Captain Korent began his search for the windward navigational sign (*kōkḷaḷ*) of Ujae, believing we had already sailed past Lae and were now located to the southeast of Ujae. He scanned the starboard horizon in search of the wave patterns of the atoll's easterly reflected wave *jur in okme* and its southern demarcation, *kāāj in rōjep*. Even though he could not discern any such pattern, he was so convinced that Ujae lay off our starboard side that he was getting ready to direct Priam to alter course to the northwest. Standing beside Captain Korent, I, too, was trying in vain to see some signs in the ocean. While Captain Korent strained his vision to starboard, I glanced port, to the south, and at that exact moment I saw something small appear on the horizon

Figure 6.1. Captain Korent Joel observing the waves on the voyage from Kwajalein to Ujae, with the yacht *Mali* under sail, 2006.

and then disappear. By this point I was thoroughly exhausted and doubting myself, thinking it was a trick of my imagination. Then I saw the faint dot on the horizon again when we topped a swell. I alerted Captain Korent, who first dismissed it as a passing ship. As we continued to focus on the manifesting image, it became clear to us that the tiny object was moving slightly back-wards with reference to us—we were, we collectively discerned, sailing past a distant island. I discretely checked my GPS and realized this was the tiny atoll of Lae—we were actually right on course since our Mejatto sighting! I could not share this knowledge with Captain Korent, of course, without jeopardizing the purity of his navigation test. Rather than dawning enlightenment, however, I instead saw confusion wash over Captain Korent's face.

A sense of panic seemed to envelope Captain Korent. This speck of land should not be there! After the Mejatto sighting, Captain Korent had mentally gauged that we were to the southeast of Ujae, having unknowingly just passed the small atoll Lae. Likely from the combined messiness of the weather systems and meandering course imposed by the still-emerging seamanship of the crew, Captain Korent felt that we had somehow sailed in the wrong direction during the night, possibly by following a circular wind pattern, and that we had inadvertently sailed back to the southern pass of Kwajalein! Thinking we were positioned where we had originally started from, he now insisted on sailing to the northwest in fervent search of Ujae.

I could not believe this was happening. In reality, we were about ten miles directly north of Lae. If Captain Korent were to realize this, it would be a more straightforward journey to the much larger westward atoll of Ujae, located about thirty miles distant on our current course. However, Captain Korent's impending shift in direction would send us on a new course far to the north of Ujae. In fact, on the slim chances of sailing close to the distant atolls of either Enewetak or Bikini some four hundred miles to the northwest, the likely trajectory would be to sail, if uninterrupted, out of Marshallese waters altogether. Captain Korent's panicked demeanor did not instill a great sense of confidence in me, so to mask my emotions and not betray my knowledge of our position, I went below deck and busied myself with confirming our position on Eric's nautical chart.

The potential ramifications of Captain Korent's impending decision were monumental. On the one hand, this voyage was serving as his final, belated navigation test that, if deemed successful by his reigning chiefs Iroij Mike Kabua and Iroijlaplap Imata Kabua, would elevate him to the famed status of a titled *ri-meto*. Becoming severely disoriented at sea and becoming lost had horrific consequences. Not only would Captain Korent fail to become a navigator, but the window to this status would, according to traditional protocols, be forever closed to him. Aside from the elderly Thomas Bokin, Captain Korent was the last hope to instigate and sustain the effort to revitalize traditional voyaging. More pressing was becoming afraid. Rongelapese navigator Lapedpedin once expressed these thoughts to Gerald Knight: "The man who is lost is afraid. He has that sinking feeling in his belly and he is in a hurry to get somewhere—anywhere—hoping he'll find his island."[5] Even worse was the possibility of *wiwijet*, which, according to oral traditions, is a crazed state of mind whereby the navigator loses his way, becomes confused and panicked, and continues to sail toward his death at sea, or, in the event of being rescued, stumbles through the remains of his life on land in a deathlike existence.

In a collection of memories from the Pacific theater of World War II,

Nathan Tartios narrates the repercussions of *wiwijet*. He and many others tried to escape Maloelap under the Japanese occupation by sailing to Aur. So many people tried to leave that most had to float in the water by holding onto the sides of the canoe, which was filled beyond capacity. When they had to take on even more people after another canoe was damaged, they could only drift. Of the some thirty-two people on that canoe, only six narrowly escaped death after hypothermic immersion in the ocean for four days to reach the shores of Aur. Many children died due to overexposure, while others drifted into a *wiwijet* stupor: "Well, some of them became dazed (crazy), the thing Marshallese call *wiwijet*, 'lost all sense of direction.' I do not know what it is in English. Their minds were damaged some from their having been in the ocean for so long."[6]

The direct translation of *wiwijet* in the *Marshallese-English Dictionary*, defined in the second epigraph as "lose the direction of; panic,"[7] does not convey the depths of meaning of becoming disorientated for Marshallese navigators. Isao Eknilang, with vast repertoires of oral traditions, summarily states that "*Wiwijet* is like getting lost, really lost, where you don't remember anything." In one section of a much longer *bwebwenato* on the origins of navigation, Isao describes how the woman Litarmelu, who had obtained her navigational knowledge from visiting navigators and ultimately passed on navigation to her son and through him the rest of the Marshallese, eventually became so lost at sea that her canoe flew upwards to the sky, where it remains obscured from sight today.[8] Through his tracing of his genealogical ties to Litarmelu, Isao describes how he witnessed *wiwijet* among his father, Turlik, and adopted father, Monaean, during their *ruprup jǫkur* sailing test:

> My father[s] Turlik and Monaean took their navigation test by sailing from Ailinginae to Wotho. From Ailinginae toward Wotho they sailed near Bikini and Rongelap and finally approached the islet of Jokdik. Between Wotho and Ailinginae they spent one week lost at sea, because they became disoriented. I rode along and learned the word *wiwijet* for navigators. All the navigators became *wiwijet*—my adopted father Monaean and Turlik, a very good navigator who conducted the navigation school on Rongelap. Everyone sailed together and became lost together.
>
> Turlik, sitting down on the canoe, showed us the navigation sign for Jokdik islet on Wotho—the male ruddy turnstone (*kōtkōt*). He said he should chant for Jokdik because we are now near Wotho. The navigation sign will reveal the island. The elder Turlik opened the chant with the lines, "The male *kōtkōt* paddles, it takes a long time to bring the canoe there, who can steer a straight course and hit Jokdik directly?"[9]

Isao's recollection of his childhood observations of dual *ruprup jǫkur* events suggests that the psychological impact of becoming lost at sea may be mitigated by the benevolent guiding of an *ekjab,* such as the ruddy turnstone of Wotho. And Captain Korent had committed to memory from Isao the various living seamarks of Kwajalein, Lae, and Ujae that might facilitate the journey with spiritual guidance. Still, the notion of sailing disorientated until expiring at sea holds tremendous weight for Captain Korent and the others. Captain Korent often joked that he did not want to become like Toshiro Jokon, who had felt the full impact of *wiwijet.* Toshiro had been the last fully trained navigator who applied his skills at sea.[10] After Toshiro returned from guiding the large Enewetakese voyaging canoe to victory at the 1992 Pacific Arts Festival in the Cook Islands, he spent considerable time at sea fishing but became disorientated during one excursion after he ran out of gas and drifted for several days. Captain Korent, then a captain leading the government's search and rescue operations, calculated Toshiro's likely position based on drifting with currents and eventually spotted and rescued him. The stories surrounding this event end with Toshiro never fully recovering from his sense of dislocation at sea, roaming the islets of Maloelap with a *wiwijet*-induced vacancy until he passed away.

Becoming a Navigator

With such descriptions of *wiwijet* firmly in mind, I began, while pondering Eric's nautical chart with our mapped position, to imagine the worst-case scenario. Captain Korent would command Priam, the helmsman, to tack to the northwest, unknowingly sailing beyond the known waters of the archipelago. Would the last *ekjab* of the western Kapinmeto seas make their presence known to Captain Korent, as they had to Turlik and Monaean? Would such spiritual guidance even help? Having mentally readied myself for whatever decision Captain Korent made, I climbed up from the cabin to the deck, and much to my relief Captain Korent had decided to sail closer to the island for a positive identification. As we sailed closer, Captain Korent and Alson discussed the probable island based on the configuration of its coconut trees. About seven miles away, Captain Korent, who as a government ship captain had seen all the atolls and their individual islets from sea, knew decidedly that it was in fact Lae.

Although the navigation test would not be complete until we sighted Ujae and sailed back to the southern pass of Kwajalein, I believe that this moment constituted the first stage of Captain Korent's *ruprup jǫkur.* With a newfound sense of confidence at sunset (although the fully overcast sky still precluded any general sense of the sun's direction), Captain Korent directed us to motor slowly at a creeping two knots to the southwest in order to avoid hitting Ujae at night. We never did detect the reflected wave patterns that should have given us directional and location clues of Ujae. More significantly, at four o'clock in the morning Captain Korent sighted the southern tip of Ujae at the same time that he and Priam observed the atoll's specific locational navigational sign in the substantiated form of an *ekjab* spirit—a named school of dolphins (*jeran kōmmaan*). Reminiscent of Turlik sighting the ruddy turnstone near Wotho, the graceful swimming of the dolphins was an oceanic sign, passed down through the stories and chants of Captain Korent's Rongelapese ancestor Lainjin and his mother, Litarmelu. Isao, Captain Korent's uncle, had chanted about this particular school of dolphins on Majuro prior to departure in his rendition of the *ikid eŋ an Lainjin,* and Captain Korent had thus embraced this navigational sign as part of his suite of strategies. While *ekjab* are known to lead some navigators astray, the benevolent act of Ujae's school of dolphins to assist us in reaching the atoll proved to Captain Korent that he had been on the right track despite his confusion.

Still, this was not the crisp intellectual transition from seasoned mariner to navigator that the stories about *ruprup jokur* had led me to believe. He had guided *Mali* 230 miles in forty-eight hours without identifying any salient navigational wave signs and without sighting any stars, and his confidence had been severely shaken through his displaced sense of location with the fortuitous sighting of Lae. Yet, he maintained a sense of dignity by jokingly asserting that at least he was not as bad as other navigators who had failed their navigation test. Once we entered the lagoon and reached the main southern islet of Ujae mid-morning, we anchored *Mali* in the calm waters, motored toward shore in a small inflatable dinghy, and walked along a path to the house of Thomas Bokin. The subsequent conversations with Thomas opened a different way of thinking about the ocean and sparked a renewed conviction in Captain Korent to complete the return voyage of his *ruprup jokur.*

After a welcome meal of cooked turtle and general comments about the voyage through the storm, Captain Korent initiated an inquiring series of questions with Thomas. Volunteer teachers stationed on Ujae had previously told me that Thomas was not very forthcoming with imparting his knowledge on others. I had thus been expecting Captain Korent to talk privately with Thomas as fellow navigators, but Captain Korent quickly drew Alson and me close to him to pose additional questions directly to Thomas. Young men, likely the community's sailors and canoe builders, stood outside craning their necks to watch their elder in action.

As we questioned Thomas on the waves, he walked outside, plucked four coconut fronds, and proceeded to weave his stick chart through the sitting mat, placing coral pebbles in various quadrants of the design (see Figure 4.1). Captain Korent was surprised to learn that Thomas' interpretation of the *wapepe,* which he literally translated as "canoe floating," was only to be used conceptually in the event that one was completely lost at sea. The important interpretation of the ocean, Thomas contended, resided in the architecture of the model. Thomas confirmed the central significance and formation of the *dilep* "backbone" wave, introduced the idea that the intersections of wave shadow effects from multiple incoming swells produce the distinctive navigation signs (*kōkḷaḷ*), and revised our understanding of the three zones of currents by placing them along the *dilep* between atolls rather than radiating outward from each atoll. In addition, Thomas declared that if direction cannot be ascertained from the waves, four celestial references of the cardinal directions could be employed. A general orientation could be determined by Jebrọ rising in the east and setting in the west, together with stationary Polaris in the north and a southern star in the Southern Cross in the opposite direction.

Based on Thomas' teachings that night, Captain Korent revised his sailing strategy for the return voyage the following day. He would follow the *dilep,* formed by the crossing of the northern and southern swells, locate the *jukae, rubukae,* and *jeljeltae* currents during the beginning, middle, and end of the voyage, and detect the reflected *kāmeto* wave "flying" back to the ocean after the western swell strikes the western edge of Kwajalein. The fundamental difference was the placement of the three zones of currents. Captain Korent also began to conceptualize the navigation signs of each atoll as the effects of wave shadows, but his emerging plan to detect these remote signatures of Ujae, then tiny Lae, and finally the extensive outline of Kwajalein had to be adjusted based on the weather conditions. In effect, he entirely reversed his mental imagery of the locations of these wave signatures. The stick chart interpretations by Isao and Thomas rest on the transformations of the trade wind–driven easterly swell. Now, the storm-driven swell was still flowing from the west, creating a dramatically reduced sea state in the lee of Ujae to the east. This area of calmer seas with refracted wave crests (*nit in kōt*) lay to the east of Ujae, not to the west. In addition, Captain Korent planned to detect Lae by sailing north of the small atoll through the wave shadow produced by a southerly swell.

As we exited the pass of Ujae in the late afternoon on September 5, 2006, the wind and ocean conditions were much more favorable. The westerly winds had calmed slightly to fifteen knots, and the swell was slightly reduced in size. Significantly, we could finally raise our sails for a pleasant downwind sail. Although this presented the dangerous proposition of jibbing in high winds if we began to run directly downwind, a series of broad reaches downwind would make for an enjoyable experience, uplifting everyone's spirits significantly. Our hosts had also loaded us with fresh fish, which Alson began to cook as we headed down the western coast of Ujae with the setting of the sun.

As we rounded the southern point of Ujae about six o'clock just before sunset, Captain Korent directed us to steer slightly north of east on a broad reach so as to sail through Lae's northern wave shadow. We immediately sensed the diminished sea state in the lee of Ujae, which was blocking the storm-driven western swell. Two hours later, with a final back-sighting to one light on Ujae, we began to notice a rising westerly swell. At ten o'clock, Captain Korent drew our attention to swells from the north and the south and felt certain vibrations that indicated to him that we were sailing through the first zone of currents, *jukae.* Three hours later, at one o'clock in the morning, Captain Korent felt another pattern of currents, *rubukae,* which he interpreted according to Thomas' explanation. A momentary break in the clouds allowed for a fragmented view of the celestial dome, and Captain Korent pointed out Jebrọ. But it was rising too far to the south, which meant we had tracked too far in a northeastern direction, and he ordered the helmsman to steer slightly more downwind to the east. This was Captain Korent's only use of a celestial referent during the voyage, as he went below to sleep for the rest of the night. The crew and I took advantage of a few more intermittent star sightings to continue sailing toward the direction of rising Jebrọ for a few more hours.

The dawn of the next morning, September 6, brought excellent sailing conditions: fifteen-knot winds from the southwest, a clear day with no threatening weather, smaller swells of three to four feet—and a sighting of tiny Lae. At dawn, I saw part of the atoll on our starboard side. We were slightly more than five miles away. The two handheld GPS units had not triggered their proximity alarms. Excited, I went below deck to awake Captain Korent in his bunk. Before I even had the chance to wish him a good morning, he stated with eyes still closed, lying prone in bed, that we were to the north of Lae, because he could feel the absence of the southerly swell.

We were on the right track! As we passed Lae and continued sailing throughout the morning, Captain Korent detected once again the south swell, and he continued to monitor the dominant westerly swell and the swell from the north. Occasional reflected waves, *kāmeto,* from Kwajalein apparently began at this point to strike the port beam, although neither I nor the rest of the crew could detect what Captain Korent pointed out to us. At four o'clock in the afternoon, we sailed through a section of currents, which Captain Korent identified as the third zone of currents, *jeljeltae,* based on Thomas' explanation back on Ujae. And the north and east swells were effectively blocked by

Kwajalein—another indication that we were on track. If we veered too far south, we would confront the eastern swell. Close to sunset, Captain Korent noticed a particular navigation sign that indicated land was nearly straight ahead. He called this *nit in kōt*, but with the conceptual reversal of the *wapepe* and *meto* as a result of the wind shift, this sign was effectively a windward *kāāj in rōjep*. A reflected swell from Kwajalein (from the east) was heaping up the intersection of the western and southern swells. We could not directly follow this wave pattern, as we would have sailed directly downwind and risked jibbing. We continued our course for several hours, and at ten o'clock at night we sighted lights.

Trying to suppress our enthusiasm, we sailed closer for Captain Korent to confirm that the lights were shining from Kwajalein's southern pass. A few miles later, with the verification of the targeted landfall through the growing luminance of the military base, Captain Korent's awakening, or "breaking of the shell," and emergence as a navigator was virtually complete. In the words of Namu navigator Alton Albious, Captain Korent's knowledge had risen (*etak in wa*, literally "light rising").

Later, back on Majuro, Alson would report to the chiefs and chronicle Captain Korent's physical and intellectual journey by sailing round-trip between Kwajalein and Ujae (Figure 6.2). With the quietness that only the Marshallese can fully appreciate, Iroij Mike Kabua and Iroijlaplap Imata Kabua deemed the trip a success, and Captain Korent was a socially sanctioned navigator. Hopeful of this verbal authentication that was to come, the full impact of what had just transpired began to settle over me and the crew as we sailed closer to Kwajalein.

The two-way voyage between Kwajalein and Ujae was a historic event. Only a few others had attempted their *ruprup jọkur* voyages after World War II, and several of those navigators are now deceased or too elderly to make such a trip. In this sense, Captain Korent was likely the last navigator who had the potential to teach others. He strongly desired to return to Rongelap, once deemed safe from nuclear contamination, and teach his young grandchildren at the coral reef training area as he had once learned from his grandfather.

Captain Korent's *ruprup jọkur* voyage highlights both the innovations and traditions that are being invoked to revitalize wave pattern navigation. The customs of Marshallese voyaging are being preserved through the maintenance of traditions relating to power and the management of knowledge, such as the personal concealment of knowledge. Inheritance continues through family lines, with the authority of the chiefs governing the use and transmission of knowledge, even though this wider sharing may ultimately erode the chiefly power and prestige of navigator-elite families. There remain requirements for

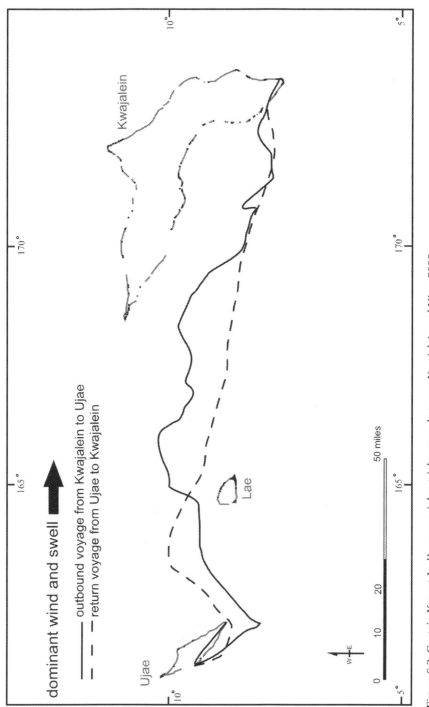

Figure 6.2. Captain Korent Joel's *ruprup jokur* trial voyage between Kwajalein and Ujae, 2006.

the demonstration of knowledge and the high value placed on experience-based learning through the *ruprup jokur* test. Formal recognition by the *iroij* still awards and socially confers the navigator's title of *ri-meto*.

These enduring forms of preserving traditions, while certainly changing, encouraged Alson and me to consider an alternate form of preservation codified in law. Following Captain Korent's *ruprup jokur* voyage, we honored him as *the* cultural expert in navigation based on legislation of the Marshall Islands Historic Preservation Office. Since the beginning of the legislation in 1992, the Historic Preservation Office can bestow a title of *ri-kapeel* on people with exceptional skills and knowledge.[11] This "person with traditional knowledge and skills" would be an individual with unsurpassed knowledge in a particular domain of knowledge, such as a *ri-kapeel* in navigation, a *ri-kapeel* in fishing, and a *ri-kapeel* in canoe building. The legislation is based on traditions of chiefs bestowing the title on their best specialists. Today, the Historic Preservation Office has the capacity to review nominations from the community and, in concert with a body of *iroij,* select one individual for this titled position akin to a national living treasure. The chosen *ri-kapeel* agrees to train one apprentice for at least one year, for which he or she receives monetary compensation. Importantly, the locally resonant *ri-kapeel* title offers a way today to continue the transmission of knowledge from elders to the younger generation. However, the legislated title has never been implemented since its inception, and our nomination for Captain Korent has remained silent. It is possible that the contemporary usage of the term may not be entirely free of negative associations, and this may have contributed to the title never being enacted. In particular, the early German ethnographies note that *ri-kapeel* were people with magical powers that could use them at their will.[12] Yet the *ri-kapeel* title and its stipend would have helped Captain Korent realize his dream of teaching his grandchildren on Rongelap, even if for a short time period, as resettlement has still not occurred.

Fallout

Although the *ri-kapeel* title was never enacted, Captain Korent had just "broken the shell" to become *the* recognized expert on navigation throughout the archipelago. In addition to our public announcement of his *ri-kapeel* nomination, Captain Korent's name ran across newspaper headlines and confirmed with the sailors and broader community what they had long suspected—that he could navigate by the waves, and that he was among the very last. Implicit in the title of *ri-meto* was the ability to officially train a protégé, even without the legislation. I was not prepared in any way to anticipate or adequately deal with what happened next.

When I returned to Majuro a year later in the spring of 2007 to visit Captain Korent, I was led, stunned, into a dark room in the hospital. Captain Korent lay in bed, blankets wrapped around his legs, looking smaller and withdrawn. We talked for a few minutes, but the tears welling up in his eyes signaled my quick departure. I visited him every day for the next three weeks to bring by some food to help out his supporting family and just to *bwebwe-nato* a little bit. I learned indirectly that he might have a prediabetic condition. But he felt his illness was caused by someone's malevolent wishes. It has remained difficult for me, even now, to fully appreciate his perception of his condition and circumstances in those days. Had we not followed certain cultural protocols? Had the *ruprup jọkur* test created hostility or jealousy? Had the psychosomatic effects of social conflict manifested a particular view of reality? How do I weigh my role in promoting Captain Korent's rise to a titled navigator given his deterioration? I returned two years later in July of 2009 to find him luckily out of the hospital but confined to his home in not much better condition. It would take the actions of his apprentice, Alson Kelen, to inspire Captain Korent to head out to sea again on a canoe voyage a year later, and this seemed to break his spell.

Chapter 7

Rise of the Apprentice

The uniqueness of an individual's accomplishments is like the distinctive wake produced by a sailing canoe (*inkan aọdde*).
—Marshallese proverb[1]

Canoe sailing is the biggest source of pride for Marshallese, and our captain has ensured that our traditional ways of navigating will not be lost.
—Ailinglaplap master canoe builder Binton Daniel[2]

~   ~   ~

The voice of the chief engineer of the M.S. *Jebro* cuts through the noise of the diesel engine as it drives us mercilessly into steepening waves. I crouch down low to cross the deck toward the cabin, mindful of the risk of being tossed overboard by a sudden deluge of water in the absolute darkness. I stumble inside, my glasses so coated with salt spray I can hardly see, and I hold onto a railing for balance as the handheld radio gets passed to me. I press the button to communicate with the canoe *Jitdaṃ Kapeel*, but I crash into the captain as a wave violently rocks the vessel. Footing regained, I try again and Alson Kelen sounds incredibly calm.

> "*Jebro, Jebro*, this is *Jitdaṃ*. Four o'clock [a.m.] check in. Do you copy? Over."
> "Hey Alson, this is Joe. Howzit? How you guys doing out there? Over."
> "Well, the guys are really cold and hungry. Over."
> "Copy that. Do you know where you are? Over."
> "We are to the east of Aur. We haven't reached Aur yet, but we are to the east a bit. Probably about ten miles or so. Over"
> "Copy that. What is your plan? Over."

"Well, we are going to keep sailing, and once the sun comes up, we will
  start searching for land to the west. We will turn downwind. Over."
"Okay Alson, sounds good. So you are going to keep going on your present
  course? Over."
"Yes, that's the plan. Over."
"Okay, you guys stay warm out there and we'll see you in the morning.
  Over."

I release the transmit button and set the radio receiver back in its holder,
holding onto the single railing in the cabin as the fishing vessel, appropriately
named *Jebro* after the cultural hero who first sailed an outrigger canoe, rolls
violently from side to side, nearly knocking down the captain as I stumble with
my footing. As I glance again at the digital map showing our position and then
out into the complete darkness through the salt spray–encrusted windows, I
cannot help but admire what Alson has just accomplished. It is June of 2015,
and what was supposed to have been a pleasant light wind sail on the heavily
rebuilt canoe *Jitdaṃ Kapeel* has turned ominous. The choppy wind-blown
waves have been so strong that most of us on the escort vessel are seasick, and
surely such a violent sea has masked any of the more subtle wave signatures
indicative of land. Yet Alson, who has begun to learn navigation from Captain
Korent, knows exactly where the outrigger canoe is located. He realizes the
canoe is racing too fast with the high winds for the rapidly diminishing distance to the approaching reef of Aur, and he needs to sail away from land to
avoid blindly crashing into the reef at night. He is doing this on his own, without navigational guidance from Captain Korent, who is bedridden with a severe ailment. Alson still has to sail through the night without the canoe ripping
apart in the high winds, and he still has to locate land with the dawn's approaching light. Binton Daniel, the master canoe builder from Ailinglaplap
who has placed his faith in Alson, relays to me through the radio that the sail's
halyard is on the verge of breaking, and the crew needs to lower the sail and
heave-to in order to tighten the weakening rope. If they can just keep going
until daylight! Alson will also have some explaining to do to his governing
chief once back home, as such a demonstration of navigational proficiency
without formal recognition of being a navigator is unprecedented. But for now,
in this moment on the open ocean, Alson has nearly found his way, returning
the canoe to his people.

This return of tradition involves shifting protocols in the use of navigational knowledge under extraordinary social conditions. Without precedent,
the apprentice navigator Alson Kelen acquired and demonstrated navigational
knowledge without the guidance of his teacher Captain Korent. The first ca-

noe voyage from Majuro to Aur in 2010 involved some radio communication of navigational information from Captain Korent, who had partly recovered from his hospitalization and thus remained on the escort vessel, to Alson Kelen aboard the canoe. Captain Korent's health took an unexpected turn just prior to departure of the second voyage to Aur in 2015, and Alson attempted the trip without Captain Korent. In this chapter, I present my understanding of this still-unfolding story as an example of the ever-shifting constraints, challenges, and opportunities of cultural revitalization in Oceania.

The "Rise of the Apprentice" is about Alson's journey toward becoming the next navigator. The opening epigraph is a Marshallese proverb that compares the uniqueness of an individual's accomplishments to the distinctive wake produced by a sailing canoe (*inkan aǫdde*). Alson's unique ability to navigate the waning but still powerful traditions in the face of emerging, critical twenty-first century issues is paramount for the resurgence of knowledge such as wave navigation. In one sense, Alson is sailing in the wake of his ancestors to, as canoe-builder Binton Daniel remarks in the second epigraph, ensure that canoe voyaging by the waves does not disappear. Invoking the proverb, Alson is also creating a new wake that will hopefully leave behind an extraordinary legacy. He is invoking the ancestral knowledge to confront and adapt to critical environmental and social concerns. The return of the outrigger voyaging canoe in the seas of the Marshall Islands provides a cautiously optimistic glimpse into the future of traditional wave navigation at a time when a restoration of traditional forms of resilience are critical for cultural survival.

Becalmed

Determined to build upon the foundational knowledge gained by observing and experiencing Captain Korent's *ruprup jǫkur* voyage in 2006 but highly constrained by constantly needing to search for supporting grants, Alson and I began planning a northern trip of sixty miles from Majuro to Aur as a navigational exercise. Alson knew he was not yet ready for his own *ruprup jǫkur* test. Without the possibility of floating in a canoe at Rongelap and having already talked-story at length with Isao Eknilang and Thomas Bokin of their interpretations of their stick chart wave models, what Alson needed was as much experience at sea as he could get.

The thirty-five-foot outrigger sailing canoe *Jitdaṃ Kapeel*, which in one translation means "searching for experiential knowledge" and proverbially means "seeking knowledge guarantees wisdom," was built to serve as the training vessel for Alson and the crew to begin to absorb the embodied knowledge of wave movements and learn directly from Captain Korent on the wa-

ter. Alson's team of canoe-building trainers and students reinforced the hull
with fiberglass for extra strength and built airtight compartments in the bulkheads to produce a virtually unsinkable vessel. After they carved a new outrigger float, relashed the outrigger complex, and purchased new rigging, we
planned on the late summer of 2009 for the canoe's first voyage. This would
serve as the first navigational training exercise, with Captain Korent guiding
the canoe, Alson learning directly from him, and the sailors internalizing as
much experiential knowledge as possible. This would be a fundamental step
to pass on Captain Korent's knowledge to Alson and another younger generation of mariners.

When I arrived in Majuro the canoe was nearly finished, and we stock-
piled food and water for the journey, confirmed that the escort vessel was on
standby, and installed some basic safety equipment. We placed an electric bilge
pump in the bottom of the canoe, secured an emergency locator beacon to the
base of the mast, hung a radar deflector midway up the side stays of the mast,
and positioned a man-overboard pole on the outrigger complex. We also flew in
Thomas from Ujae to conavigate with Captain Korent. Although seventy-nine
years of age at the time, he was still amazingly active and yearned to be at sea
once more. We anticipated that it would be a wonderful blend of experiences on
the canoe. Then we waited.

We had scheduled the voyage during the latter part of the summer voyaging season (*rak*), and that year the light winds had become erratic and
highly variable and then dropped to nothing. Inexplicably, there were virtually no winds for nearly a month, which left us gazing, day after day, at a
glassy ocean from shore. Every day Alson and I drove to Thomas' house and
brought him to the canoe building site, and we talked under the shade of a
tree. Sometimes Captain Korent and Isao would join us. With a malaise building in all of us, staring at the flat sea day after day, we eventually decided to
tow the canoe to the far northern pass of Majuro to conduct a floating classroom lesson. Thomas had been describing the much anticipated trip to Aur,
and he said that at the northern pass of Majuro he would be able to immediately show us the *dilep* path of waves extending northward toward Aur.

The faintest breath of wind encouraged the sailors to raise the sail, but
we still had to be towed the seventeen miles to the deep pass. Thomas sat
perched on the navigator's lee platform, talking to Isao and Alson. As we
passed the last islet and drifted in the pass, we felt some strengthening of the
wave energy, as we were nearly out of the calm lagoon and into the deep
ocean. Thomas confidently demonstrated by gesturing with his hands to Alson and Isao the crossing of east and west swells at this location. We could all
see the intersections of the waves flowing from the east and the waves flow-

ing from the west. The waves struck each other with a heaping-up effect. Thomas indicated that a navigator would start with this crossing of waves and sail northward toward distant Aur, searching for the next such intersection or "knot" along a path.

Radio Silence

A year later, in May of 2010, *Jitdam̧ Kapeel* made her first water crossing from Majuro to Aur and back under sail with strong winds, but with a novel way of navigating. The crew faced high wind-generated seas that were part of the normal ending of the windy season (*añōneañ*). With the winds blowing from the east, the canoe could track northward to Aur on an ideal beam reach without the need for shunting. Captain Korent, with recovering health, did not feel up to the task of sailing on the canoe. He decided to stay aboard the escort vessel while Alson commanded the canoe with six experienced sailors from Ailuk, and the two vessels would maintain radio contact so that Captain Korent could help guide Alson. This was an unprecedented plan. Never before in the Marshall Islands had the navigator given directions to his apprentice through radio waves.

Shortly after departure, the handheld VHF (very high frequency) radio onboard the canoe malfunctioned, with depleted batteries. Captain Korent strained in vain to yell directives to Alson above the wind and across the seas between the two vessels. Communication stopped amidst the heaving of the vessels, salt spray drenching Captain Korent on the escort vessel and waves inundating Alson and the Ailuk sailors on the canoe. In practice, Alson, as captain of *Jitdam̧ Kapeel,* was on his own to guide the canoe, but at least he had the visual comfort of the escort vessel with the daylight. But most of the voyage took place at night, when it was too easy to lose sight of the escort vessel's lights. Stories from Alson and the crew relate how at times the waves washed over the entire canoe—and crew! One crew member fell overboard and the inexperienced crew could not quickly reduce the speed of the canoe, but fortunately he was picked up by the chasing escort vessel. The return voyage was characterized by even higher seas, forcing the crew to lower the sails several times. Tension mounted on the canoe without Captain Korent's guidance and leadership as Alson and Tem Alfred, the most experienced of the Ailuk sailing crew, challenged each other's authority. Yet, they made it safely to Aur and back to Majuro. Alson shares his view of the voyage:

> Captain Korent was still very weak from his sickness and had to be helped on board the escort vessel. The plan was for Captain Korent to radio directions to me on board the canoe. We got to the pass leading out of Majuro

around midnight, with blowing winds and white-capping seas. There was much discussion amongst the crew from Ailuk whether to go or not. Tem told me that the sail would not withstand the wind, and to abort. I told Tem that I knew the integrity of the canoe, and that it would not break. I radioed to Captain Korent to give me the swell to Aur, and he said, "No. It is too rough and the trip should be aborted." I told Captain Korent that I wanted to test the canoe, as it had never before sailed in the ocean. I reminded the crew that it was reinforced with fiberglass and had airtight bulkheads, so that it could not sink. In the event of capsizing, I advised the crew to grab a line and get out of the way of the hard fiberglass, and once it settled in the water to grab on. Tem told me that Captain Korent alone knew the seas, but I was determined to make the trip. Wanting to experience the sea, even in the high winds and seas, made me continue. Tem reluctantly raised the sail, and we flew out of the pass away from Majuro. We had sustained speeds of twenty knots, faster than powerboats I have been on. We just flew! Sometimes the canoe would arch out of the water and ride down the next swell.

As we sailed, Tem challenged my knowledge and ability, since Captain Korent was not giving active instructions. The plan was that Captain Korent would only radio me if the course needed to be corrected. The rest of the crew kept quiet and trusted me, stating that I wouldn't put their lives at risk, but Tem continued to have his doubts. The distance between Aur and Majuro is sixty miles, and we would have made it to Aur by sunrise but we had to repeatedly wait for the escort vessel during the night. At about nine in the morning we spotted the first signs of Aur, but I didn't know where on Aur we were approaching. I asked Tem, who, having sailed these waters, pointed out the pass ahead. But rather than sailing straight through, I had the sail lowered and the escort vessel towed us in to avoid risking hitting the reef in the narrow pass. We finally reached the mayor's house, who came out and was surprised to see that we had sailed through the high winds.

We stayed a few days, and Tem led the strengthening of the outrigger with some additional lashings, and then set sail again at seven o'clock, with still strong winds and seas. This time, though, a strong westerly current and a strong easterly wind made for very turbulent seas, making steering very difficult, and sometime in the night, about three o'clock in the morning, I finally told everyone to just take down the sail and sleep. The current would eventually bring us to some calmer seas. At dawn, we raised the sail again, and sailed within sight of the pass of Majuro. Having accomplished the navigation, the escort vessel towed us in.

On the Aur trip there were six crew plus myself. All of us fit comfortably on the canoe, with three actively working as crew while three slept. We could also cook. One would be below deck, cooking rice and brewing coffee and tea, while we sliced through the ocean. The canoe was also packed with gallons of water for ballast. As the waves came pouring over the canoe, the one below would calmly ask everyone how they wanted their coffee!

This trip strengthened Captain Korent. He had to be helped on board the escort vessel by hand, and I told the other captain to not let him do anything. But by the time we had completed the trip, Korent's health had returned and he was doing some of the work, such as dropping the anchor. I couldn't believe it, but then I realized that Captain Korent was a person of the ocean, and that is where he belonged. If such a person stays on land too long, their health begins to deteriorate.[3]

The 2010 Aur voyage accomplished a lot of things. It allowed the sailing crew to handle the canoe in severe weather conditions for the first time. It served as a quick remedy for Captain Korent's deteriorating health. The tension caused by the unprecedented navigation via radio contact worked to eventually unite the crew. It also allowed Captain Korent another opportunity to navigate by the waves on his own aboard the escort vessel. While admiring Alson's determination to reach Aur, Captain Korent recognizes that Alson did not follow his directives. Captain Korent reflects on his experience:

I felt the *dilep* all the way to Aur. I also felt the *kāāj in rōjep* to the southeast of Aur some fifteen miles away. The canoe had a lot of leeway and veered off to the left of the course. We could see Polaris intermittently, as it was partly overcast with lots of rain and strong winds from the east. We sighted one of the far western islets of Aur rather than the main islet, but got there nonetheless. On this outbound trip, Tem wanted to steer more upwind, more northward, but Alson persisted in sailing west of north. I did radio to Alson a few times to tell him to alter the course, but he did not.

On the return trip, I also felt the *dilep* from the east and west waves, but the canoe this time drifted too far to the west. There is a shallow wave connecting Arno and Aur, and we ran into this very choppy water. Eventually we made our way onwards but actually sighted Arno first. We came back toward Majuro. It was a good trip. It could have been better, with a straighter course, but at least we got there and back. I did not plot anything. The course is so short there is no need.[4]

Tem Alfred did not agree with Alson's choice to sail with the high winds and did not have confidence in Alson's knowledge of the sea. He also felt that the design of the canoe was inappropriate. With a relatively horizontal keel, the vessel did not track well. When minor adjustments to the course heading were made with the steering paddle, the canoe would keep shifting direction, and then only brute strength would bring the canoe back on course. Incredibly muscular and much older and more experienced than the younger Ailuk crew, Tem steered the canoe for most of trip, causing immense pain in his back that he would feel years later.

When I had first talked to Alson in 2005 about his plans for the canoe revitalization, he stated that he envisioned his role to be like that of Nainoa Thompson in the Hawaiian renaissance. He shared with me that he felt a calling and deep responsibility to serve as the link between the ancestral knowledge, embodied now in Captain Korent, and the future generations of sailors under his tutelage at Waan Aelōñ in Majol. Alson had first sailed with Thomas from Ujae to Majuro in 1996. Then, in 1999, he sailed with Hawaiian navigator Shorty Bertelmann and legendary Satawalese navigator Mau Piailug from Hawai'i to Majuro on board the Hawaiian voyaging canoe *Makali'i*. It was this journey that deepened his commitment to, as he stated, "becoming the Nainoa Thompson of the Marshall Islands." With the first traditional passage from Majuro to Aur aboard *Jitdaṃ Kapeel,* Alson had taken his first step in realizing his vision.

Searching for the Waves

The name of the thirty-five-foot outrigger sailing canoe—*Jitdaṃ Kapeel* —has another meaning in addition to "searching for experiential knowledge" and proverbially "gaining wisdom." Alson describes how it can also mean "exchanging of experiential knowledge," with the idea of face-to-face interactions. In 2015, the search for a more complete understanding of the waves— notably the still enigmatic *dilep* wave path—included a complex exchange of knowledge, experiences, and perspectives. A year earlier Alson and I had invited John Huth, a particle physicist at Harvard University with a passion for traditional navigation, and Gerbrant van Vledder, a wave modeler from Delft University in the Netherlands, to accompany Captain Korent when he would guide *Jitdaṃ Kapeel* on a repeat voyage northward to Aur and back to Majuro.[5] While the wave transformations near an atoll made sense to both scientists, the foundational "backbone" wave—the *dilep*—between atolls remained problematic from a Western scientific perspective. They traveled halfway around the world to meet Captain Korent and observe his navigational prowess in action and to feel for themselves this critical path of waves.

When I had first met Captain Korent in 2005, his foremost request was that he wanted a scientist to validate what he had been feeling at sea for the past four decades. The presence of a physicist and oceanographer on Majuro fulfilled my promise to Captain Korent, but more importantly it would allow them to inquire for themselves about the *dilep* wave and for Captain Korent to corroborate or possibly improve his experiential knowledge. Like the 2010 voyage to Aur, Alson strategized that Captain Korent would remain on the escort vessel and radio navigational information to Alson on board the canoe. Alson and the sailing crew would become immersed in sailing the canoe on the ocean, while Captain Korent would demonstrate to John and Gerbrant the waves he was using to pilot the escort vessel toward Aur. Heightening the significance of this journey for Captain Korent and Alson was the coverage by the *New York Times Magazine*. A writer and photographer came to document this collaborative, interdisciplinary search for the wave that would finally validate the idea of wave piloting.[6] Days before their arrival in Majuro, however, the search for the *dilep* wave became nearly unattainable.

Captain Korent had developed an infection in his leg. When Alson and I visited him at his home immediately upon my flight's arrival in Majuro, we first met his wife who instantly shared with us that he was sick. Alson and I looked at each other, dreading what was about to come next. She explained that a few weeks ago he had been fine, and then his leg began to hurt. A combination of traditional and Western medicine did not seem to be helping. We spoke with Captain Korent briefly. He was happy to see us but could not get up from a prone position in bed. We tried to stay positive and hint that perhaps if he felt better he could show the scientists the *dilep* at the Majuro pass like Thomas had done in 2009, but we both comprehended that he was not going to be sailing with us to Aur. Still, Captain Korent tried to engage the scientists. "Do you believe in the *dilep*?" he asked them, and the next few moments was a hurried exchange of ideas as the scientists asked him questions about the currents and provided their own insights, as well as diagrams of the possible wave conditions to Aur (Figure 7.1). I felt an eerie repeat of his condition and our attempt to go sailing several years ago, as Alson asked, "What are we going to do now?"

Without Captain Korent, Alson's options narrowed. We could try to enlist the navigational guidance of Thomas or Isao. But Thomas was now eighty-five years old and away on remote Ujae, with no regular airline service to Majuro. I met Isao several times as he sat in front of the Rongelap Atoll local government office, but when asked, he humbled his abilities by stating he "would get us lost." This was not his moment. Without a navigator, one emerging option was to go ahead with the trip and install a GPS on the canoe for guidance so that the voyage would serve as a training exercise for Alson and the sailing crew on how to handle the canoe on the open ocean. With fierce determination, Alson decided to attempt the voyage. He would lead the

Figure 7.1. Captain Korent Joel at his home in Majuro, looking at a wave map prepared by John Huth, 2015 (photograph courtesy of Mark Peterson/Redux).

canoe as the navigation apprentice, absorb as much information from the ocean as possible, and relate this to Captain Korent upon our return. Three independent GPS systems aboard the escort vessel would adequately serve as navigational help if he needed it.

This breach of protocol in the use of navigation was yet another move without precedent. This was certainly not Alson's *ruprup jọkur* navigation test. If pushed, he would admit to others that he was a navigation apprentice, but he preferred to avoid any suggestion of his growing knowledge of the waves. He prefaced the trip when talking with the community that he would be "guessing" along the way. Taken at face value, it would appear that he would in fact be trying his best to comprehend and interpret the waves. But humbling of one's knowledge is an older, distinctive Marshallese form of communication. By telling others that he would be guessing his location on the canoe, the elders in the community might conclude that he in fact knows how to navigate. As this had not meant to be Alson's time to rise to the status of navigator, he would simply tell people, when asked, that he and the sailing crew were going on a fishing trip and would guess their way northward.

At least the canoe was ready, but just barely. For two months in the late spring on Majuro, Binton Daniel, the master canoe carver from Ailinglaplap, Waan Aelōñ in Majol trainers Sear Helios and Elmi Juonraan from the same atoll, and their students rebuilt and strengthened several components of the outrigger voyaging canoe that had failed during the 2010 trip. They carved a new outrigger float, heightened the deck, cut new supports for the outrigger complex, added fiberglass for reinforcement, relashed the entire canoe, and sewed and attached a more durable sail to the booms. Once the canoe was launched in the protected lagoon, they lashed a protective guard to the bottom of the hull and installed safety equipment, including an electric bilge pump, a radar deflector, and a man-overboard pole. During this construction and maintenance period, the twenty-five Waan Aelōñ in Majol students were heavily involved in the work, learning directly from their teachers and through quiet observation. Alson wanted Binton to be his next in command on the canoe out of respect for his wisdom as an elder, but also because he knew every modification that had been done to the canoe over the years. Sear and Elmi readily agreed to crew the canoe, and Alson also requested the assistance of former Waan Aelōñ in Majol trainer Ejnar Aerok from Arno and Jason Ralpho from Namdik. Due to light and variable winds, the sailors had only one day to conduct sea trials. But the canoe performed well in the lagoon, with no mandated adjustments. We secured the use of the escort vessel, stocked it and the canoe with food and water, and brought in the sailing crew from their homes.

During the predawn darkness on the day of our tentative departure, on June 17, 2015, Alson walked to the oceanside reef of Ejit island on Majuro and felt the stirring of the easterly wind. With steady ten-knot winds arriving by mid-morning, Alson made the decision to set sail in the afternoon. He readied the sailing crew on *Jitdaṃ Kapeel* while I organized the research and documentary teams on the M.S. *Jebro*.

The canoe, having sailed almost straight downwind westward across the lagoon, reached the pass about six o'clock, an hour before sunset (Figure 7.2). Remembering how Thomas pointed out the westerly swell that combined with the easterly swell to form the *dilep* heading to Aur, the scientists and I searched for a westerly wave to accompany its eastern counterpart, but we could not detect it. As soon as the canoe turned upwind and got out of the protected lagoon waters, the easterly wind increased to about fifteen knots and we were greeted by its wind-driven wave. After sunset, the seas became rough. When the canoe sliced downward through a wave, the entire hull in

Figure 7.2. *Jitdaṃ Kapeel* outward voyage from Majuro to Aur, 2015 (photograph courtesy of Mark Peterson/Redux).

front of the mast became submerged. With its rounded hull, the escort vessel fared much worse. It began rocking so violently from side to side that all but one of the research and documentary team became violently seasick.

As the sun sank beneath the horizon, Alson guided *Jitdaṃ Kapeel* north-ward, with fifteen-knot, wind-driven, choppy waves from the northeast and still no indication of a westerly swell. A waxing crescent moon appeared above the setting sun, along with the bright planet Venus. As we continued to sail northward, the stars were clearly visible. For most of the night I was able to sight stationary Liṃanṃan. With the approaching dark, we began to track slightly east of north and kept this course well into the night. Alson, on the other hand, faced mostly astern and kept track of his northeastern movement in terms of the southern position of kite asterism Liṃaakak. The waves be-came bigger, violently rocking the M.S. *Jebro* from side to side. With the higher winds, now gusting to twenty knots, Alson realized that he should have waited longer at the pass before blazing across the sea, because he was going to arrive at the southern reef of Aur before sunrise. He knew the approximate arrival time based on the strong winds during the previous 2010 Aur voyage and from stories shared by fishing ship captains who timed their arrival with the rising sun to avoid crashing on the reef in the dark. Thinking of the safety of his crew, Alson sailed northeast as close-hauled into the direction of the incoming wind as possible to intentionally overshoot Aur so that in the morning Aur would lie downwind to the west of the canoe.

Around midnight, the halyard holding up the sail against the mast began to stretch so that the upper boom began violently hitting the mast. The stretching rope left a three-to-four-foot gap that separated the mast from the sail. Under Binton's directives, the sailors lowered the sail, hove-to, and examined the rope, and then tried to pull it tight before raising the sail. They repeated this procedure several times during the night. During this time, Alson felt a spiritual power help the canoe along the route: "We took down the sail because the rope that connected the sail to the mast was about to break. I believe a spirit was with us helping us to reach our destination. The rope could have broken and the canoe could have had some serious issues. Some might have died, but a spirit stretching from the ocean to heaven helped us so that none of these events happened."[7]

We lost contact with the canoe at two o'clock in the morning. The crew had forgotten to install a light at the top the mast. They did bring along a radar deflector so that passing ships could detect the canoe with their radar, but the sailing crew hung it so low in the rigging that even the nearby M.S. *Jebro* radar could not discern the canoe from the background scatter of waves. Because the escort vessel could not detect the canoe with radar, visual sightings were required even in the darkness. The sailing crew would periodically project the beam of a flashlight onto the sail, and then the captain of the escort vessel would shine his high-powered searchlight at the canoe to signal we knew where they were. We did communicate by radio, but to conserve batteries Alson shut his handheld VHF radio off after each use. We motored across the incoming swells, salt spray coating the cabin windows, waiting for the radio contact and searching in vain for a glimmer of light. Finally, the call came.

> "*Jebro, Jebro*, this is *Jitdaṃ*. Do you copy? Over."
> "Copy. This is Joe. How are you guys doing, Alson? Over."
> "Crew doing well, canoe holding up. Eating some rice Elmi cooked in the teapot. How you guys? Over."
> "All us *ri-pālle* [foreigners] are throwing up. Otherwise okay. Over."
> "Funny. Over."
> "Alson, we can't see you guys anywhere. Can you see us? Over."

"Yeah, we are at your one o'clock, can see you fine. I'll check in an hour
    from now. Gotta save power. Over."
"Okay. Over."

An hour later, Alson described to me over the radio where he believed
the canoe was located. I did not want to alert him to his position unless he
started to approach too close to Aur, and currently he was safely about fourteen miles to the southeast of the atoll. And even during the high winds and
rough seas, I needed to ask about the safety of the crew. His response was
both reassuring and startling for its accuracy. He described our exact position
as displayed on the GPS display in the cabin of the M.S. *Jebro.* With no dis-
cernable wave patterns, Alson determined his location from a solitary focus
on sighting the kite asterism of Liṃaakak and maintaining a tight angle to
the wind.

With the dawn's first glow at five o'clock, the canoe was about fifteen
miles due east of Aur, five miles too far to sight land. Alson knew his approximate location and needed to turn downwind. Once they sighted one or
two of the islets of Aur, they could triangulate their position and then return
southwest to enter the lagoon on the southern pass or shift northward and enter the northwestern pass. Yet they continued sailing into the wind for several
hours with complete radio silence. Then, about seven o'clock, Alson radioed
the escort vessel, stating that they were having a really hard time turning
downwind.

After the 2010 voyage to Aur, the master canoe builder, Binton, had
remedied the problem of not tracking well, but with no opportunity to conduct proper sea trials, he and the crew now realized the opposite problem—
they could not get enough leverage in the steering paddle to turn the bow of
the canoe downwind. Exhausted, cold, and hungry, the crew still trusted in
Alson's leadership as they tried in vain for several hours to turn the canoe
downwind.

Binton asked Alson about the location of land. With the rising sun directly behind him, Alson pointed to a dramatic rainbow diving into the ocean
to the west. He had no way to verify it at the time, but I was looking at the
same rainbow and later would realize that Alson once again knew exactly
where he was—fifteen miles east of the northeastern islet of Aur called Tabal.
But they could not get there. Binton reverently looked up to the sky and said,
"The spirit will guide us." As the crew could not steer the canoe downwind,
Alson suggested that the escort vessel tow them the remaining distance to
Aur. Binton was relieved and astounded when a few miles later, after chasing
the rainbow for an hour, he spotted the distant trees on Tabal. From then on

and with quick rejection by Alson, Binton has quietly referred to Alson as "captain," the adoption of the English word to mean a local navigator: "During the voyage I put all my faith onto my captain and trusted that we would make our destination, although I was a bit worried because that was my first time sailing between islands in an outrigger canoe. It took time to sail, but we managed to reach our destination."[8]

Ailinglaplap sailor Elmi similarly refers to Alson as the respected captain: "I wasn't worried about the canoe or anything. I just sat and saw how smooth we sailed with the wind. I had no concerns at all. I had no doubt in the captain because he knew the route."[9]

After a ceremonial welcoming of singing and sharing of food with the Tabal community in the shade of a thatched open building, the sailing crew enjoyed some much-deserved rest. The following day they repaired the canoe, which suffered minor problems during the outward voyage. They replaced the sailing sheet and the halyard that hoists the sail, as the original rope had stretched too much during the voyage, and relashed part of the outrigger complex, as one of the horizontal pieces had become loose and shifted downward toward the outrigger. After church service the following morning, on June 20, with coconut leaf baskets laden with food and fresh coconuts to drink, the sailing crew hoisted sail. A steady ten-knot wind out of the east filled the lateen sail of *Jitdaṃ Kapeel* as it headed southward across the lagoon toward the southern pass. Rather than shunting the canoe to reach the pass, Alson guided the canoe right across the shallow reef, scraping the bottom as they headed into the open ocean in the late afternoon.

Compared to the outbound voyage, the sea and wind during the return voyage afforded excellent sailing. Gently rolling swells from the east, about three to five feet in height with a six-second period, characterized most of the voyage. As the canoe left Aur, the swell was flowing from slightly south of east, and the canoe's track was roughly perpendicular to the swell, tracking slightly west of south. Before sunset, Alson observed the wake of the outrigger float and extrapolated that they were experiencing a slight current flowing to the west (Figure 7.3). A few hours later the winds began to lighten, and by midnight there was barely a breath of wind, somewhat variable in strength. The easterly swell had shifted to flowing directly from the east, but with such light winds, the canoe had difficulty heading close to the wind and continued drifting westward. The ocean was barely moving as Alson peered over the outrigger complex and shone his light over the side—"moving about as fast as a turtle!" At two o'clock in the morning the winds picked back up, eventually to about fifteen knots, and at that point Alson was able to turn the canoe more into the wind and veered more east of south. The direction of the incom-

Figure 7.3. Alson Kelen (and Elmi Juonran and Binton Daniel), return voyage from Aur to Majuro, 2015 (photograph courtesy of Mark Peterson/Redux).

ing swell had also shifted slightly to flowing from north of east. Looking at the GPS map in the cabin of the M.S. *Jebro,* I realized that with the shift in direction Alson was guiding the canoe directly toward Rongrong, the farthest northwestern islet of Majuro.

Dawn broke with a brilliant sunrise. The canoe was about twenty miles to the northwest of Rongrong islet, heading straight for it, but still a third of the overall distance left to cover. About ten o'clock, Alson made radio contact.

> "Good morning, Joe. Do you copy? Over."
> "Hi Alson, this is Joe. How you guys doing? Over."
> "The guys think they see land. Over."
> "Okay, copy that. Over."

I had just spotted Rongrong myself and had confirmed our location on the GPS map, but based on Alson's comment that they might have seen land, I did not want to give away any information even though I desperately wanted to congratulate him. In fact, Elmi had already spotted land and the crew had already burst into cheers, shouting with excitement. After another hour, the crew triangulated their position. They could just barely make out two islets, and Alson pointed out that there are only two places on Majuro that look like that. He wanted to give the crew a chance to figure this out. It was Sear who recognized one of the islets after remembering that he had once gone spearfishing there, and with that confirmation Alson went to sleep as the crew sailed straight toward the pass, completing the voyage on the open ocean in about twenty hours. Without Captain Korent, we were still not that much closer to understanding the *dilep* wave path, although the scientists gained adequate experience to begin to revise their computer models and simulations. It was actually on the escort vessel where the practical experience of navigation lay hidden and untapped.

With another moment of extreme humbling of knowledge, the realm of maritime knowledge and navigational experiences among noncanoe sailors—the crew of the interisland transport ships—became acutely apparent to me during the voyages between Majuro and Aur. I chatted with Joseph Junior Lanwi, a young man in his mid-twenties serving as chief engineer aboard the M.S. *Jebro,* while cooking a pot of chicken and potatoes in the tiny galley and while searching for the dim light of *Jitdaṃ Kapeel* throughout the nights. What I learned astonished me.

Junior had anticipated the sea conditions and the canoe route of both the outbound and return trips based on accumulated practical knowledge of the sea and wind conditions along with local forecasting. His parents are from Majuro and Tabal islet on Aur. In elementary school he sometimes cut class and hopped on a boat to Aur, and he has continued sailing that sixty-mile route ever since. He has also sailed to nearly all the atolls within the archipelago. This voyage seemed like a well-known path to him, and after our return he would wait only one week before heading out again to bring fishing supplies to the Tabal community. He said if I had asked him prior to our departure from Majuro, he would have told us we would throw up! While calm in the lagoon, he stated, it was going to be rough conditions in the open ocean. He pointed to the waxing crescent moon and explained how the phase of the moon influences ocean conditions. During the moon phases that span a new and quarter moon, the sea will be really rough at low tide. On the other hand, a high tide coupled with the moon phases between first quarter and third quarter is characteristic of calmer seas. Indeed, we left at low tide and it was rough. And we returned when the moon was a bit bigger, almost quarter moon, and at high tide, and it was calmer.

In addition to anticipating the sea conditions, Junior predicted Alson's course based on experience of the local winds and currents. At sunset, while leaving Aur, the canoe had begun to track to the west, and this caused some anxiety among the scientists, as the extrapolated course would take us west of

Majuro well out of visual range of sighting the islands. Junior suggested that Alson would continue on his course, but a few hours later, after midnight, he would start to arch back toward Rongrong, the northwestern tip of Majuro. He explained that most of the time there is a slight westerly flowing current, and when leaving Aur the easterly wind shifts to blowing from just south of east, so that even close-hauled the canoe would at best sail west of south. About halfway to Majuro the winds would shift back to blowing from the east, which would allow the canoe to sail directly southward. Closer to Majuro the winds would shift again, blowing from slightly north of east, which would allow Alson to sail a bit east of south and head straight for Rongrong. While Junior had explained the explanation of the moon phases after the journey had started, now he was predicting the course based on wind and current conditions at the onset of the journey. And the canoe traced the exact route he had predicted!

Junior's story of practical seafaring knowledge is not unique. The professional sailors of the Marshall Islands spend considerable time at sea and have surely amassed similar local knowledge of the winds, moon phases, currents, and the waves. This vast practical experience, combined with a renewed community interest in the canoes that is symbolized by the recent flight of *Jitdam Kapeel* to Aur, as well as the continuity of sailing with comradery and spirituality, brings hope that the ancient art of navigating by the waves will not vanish.

The path forward to keep searching for the waves rests on the forging of trusting relationships. Unlike the 2010 voyage that was characterized by some tension among the sailors, the 2015 journey was filled with comradery. Although the sailors hailed from different atolls, they worked well together. Alson believes it was the best crew he had worked with—hard working, determined, and cheerful:

> In comparing the voyage of 2010 and this voyage of 2015, I tell people that the voyage now is way better than the first one. Before I had guidance from a captain. This time I was very scared because lives depended on me. I was trusted by many to guide us safely to Tabal and I cannot thank them enough for trusting me with their lives. As we sailed, there were a lot of obstacles and many dangers—dangers with the sea and with the rain, but they still trusted me. A lot could have happened and there could have been disasters. I was so happy on how things turned out. It was due to the hard work of the crew. Binton took responsibility for the functioning of the canoe. Sear took responsibility for steering, and Elmi was the cook and engineer. Everyone worked together.[10]

The shift from the strain of the 2010 voyage to the solidarity of the 2015 voyage is reminiscent of the shifting dynamics on board *Hōkūleʻa* between the inaugural 1976 voyage and return voyage in 1980 to Tahiti, and both the Marshallese and Hawaiian voyages of rediscovery also shared a spiritual journey. Alson Kelen, like Nainoa Thompson during his navigation to Tahiti, journeyed back to the spiritual world of his ancestors.[11] Previously, while standing in a small circle on the cement platform looking out to the moored canoe in Majuro, Alson had led the crew in a prayer. He had asked for a smooth deliverance to Aur and for the crew to place their lives with him. They did have complete faith in Alson's abilities to find land. During the early morning on the outbound voyage to Aur, Binton had looked skyward and asked for guidance when the crew could not turn the canoe downwind. He had asked Alson about the location of Aur, and Alson pointed to the direction of a rainbow. Although the escort vessel had to tow the canoe, we still sailed straight toward the rainbow when Binton saw land. On the return voyage, when Elmi spotted the islands of Majuro, a booby flew overhead. One of the crew members chanted about Litakpoki, the name of the navigation sign for Majuro. The idea of an *ekjab* in the form of a seabird guiding the canoe toward Majuro was not unexpected—a school of dolphins known to be the *ekjab* for Ujae had been spotted just as Captain Korent had sighted land during the 2006 voyage.

During the night on the return voyage to Majuro, the crew, more relaxed than during the wild outbound voyage, enjoyed the fellowship of song. With the water flowing past the hull, the supports of the outrigger creaking against their lashings, and Alson giving occasional directions to fall off the wind or turn into the wind, an old song filled the night. Ejnar Aerok led the song with his sweet tenor, and Jason Ralpho accompanied him with a deep baritone voice. The song speaks poetically of a heroic voyage from Aur southward to Majuro.

> Calm wind and the clapping rhythm on the sail
> The wind that guides the canoe to the islands in the distance
> Land ho! Land ho! A small island appears on the bow
> Aim at the island and don't get off the course, Majuro is on the bow
> Aim at the island and don't get off the course, Majuro is on the bow
> We have accomplished what we've worked hard for
> It was not by luck that this happened
> I see the island and the magnificent surrounding sea, nurturing us
> I will stay on Majuro where I will enjoy a beautiful life
> I will stay on Majuro where I will enjoy a beautiful life[12]

"Staying on Majuro where I will enjoy a beautiful life" eloquently cap-tures the cultural significance of the *Jitdaṃ Kapeel* voyage. The return of the canoe is much more than the reforging of an identity of an ancestral seafaring people. It is about the reawakening and renewal of traditions that will build cultural resilience in such a way as to allow the Marshallese to stay on their precious islands. Against an uncertain future of climate change–induced ris-ing sea levels and other emerging environmental and social issues, the return of the canoe may afford not just cultural survival but a right to enjoy a beauti-ful life.

Epilogue:
Return of the Canoe

A little girl runs out to the water's edge on the lagoon side of Tabal islet on Aur and asks, "What's that?" Having never seen a real sailing canoe, the lowering of the sail of *Jitdaṃ Kapeel* upon its arrival must seem like the materialization of Lōktañūr's legendary first sailing canoe. Bollon Boklon, the community leader of Tabal and younger brother of Iroij Jackious Boklon, who had extended the invitation to host our sailing crew, welcomes our fellowship with a feast. He describes in a formal speech how two weeks of local wages had been used to purchase the gasoline required to drive an outboard motorboat to the best reefs to hunt the lobster and spearfish the catch we are consuming. Copra and handicraft production earns the residents of Tabal about $1 per day, he explains, but the price of gasoline hovers at $10 a gallon. Ending his formal remarks, Bollon invokes the proverb, "*Wa kuk, wa jiṃor. Waan kōjipañ koj, waan kọkkure kōj. Waan jokkwier*" ("Canoe to bring us together, canoe belonging to everyone. Canoe to help us, canoe to destroy us. Canoe to give meaning to our lives").

I imagine that my deceased Marshallese host-father Kilon Takiah might have similarly invoked this proverb in the ending of his grand *bwebwenato* of Captain Korent's quest to become a navigator. The 2015 *Jitdaṃ Kapeel* voyage has left a strong impression of the value of traditional maritime practices and deep cultural meanings of the Marshallese canoe on the Tabal community of Aur. And symbolic of the broader cultural revitalization, the canoe is quietly awakening the spirit of the sea for the Marshallese, reforging an ancestral identity.

Breaking the Shell: Voyaging from Nuclear Refugees to People of the Sea in the Marshall Islands, the story of Captain Korent's quest to relearn his Rongelapese ancestors' methods of navigating by the waves, is a testament to the resilience and adaptability of tradition. Gendered genealogies and histories trace the learning on Rongelap from Lijon Eknilang's learning as a little girl in the mid-1900s back to Litarmelu's comprehension of the waves, and from Lōktañūr's invention of the sail to Jineer ilo Koba's expanded creation of an island world. The sleek outrigger canoe originated on Bikini, the ground-zero site of the apocalyptic thermonuclear Bravo test that forever transformed the lives of the Rongelapese in ways so fundamental as to alter their genetic codes for untold generations yet to come. The nuclear testing distanced Captain Korent and his elders from the chance to "break the shell" (*ruprup jọkur*) on a trial voyage for nearly half a century. Although continuing to live in exile from their irradiated home islands, the Rongelapese rallied together, the supporting elders imparting their precious knowledge to Captain Korent but in the process losing a fundamental component of their prestige as the last custodians of Rongelapese navigation. With their help, Captain Korent became a socially sanctioned "person of the sea" (*ri-meto*), and despite several years of illness, which he attributed to his rise in fame as a titled navigator, he helped his apprentice, Alson Kelen, guide a voyaging canoe at sea under extraordinary, shifting protocols in the use of navigational knowledge. A long-distance canoe voyage navigated by the waves like this has not happened in the Marshall Islands for decades.

Reclaiming ancestral maritime heritage by awakening a voyaging spirit is but one way the Marshallese have combatted the dark history that has loomed over them. Efforts to move past an identity of victimhood and heal from the nuclear testing and broader militarization of the islands are represented in language, songs, and poetry. The Rongelapese who were entered into Project 4.1 composed humorous songs to ease the emotional trauma of their dehumanizing experiences, and contemporary Marshallese poets continue to compose lyrical pieces about their ancestor's experiences and to raise awareness beyond the Marshall Islands. Refusing to let the violence of the nuclear testing be forgotten or easily explained away, for example, Kathy Jetnil-Kijiner's slam poetry piece, "History Project," describes her pain and anger in trying to share the experiences of her people to an audience of insensitive judges in a high school history fair. As she demonstrates in other prose, the legacy of the nuclear testing is one of many critical issues the Marshallese are confronting today.[1]

The ability to deftly negotiate the waning but still powerful traditions in the face of emerging twenty-first-century issues is paramount for the continuation of wayfinding knowledge, but such knowledge, grounded in a deep ancestral past, can also be invoked to confront those challenges. The Marshallese, with the strategic defensive security that their islands afford the United States, are deeply connected to global militarized currents. New challenges emerge not only at home but in the far-flung diasporic communities. And it is such visible demonstrations of navigating tradition as the return of the Marshallese canoe *Jitdaṃ Kapeel* that provide metaphorical and literal means to ensure cultural survival.

In 2011 the *Civil Beat* newspaper headline screamed, "No Aloha for Micronesians in Hawaii," voicing an escalating undercurrent of racism in the Aloha State toward its newest arrivals.[2] With free visa entry into the United States under the Compact of Free Association, relocations have focused on Hawai'i, with its geographical and cultural proximity to the Marshall Islands. The enticements to leave home for education and employment opportunities, as well as medical services, are heighted for the nuclear survivors and their descendants. Without deep cultural awareness from both sides, mounting tensions exist between the incoming Marshallese (and other Compact of Free Association migrants) and Native Hawaiians and other local residents, giving rise to mutual stereotyping, racism, discrimination, conflict, and violence. Quite noticeable in urban Honolulu, these tensions are more subtle but still present on the neighbor islands. Notably, a growing number of Enewetakese, dissatisfied with their disrupted life on their ancestral atoll, have settled in the rural community of Ocean View on the southwestern side of Hawai'i Island, while a smaller population of Marshallese in the town of Hilo is largely comprised of islanders connected by heritage to Bikini and Rongelap. In both places, the newly settled communities strive to avoid direct conflict as they adjust to their new home.[3] Discussions are underway by such community organizations as Micronesians United–Big Island (MU–BI) to build a sailing canoe to help bridge this divide and to restrengthen the diasporic communities by using their traditional skills. The actual use of such a canoe could also directly shape the destiny of their family members who have remained in the Marshall Islands.

Along with other low-lying atoll communities throughout Oceania, the inhabitants of the Marshall Islands face an imminent threat to their survival as a people culturally and historically connected to the sea: climate change–induced rising sea levels. The estimates are alarming—a near certainty that rising seas will disrupt the precious freshwater lenses, inundate coastal sites, and ultimately submerge the atolls. The Marshall Islands are projected to be among the first nations in the world to experience the synergistic impacts of climate change.[4] Threats to livelihood security include coastal effects of sea level rise, reduced quality and quantity of water resources, coral reef degradation, diminished agricultural sustainability, and various impacts on human health such as waterborne diseases. In response, individuals, families, atoll representatives, and national government officials are considering community relocation and migration. And despite the fact that the Marshall Islands contributes minimally to anthropogenic climate change, its leaders are attempting to catalyze the world to slow down the increasing global emissions and concentrations of tropospheric greenhouse gases.[5] In particular, the foundational Majuro Declaration of 2013 captures the political commitment of island nations in the Pacific to transition to renewable and sustainable energy.[6] To do their part in this proactive mitigation to keep global warming below a 1.5-degree threshold, the Marshallese government is looking for ways to reduce its national energy expenditure, 70 percent of which went to sea and air transportation in 2013.

At a time when the Marshallese and other island communities are examining their options to optimistically galvanize a global response to climate change and pragmatically search for ways to stay or migrate to higher land in another country, Alson Kelen, as director of Waan Aelōñ in Majol, is returning to his people's seafaring heritage to confront the encroaching seas. Drawing inspiration from his grandfather's proverbial expression "*Malene ilju pādpād ion inne*" ("Shape the future based on the past"), which he incorporated into the motto of Waan Aelōñ in Majol, Alson envisions a return to sustainable sea transport. More voyaging outrigger canoes that harness the power of the wind, even with reliance on GPS for navigation, means lessening dependence on fossil fuels. The canoes—essentially water taxis—could transport materials and people within each atoll and even between its scattered atolls rather than rely on government transport ships. This would reduce socioeconomic vulnerability to external rises in oil prices and help move the nation toward increasing energy independence, as well as lowering carbon emissions in the global mitigation of climate change.[7] Such efforts would strengthen cultural resilience.

This ultimate return of tradition has yet to be achieved in the Pacific, but it is close. The conception to return to outrigger voyaging canoes is part of an emerging broad initiative called the Micronesian Sustainable Transport Center. Consistent with the 2013 Majuro Declaration and other regional policies, this initiative—which expands beyond canoes to innovative technological solutions such as wind-powered interisland freighters, ground-effect vehicles or "wingships" that use the aerodynamic interaction between the wings and the surface of the sea for sustained flight, rotor ships propelled by spinning airstreams, and marine-based renewable biofuels—would assist the Marshallese government in achieving its policy target of reducing its transport emissions 16 percent by 2025.[8] Other initiatives are more symbolic. Notably, the Polynesian Voyaging Society's current Mālama Honua Worldwide Voyage is symbolically using *Hōkūleʻa* to raise global awareness of nurturing sustainable environmental practices based on indigenous principles.[9] But a literal return of the canoe as a means of cultural survival might just give the Marshallese an edge in their battle against the rising ocean and allow them to celebrate their existence as a people born to the rhythms of the sea. Ultimately, however, such a cautiously optimistic glimpse into the future of voyaging in the Marshall Islands must recognize the cultural imperative to navigate the dampened but still powerful protocols of traditional knowledge.

This story began with Captain Korent symbolically embodying the century-long decline and more recent resurgence of the traditions of the ocean by "breaking the shell," and it ends with his rising navigation apprentice Alson Kelen representing another layer of "breaking" from tradition by sailing *Jitdaṃ Kapeel* by the waves without his teacher. How they continue the revival remains uncertain. After our return voyage from Aur in 2015, Alson and I quickly sought Captain Korent at his home only to discover he had been admitted to the hospital in Majuro, a place his despairing family felt was not for recovery but a path toward certain death. The infection became so serious that a few days later his wife accompanied him to a hospital in Honolulu. By then, gangrene had spread upward to just below his knee, and a team of doctors amputated his leg without delay to stop a life-threatening systemic infection. Amazingly, this medical trauma, coupled with decades of living in exile and now the rising ethnic tensions abroad and uncertainty about the fate of the islands, had not dampened Captain Korent's resilient spirit. He still wanted to see his people navigating by the waves again. When I visited him following the surgery, we spoke little, mostly just enjoying each other's presence. He shared a few stories in his broken English with a twinkle in his eye, and we reminisced about our adventure together. When I last saw him just before leaving the hospital room, he reminded me that we still have to finish understanding the waves.

Notes

Introduction: From Nuclear Exodus to Cultural Reawakening

1. In response to Hauʻofa's (1994, 2001) vision that the ocean is a cultural space and part of the identity of Pacific Islanders, D'Arcy (2006) provides a nuanced historical survey of Pacific Islanders' intimate connections to the sea, especially those that self-identified themselves in their own speech communities as "people of the sea." The Marshallese did not historically use a term like this in reference to their entire culture, but the term *ri-meto* (navigator) literally means a "person of the sea."

2. Nuclear testing also occurred by the United States in Kiribati from the late 1950s to early 1960s, by Great Britain in Australia and Kiribati in the 1950s, and by France in Moruroa and Fangataufa in the Tuamotu Archipelago of French Polynesia from 1966 to 1996. Genz et al. (2016b) detail these and other practices of militarism in Oceania.

3. Johnston (2016).

4. Niedenthal (2001, 21).

5. Katerina M. Teaiwa (2015, 24).

6. In addition to Olopai's (2005) reflections, other notable biographies, life histories, and memoirs include accounts of Tosiwo Nakayma, the first president of the Federated States of Micronesia (Hanlon 1998), Queen Sālote Tupou III of Tonga (Wood-Ellem 1999), and Right Honourable Ratu Sir Kamisese Mara (1997) of Fiji; however, Captain Korent did not hold similar political status or recognition as these leaders. In many ways, Captain Korent's quiet quest for social justice for his people of Rongelap complements the lifelong advocacy work of Darlene Keju, whose story is captured as a personalized biography by her surviving husband Giff Johnson (2013).

7. Low (2013).

8. Kovach (2009) discusses story as a form of indigenous methodology for decolonizing research.

9. This follows Hanlon's (2003) call for decentering the practice of history in Oceania.

10. In addition to Finney (1979) and Gladwin (1970), other notable works of voyaging and navigation with this holistic approach include Feinberg's (1988) ethnography of Anutan voyaging, Thomas's (1987) reflexive study of Satawalese navigation, Ammarell's (1999) ethnography of Bugis navigation in Indonesia, and DeLisle and Diaz's (1997) documentary film of the revival of Polowatese voyaging on Guam.

11. Turnbull (2000) and Agrawal (1995) launched comparative studies in the sociology of Western scientific and indigenous knowledge systems, and Meyer (2001), Gegeo and Watson-Gegeo (2001), and Lauer and Aswani (2009) produced foundational ethnographically focused studies on epistemology in particular island communities in Oceania.

12. Lassiter (2005) and Field and Fox (2007) provide overviews of the emerging disciplinary shift within anthropology toward collaborative ethnography, and Finney et al. (2015) provide ethnographic examples in Oceania for the collapsing distinction between cultural insider and outsider.

13. Lewis (1994).

14. D'Arcy (2006, 176).

15. D'Arcy (2006, 90) summarizes the gendered dichotomy of maritime activities and provides additional historic examples of women navigators from the Marshall Islands and Kiribati.

16. Australian Bureau of Meteorology and CSIRO (2014); Nurse et al. (2014).

Chapter 1: Born from the Sea, Coming across the Sea

1. Davenport (1953, 221).

2. Kirch (2000, 2).

3. Kirch (2010) provides an excellent example of this approach of blending oral traditions with archaeology for ancient Hawai'i, and Kirch and Sahlins (1992) provide another example of this approach for the recent historical community of Anahulu on the north shore of O'ahu.

4. English translation by Tobin (2002, 11).

5. Davenport (1953); Dobin (2011, 242n23); Erdland (1914, 308–309).

6. Tobin (2002, 48).

7. Dobin (2011, 131); Erdland (1914, 311).

8. Knappe (1888, 3).

9. Although contained in a different story, one of the first usages of the term "vault" to describe the essence of the heavens comes from Erdland's (1914, 311) use of the term *das Himmelsgewölbe* (the Heaven vault).

10. Tobin (2002, 15).

11. Jineer ilo Koba's names for winds include *jonin itok i rear* (wind comes from the east), *jonin ketak* (wind comes from the west), *jonin kitak* (wind comes from the south), and *jokļā* (wind comes from the north); terms for currents include *aeto* (current flowing westward), *aetak* (current flowing eastward), *aeniñeañļǫk* (current flowing northward), and *aerōkeañļǫk* (current flowing southward); terms for swells include *buñto* (east swell, lit. swell flowing westward), *buñtak* (west swell, lit. swell flowing eastward), *buñtokrōk* (south swell, lit. swell coming from the south), and *buñtokeañ* (north swell, lit. swell coming from the north) (Tobin 2002, 15–17). See Genz (2008) for a more detailed description of how the Marshallese grammar modifies the base terms for winds, currents, and swells.

12. Carucci (1997a, 110).

13. Beckwith (1951); Lili'uokalani (1978).

14. Beckwith (1951, 125; 2007, 192); Malo (1951, 244).

15. Tobin (2002, 20).

16. Dobin (2011, 129–131).

17. Erdland (1914, 310–311), translated from German by Joseph Genz.

18. Carucci (1995, 30); I have used the modern spellings for Kapilōñ and Kapinmeto.

19. Davenport (1953).

20. Kirch (2010).

21. Bernarik, Hobman, and Rogers (1999); Thorne and Raymond (1989).

22. Irwin (1992) theorized that mariners strategically sailed in an upwind direction for a more successful downwind return, an idea predicated on technological innovations of canoe design. One possibility is that the early rafts were rigged with a triangular sail. This rig would have likely been framed by two booms supported on a loose prop without a fixed mast. When this design was eventually transferred to an outrigger canoe, it could have been tilted fore and aft to control the direction of the craft relative to the wind, just like a modern windsurfer (Horridge 2008). The presence of shell adzes in coastal sites in Indonesia and the Bismarck Archipelago suggests that the technology was available to hollow out logs for dugout canoes, which, if used, would have improved buoyancy and ease of paddling over rafts and, with the development of an outrigger attachment, provided roll stability (Irwin 2007).

23. Green (1991).

24. The term "Micronesia" was part of an artificial tripartite division of the Pacific popularized by Dumont d'Urville in 1832. Although the term is often used today by residents of the islands stretching from Kiribati and the Marshall Islands in the east to Palau and the Mariana Islands in the

west, it is a colonial construct that does not reflect the migrations, histories, and cultures of diverse speech communities (Hanlon 2009).

25. The congruence of the widespread distribution of Austronesian languages and ocean sailing canoes at the time of European contact and the historical reconstruction of ancient canoe terms based on contemporary Austronesian languages strongly suggest the advancement of an outrigger sailing canoe complex (Pawley and Pawley 1994). The one Austronesian language that apparently lost this canoe terminology is Formosan, spoken on the island of Taiwan, which lies seventy miles off the Fujian coast of southern China. As sailing technology would have been required to cross this gap due to a strong northward-flowing current, linguistic and archaeological evidence suggests that either the Austronesian speakers on Taiwan had this technology and later lost it with the influx of the Han Chinese, or they made it to Taiwan by sailing on bamboo rafts and then either adopted the technology from indigenous inhabitants in the Philippines or developed it there (Bellwood 2000; Blust 1995; Pawley and Pawley 1994). Alternately, the Austronesians could have developed the outrigger canoe complex more to the south in the Philippines as a trade language that made its way north to Taiwan and the Chinese mainland (Meachem 1984; Solheim 1984–1985).

26. For instance, limited direct archaeological evidence of canoes from wetland sites in eastern Polynesia indicate composite construction, with such components as dugout logs with lashed-on ends, planks with lashing holes, thwarts, cordage, and steering paddles (Cassels 1979; Irwin 2004; Sinoto 1983).

27. Haddon and Hornell (1975); the sails are typically categorized as lugsails, spritsails, and lateen sails.

28. Finney (1994); Irwin (2008, 2011); but see Anderson (2000) and Anderson et al. (2006) for arguments of severely limited upwind ability.

29. See Finney (2007) for a review of historic observations of voyaging canoes. The knot is a unit of speed equal to one nautical mile per hour, approximately 1.151 miles per hour or 1.852 kilometers per hour.

30. Ammarell (1999); Lauer (1976); Lewis (1994).

31. It is entirely possible that double canoes were used along the Lapita trail before arriving in Polynesia, but linguistic reconstruction of double-hulled canoe terminology suggests that it was a uniquely Polynesian innovation that occurred after the settlement of western Polynesia. For instance, *paquurua*, a reconstructed term for double-hulled canoe in the hypothetical Proto Eastern Oceanic language translates as "bind, lash, or construct by tying together" (*paqu*) and "two" (*rua*), which suggests that double-

hull technology was in place during the expansion to eastern Polynesia (Blust 1999).

32. Rieth et al. (2011); Wilmshurst et al. (2011).
33. Jones et al. (2011).
34. Anderson and O'Regan (2000).
35. These investigations were in direct response to arguments by experimental archaeologist Thor Heyerdahl (1953) and historian Andrew Sharp (1956) that ancient Polynesian canoes could not have sailed against the direction of the prevailing easterly trade winds and that their poor navigational methods, coupled with unseaworthy canoes, would have been inadequate to intentionally sail and navigate distances longer than 350 miles. To assess the performance characteristics of the ancient double-hulled canoes that set forth from Hawaiki to settle the far reaches of Polynesia, as well as ascertain the possible sailing strategies and long-distance navigational abilities, several canoes were built and sailed in the 1960s and 1970s. In the wake of Heyerdahl's reconstruction of a balsa raft, *Kon Tiki*, to demonstrate possible drift voyages from Peru to Polynesia, anthropologist Ben Finney (1979) constructed a forty-two foot Hawaiian double-hulled, crab-claw spritsail-rigged canoe based on the drawings of Kamehameha III's canoe from the mid-1800s. This canoe, named *Nālehia*, could sail within 75 degrees of the wind with speeds averaging about five knots in moderate trade winds. *Nālehia* could be paddled in calm water, but the physiological costs to the paddlers were too high compared to the amount of water and food that could be stored to sustain long-distance paddling. Drawing from historically recorded designs, Finney, in collaboration with Hawaiian sailor Tommy Holmes and Hawaiian artist Herb Kāne, then built a nineteen-meter double-hulled canoe with twin crab-claw spritsails that represented an archaic Polynesian canoe design, in order to replicate a postdiscovery crossing of 2,400 miles between the Hawaiian and Tahitian archipelagoes. During the first voyage in 1976 and subsequent crossings, *Hōkūleʻa* averaged a little over four knots or 115 miles per day. Anderson (2000) argues that *Hōkūleʻa* is too fast to represent the canoes of the migration from western to eastern Polynesia, to which Finney (2007) provides evidence that *Hōkūleʻa* is in fact very slow for its size.
36. Feinberg (1988); Gladwin (1970); Lewis (1994); Thomas (1987).
37. Alkire (1970); Frake (1995); Gladwin (1970); Goodenough (1953); Sarfert (1911); Thomas (1987).
38. Hutchins (1995).
39. George (2012).
40. Riesenberg (1976).

41. Finney et al. (1986); Lewis (1994).

42. Based on extensive work with the late navigator Koloso K. Kaveia and building from previous research conducted by David Lewis, George (2012) discusses the characteristics and possible explanations of *te lapa* in the Santa Cruz Islands, including theories about bioluminescence, electromagnetic phenomena, and the effects of swell shapes on light.

43. Another scenario for crossing the navigational threshold into Remote Oceania by the Lapita seafarers rests on strict downwind sailing or drifting, in which canoes with limited upwind capability could have harnessed prolonged westerly wind events associated with major El Niño–Southern Oscillation (ENSO) episodes. Experimental voyaging with *Hōkūle'a* involved the exploitation of several kinds of westerly winds, including El Niño westerlies that extended quite far into eastern Polynesia, and such episodes are known to have increased in frequency from about 1300 to 500 BCE during the Lapita settlement of western Polynesia (Anderson 2000, 2001; Anderson et al. 2006). Computer simulations also indicate that the deliberate exploration and discovery of the islands of Remote Oceania during the Lapita dispersal did not require any windward ability or advanced exploration strategies (Avis, Montenegro, and Weaver 2008). While this downwind colonization model is possible, it does not match the current archaeological record and rests on an assumption of limited canoe performance (Irwin 2007, 2008, 2011).

44. Beaglehole (1955); Biggs and Biggs (1975).

45. Finney et al. (1989); Finney and Kilonsky (2001). Siers' (1977, 1978) description of how easterly trade wind–driven seas battered an experimental Kiribati canoe serves as a cautionary tale of what can happen when attempting long-distance voyages upwind without exploiting westerly wind shifts.

46. Irwin (2007); Lewis (1994).

47. Beardsley (1994); Weisler (2000); Rainbird (2004, 231).

48. Peterson (2009, 39–44). A distinctive trolling lure of pearl shell, excavated in a cemetery on Majuro and dated to between two thousand and one thousand years ago, is suggestive of contact with the Solomon Islands and may be associated with the direction of arrival of the first settlers in the Marshall Islands (Spennemann 1999; Weisler 2000).

49. Rainbird (2004, 95–96) finds a possible indication of seeding on Kosrae, a high island to the west of the Marshall Islands. From settlement dates and evidence of charcoal deposits, Rainbird suggests the possibility of a precolonization seeding process of coconut and breadfruit on Kosrae, with origins likely in the Marshall Islands.

50. Tobin (2002, 315).
51. Lessa (1961).
52. Downing, Spennemann, and Bennet (1992, 36–38).

Chapter 2: Sailing in the "Sunrise" and "Sunset" Islands

1. Knight (1999, 109); I have slightly modified the original wording, which Knight had translated in broken English, without changing the meaning of Lapedpedin's narrative. Following the original wording is difficult, and I feel that leaving Knight's original English rendition of Lapedpedin's story delegitimizes Lapedpedin's intellect.
2. Interview with Alson Kelen, July 24, 2014.
3. D'Arcy (2006, 113–116).
4. The Marshallese term *ri-meto* (navigator) is a cognate of *remethau* or *re metau*, which among the outer-island languages between Yap and Chuuk Lagoon in the Federated States of Micronesia refers to their entire island communities as "people of the ocean" (Thomas 1987, 58). This term has strong contemporary relevance—the Remethau community of Hawai'i (approximately one hundred community members) annually celebrates their students' graduation from college, high school, middle school, and elementary schools throughout Hawai'i and the U.S. mainland in a ceremony held at Wow Wow Park in Kailua-Kona, Hawai'i Island.
5. Spennemann (1993, 155–156).
6. Barclay (2002).
7. A film called *The Land of Eb*, written by John Hill and Andrew Williamson (2012), draws inspiration from this mythological island of the dead to portray a better life for Micronesian migrants in Hawai'i.
8. Tobin (2002, 14–15).
9. This Marshallese phrase and translation are from Miller's (2010) paraphrasing of Tobin's (2002) recorded version, compilation of other sources, and personal translation.
10. Tobin (2002, 15).
11. Kowata et al. (1999, 4).
12. Downing, Spennemann, and Bennet (1992, 23).
13. See Finney (2007, 130–131) for a review of historic observations of voyaging canoe speeds. The speed estimate of fourteen knots comes from an early historic account from Guam that detailed the Chamorro lateen-rigged shunting outrigger canoes. Of comparative note is that the Marshallese and other Micronesian canoes were so efficient in harnessing the power of the wind that some of the descendants of the Lapita explorers adapted the sail and rig design to produce lateen-rigged shunting double-hulled canoes.

This innovation, which was occurring in the late eighteenth century at the time of European contact in Fiji, Samoa, and Tonga, produced massive double-hulled canoes that reached sustained speeds of fifteen to seventeen knots. One of the most unique modifications of this technology, according to Feinberg and George (2008), comes from the Polynesian outlier community of Taumako in the southeast Solomon Islands with the development of the *te puke*, a design utilizing almost entirely submerged hulls when under sail that minimize surface tension and wave action to produce faster speeds than conventional hulls.

14. Alessio and Kelen's (1995) documentation of the measuring, lashing, and construction techniques of an outrigger voyaging canoe of Ujae provides detailed descriptions, vivid illustrations and photographs, and an exhaustive explanation of Marshallese terminology for the outrigger canoe features.

15. Tobin (2002, 56–61).

16. Interview with Isao Eknilang, December 5, 2005.

17. See Knight (1999, 4–8) for an elaborate version of the story of Jebrǫ and Tūṃur. The concept of seasons associated with stars "falling into the sea" or disappearing from view is in contrast to other systems of weather forecasting in Oceania that focus on observing a star's annual appearance rising on the eastern horizon at sunset.

18. Carucci (1997, 85).

19. Krämer and Nevermann (1938); the hard wood is from the tree called *kōñe*.

20. Stone, Kowata, and Joash (2000, 7).

21. Alessio and Kelen (2004).

22. Carucci (1995, 21); also see Miller (2010, 66–67).

23. Miller (2010, 66–70); see also Alessio and Kelen (2004).

24. Krämer and Nevermann (1938).

25. This translation and location of Kapinmeto comes from an interview by Tobin (2002) with Jelibor Jam in 1975.

26. Interview with Isao Eknilang, August 14, 2006. Krämer and Nevermann (1938, 51) mention the sea Metoëríkerik (Metodikdik).

27. The term "Lōluiébleb" is documented by Erdland (1906, 172; 1914, 4); I use the spellings provided by Spennemann (2005). The term "Joiiaenkan" is documented by Nakayama and Ramp (1974, 85).

28. Spennemann (1993, 120–136) diagrams the traditional *wāto* land division.

29. Erdland (1914, 317).

30. Krämer and Nevermann (1938, 37); Erdland (1914, 248) names the "island of the dead" as Eoereak.

31. See Alkire (1965) for a discussion of long-distance voyaging in other parts of Micronesia.

32. Marck (1986); Rehg (1995).
33. Weisler (1997; 2001).
34. Krämer and Nevermann (1938, 30); Spennemann (2005, 44).
35. Spennemann (1993, 50–63, 70).
36. Eisenhart (1888); see Spennemann (2005, 36) for estimates of the voyage to Aur and description of historically documented food items that were exchanged.
37. Tobin (1956, 57); see D'Arcy (2006, 104–109) for the sea as a zone of conflict.
38. Kotzebue (1821, 2:87).
39. Kotzebue (1830, 317–318).
40. Lewis (1994, 196–197).
41. Schück (1884); Krämer and Nevermann (1938, 240).
42. Byran (1972, 149).
43. Stone, Kowata, and Joash (2000, 3–4).
44. Erdland (1910, 20; 1914, 81–82).
45. Krämer and Nevermann (1938, 217); Stone's (2001a) compilation of the early German ethnographic documentation of astronomy similarly limits the navigational use of stars to short voyages but elaborates on how weather forecasters would predict storms as well as mark the calendrical shift in the seasons.
46. See Spennemann's (2005, 35) visual coverage of Schück's (1902) compilation.
47. Carucci (1995, 24–25).
48. Carucci (1995, 25).
49. Hambruch (1912, 37).
50. Spennemann (2005, 38–39).
51. Emory (1965, 53–55); Krämer and Nevermann (1938).
52. Krämer and Nevermann (1938, 217); Nakayama and Ramp (1974, 6–7, 84).
53. Chamisso (1836); Finsch (1893, 166); Giesberts (1910); Krämer and Nevermann (1938, 3, 35); see Spennemann (2005, 42–43) for a more detailed description of drift voyages to and from the Marshall Islands.
54. Spennemann (2004); Hezel (1983).
55. Spennemann (2004) provides a detailed account of the voyages of Captain Marshall and Captain Gilbert through the southern Marshall Islands, including their original journal entries. In addition to the naming of the Marshall Islands, the Gilbert Islands, now pronounced locally as Kiribati, were named after Thomas Gilbert.
56. Kotzebue (1821).
57. Chamisso (1836); Choris (1822, 1826); Kotzebue (1821).

58. Salmond (2005).
59. Chamisso (1836, 138).
60. Chamisso (1836, 132) noted that Kotzebue did not remark in his journal on the building of the Wotje model canoe.
61. Kotzebue (1821, 1:174–176).
62. Kotzebue (1821, 2:148–149).
63. Kotzebue (1821, 2:70, 83–84).
64. Chamisso (1836, 140).
65. Kotzebue (1821, 2:108, 118).
66. Kotzebue (1821, 2:143–145).
67. Kotzebue (1821, 2:136).
68. Kotzebue (1821, 2:146); Kotzebue (1821, 2:132–133) also worked with Edock, a native of Woleai who had storm-drifted eight hundred miles to land on Aur in the Marshall Islands, to understand the geography of the Carolinian atolls. Edock, like his Ratak counterparts, gestured the number of days a certain voyage would take from a particular atoll. Interestingly, Kotzebue marked the sailing courses and their number of required sailing days on the chart itself, and he also acknowledged Edock's knowledge in the title of the Carolinian map, "Chart of the Caroline Islands, after the Statement of Edock."

Chapter 3: Exodus from a Stronghold of Navigation

1. Interview with Alson Kelen, November 23, 2005.
2. Knight (1999, 160); Here again I slightly modify the original wording without changing the meaning of Lapedpedin's narrative.
3. D'Arcy (2006, 94–97).
4. Erdland (1914, 99–101).
5. Tobin (2002, 388).
6. Alkire (1965); Peterson (2009, 115).
7. Carucci (1997b, 207); Erdland (1914, 99–101).
8. Tobin (2002, 114n8) notes that his elderly informant used the English loanword "appoint" and describes the ritualistic manner in which commoners would ask their chief for permission to learn navigation (386).
9. Interview with Alson Kelen, June 25, 2015.
10. Davenport (1960, 23); Erdland (1914, 77); Krämer and Nevermann (1938, 215).
11. In 1972 Mark Juda shared with Jack Tobin (2002, 113) that the two main regions of navigation were Rak in Meto and En in Meto in the Rālik chain.
12. Metzgar (2006).
13. Krämer and Nevermann (1938, 221).

14. Carucci (1997b).
15. Knight (1999, 109).
16. Alkire (1978, 141); Hezel (1995, 108).
17. Lewis (1994, 17).
18. Carucci (2001); Walsh (2003).
19. The inversion of tradition is discussed by Thomas (1992).
20. Spennemann (2005, 33).
21. Kotzebue (1830, 1:269).
22. Spennemann (2005).
23. Spennemann (2005).
24. Giesberts (1910).
25. Alkire (1978, 141); Hezel (1995, 108).
26. Falgout, Poyer, and Carucci (2008, 95, 141).
27. Falgout, Poyer, and Carucci (2008, 159–165).
28. Carucci (1989).
29. Carucci (1989); Walsh (2003).
30. Carucci (1989, 91–92); McArthur (2000, 92).
31. Narrated by Isao Eknilang, September 5, 2006. Another version recorded by Tobin (2002, 115–125) from Jelibor Jam in 1975 describes in detail how the foreign navigators taught Litarmelu by towing her around an islet on Jaluit. An alternate version recorded by Krämer and Nevermann (1938, 47) from Ḷotop in the 1930s reveals different family relationships: Lainjin, who died in 1895, was Ḷotop's uncle, and Lainjin had learned from Likijoan, the mother of Litarmelu.
32. Chanted by Isao Eknilang, July 10, 2006. Knight (1999, 68–74) recorded a version of the *ikid eņ an Lainjin* from Lapedpedin; Krämer and Nevermann (1938, 254–266) documented a version from Ladap Lanbulien; and Tobin (2002, 131–142) recorded a version from Jelibor Jam. See Genz (2008) for Lijon Eknilang's sung rendition in a series of verses.
33. Erdland (1914); Krämer and Nevermann (1938).
34. Tobin (2002, 91).
35. Kiste (1974, 17–18).
36. Knight (1999, 115–117).
37. Interview with Alson Kelen, November 9, 2005.
38. Erdland (1906, 190); see also Krämer and Nevermann's (1938, 216) similar description of *ruprup jǫkur.*
39. Interview with Alson Kelen, June 25, 2015.
40. Gladwin (1970, 132–133).
41. Mason (1948) and Tobin (1953) documented and advocated for the Bikinians following their relocation to Rongerik in 1946, and Kiste (1974) pro-

vided a look at the long-term social implications of their exodus; Barker (2013) provides a recent synthesis of this early and later material, including information from recently declassified documents.

42. Johnston and Barker (2013, 17n5) note that near-lethal doses of radiation from the Bravo event also affected twenty-eight U.S. weathermen on Rongerik and the twenty-three-man crew of the Japanese fishing vessel *Fukuryu Maru.*

43. The excerpts by John Anjain are from "The Fallout on Rongelap Atoll and Its Social, Medical and Environmental Effects," edited and translated by Richard A. Sundt (unpublished manuscript, 1973), on file at the Nuclear Claims Tribunal, Majuro, cited in Johnston and Barker (2008, 11–12).

44. Barker (2013); Johnston and Barker (2008).

45. Barker (2013) documents testimonies from Ailuk and other communities not recognized by the U.S. government as having been irradiated by the Bravo test.

46. Teaiwa (1994).

47. Waibel (2012); "Project 4.1 Zombieland" (2012).

48. "Project 4.1 Morphs to Haunted House" (2012).

49. Barker (2013); Johnston and Barker (2008).

50. Interview with Captain Korent Joel, September 1, 2005; a smaller portion of this interview quote appears in Genz (2011, 12–14).

51. Interview with Captain Korent Joel, November 9, 2005.

52. Interview with Captain Korent Joel, November 9, 2005.

53. Knight (1999, 160).

54. Interview with Alson Kelen, June 23, 2015.

55. Marshall (2004, 62–65).

56. Miller (2010, 99).

57. Carucci (1995, 17).

58. Carucci (1995, 18–19).

59. deBrum (1959, 1961, 1962); "Signs and Weather" (1959); Lewis (1994, 27); Winkler (1898).

60. Smith-Norris (2016, 111–124) details the buildup and consequences of these "sail-ins." For example, the first "sail-in," which the United States believed to be a bluff, caused the cancellation of two missile tests with an estimated loss of approximately $2 million.

61. Using the canoe as a symbol of protest and resistance has been effectively used in other places in Oceania, especially Hawai'i. From its inception, *Hōkūle'a* meant to challenge the colonial knowledge regimes that cast doubt on the ability of the ancient peoples of Oceania to make intentional, long-distance voyages. And some crew members discussed sailing to

Kahoʻolawe as a symbolic sign of protest before undertaking their inaugural voyage to Tahiti in 1976. That same year, protectors of Kahoʻolawe had made their first landing in their attempt to stop the U.S. military's use of the island as a bombing target. Still another act of resistance played out on board the canoe itself on the way to Tahiti. A deep schism had developed during the genesis of the project about struggles over authority that erupted during the voyage. In one interpretation of the various confrontations that led to physical violence, Walker (2011, 115–122) argues that one Hawaiian validated his authority by expressing his identity as a person intimately connected to the ocean rather than to a mindset represented in his colonial oppressors. Alternately, more nuanced understandings of the mounting tensions aboard *Hōkūleʻa* during the 1976 Tahiti voyage come from Finney (1979), who provides a firsthand account of the events, and Low (2013), who reconstructs the episode from extensive interviews with the entire crew.

62. Johnston and Barker (2008).
63. Barker (2013); see also Schwartz (2012) for an in-depth look at Rongelapese musical activism through the singing voice of Lijon Eknilang.
64. Jetnil-Kijiner (2012).
65. Johnston and Barker (2008).

Chapter 4: Navigating the Cultural Revival of Voyaging

1. Tobin (2002, 386).
2. Interview with Alson Kelen, November 23, 2005.
3. Alessio (1989, 1990, 1991a, 1991b, 1991c, 1993); Alessio and Kelen (1995).
4. Finney (2003, 44–45).
5. Carucci (1995, 29–30)
6. Carucci (1995, 30, 31n1).
7. Finney (2003, 47–48).
8. Alessio (1991d) conducted an economic survey on Ailuk in the early 1990s and documented that once the construction of a canoe is completed, the main advantage of the sailing canoe is the obvious ability to harness the power of the wind; Miller (2010) explores the importance of canoe culture on Namorik.
9. Miller (2010).
10. Kabua (2004).
11. Miller (2010).
12. Johnston and Barker (2008).
13. This section is based on Genz (2011).

14. Carucci (1997b).
15. The shifting use of Rongelapese navigational knowledge without precedent—first with Captain Korent sharing his knowledge with Alson Kelen in 2005 and then by Alson demonstrating his knowledge in 2010 and 2015 without Captain Korent—is elaborated in Genz (2017).
16. Lewis (1978, 176).
17. Interview with Captain Korent Joel, January 1, 2006.
18. Abo et al. (1976).
19. Translations of this proverb are found in Abo et al. (1976); Miller (2010, 145); Stone, Kowata, and Joash (2000, 67).
20. Stone (2001b) argued that the knowledge systems in the Marshall Islands do not hold the same prestige as they once did.
21. Davenport (1960, 23).
22. Peterson (1993).
23. Simpson (2007).
24. Rubinstein and Limol (2007); Rubinstein (2009).

Chapter 5: Maps, Models, and Simulations

1. Ascher (1995, 366).
2. Ingold (2000, 25).
3. Lewis (1994).
4. There are strong cultural and archaeological ties between the main Marshall Islands and Enen-kio, but the atoll is currently a territory of the United States that is managed by the United States Air Force.
5. Lagerloef et al. (1999).
6. Ammarell (1999).
7. Erdland (1910).
8. See Garrison (2001) for an overview of swell transformations through the process of reflection, diffraction, and refraction, and Wright (1995) for current-induced wave refraction.
9. Ae'a's (1947) Hawaiian manuscript was originally written but not published in 1862–1863; Gulick (1862); Meinicke (1863, 403).
10. Schück (1884); Schück (1902, 8–9).
11. Finney (1998, 489–492).
12. Winkler (1898).
13. Krämer and Nevermann (1938).
14. Ascher (1995).
15. de Laubenfels (1950); Ascher (1995, 364).
16. Winkler (1901, 493).
17. According to Krämer and Nevermann (1938, 222), Hermann Grösser

states the meaning of *dilep* as "sailing route" based on the testimony of a navigator from Ailinglaplap.

18. This section on contemporary explanations of the stick charts is summarized from Genz (2016).

19. Isao Eknilang also constructed a model called *niñeañ kab rōkeañ* that differs from the *wapepe* only in its level of inclusiveness. The modeling of *niñeañ kab rōkeañ*, which literally means "northward and southward," is limited to voyages in a north-south direction, whereas the symmetrical modeling of the *wapepe* can be applied to voyages in these and other east-west voyages. The *niñeañ kab rōkeañ* was traditionally used to teach novices on Rongelap how to guide their canoes southward to Kwajalein and back, a distance of about one hundred miles. Kwajalein is the largest atoll in the world, measuring ninety miles from east to west, and Rongelap measures about fifty miles. These atolls would effectively block the southern and northern swells that a navigator would expect to encounter on the open ocean. As a result, the training and modeling of the *niñeañ kab rōkeañ* became focused on the swell transformations of only the east and west swells.

20. See Genz (2014) for a description of the cognitive and experiential ways of knowing the ocean in Marshallese navigation. In Marshallese navigation, a powerful dynamic emerges in the complementarity of information-processing modes, including mentally recalling information from the models and maps but emphasizing the perception of the movement of waves. Swells and other terminology contribute to an "absolute directional frame of reference" (Frake 1995) to name the cardinal directions, but the terms do not form a conceptual swell compass for spatial orientation analogous to how the Carolinian star compass (Gladwin 1970) and the "wind bearing system" of the Santa Cruz Islands (George 2012) allow for correlating winds, celestial bodies, seasons, calendrics, and interisland voyaging routes. Instead, directions for voyages are expressed with oppositional terms that describe direction in relation to the canoe and wind in a "contingent or relative directional frame of reference" (Frake 1995).

21. Alessio and Kelen (1995).

22. Genz (2016) details the differences between Isao Eknilang's *wapepe* and Thomas Bokin's *meto*, including expanded illustrations that feature Thomas' *meto*.

23. Lewis (1994, 228–230).

24. Grimble (1931, 220).

25. Tobin (2002, 117).

26. Davenport (1960); Spennemann (1993).

27. This section on wave modeling is a condensed version of Genz et al. (2009).
28. George (2012, 163–165).
29. Huth (2013).
30. Personal communication with Huth; Hein, Wong, and Mosier (1999) depict underwater bathymetry and locations of named seamounts.

Chapter 6: "Breaking the Shell"

1. Gladwin (1970, 127–128).
2. Abo et al. (1976).
3. The description of this voyage is based on, but elaborated from, previous accounts in Genz (2014, 2015, 2016). The phrase "voyage of rediscovery" is borrowed from Finney's (1994) description of *Hōkūleʻa's* two-year cultural odyssey through much of Polynesia between 1985 and 1987.
4. Finney (1994); Low (2013).
5. Knight (1999, 113).
6. Falgout, Poyer, and Carucci (2008, 165).
7. Abo et al. (1976).
8. Knight (1999, 67) translates Lapedpedin's explanation of *wiwijet* as "crazy from too much sky and ocean."
9. Interview with Isao Eknilang, September 1, 2006.
10. Finney (2003, 44–46).
11. Spennemann (1992, 29–31).
12. Petrosian-Husa (2004, 52) draws from Erdland (1914); and personal communication, 2006. See Genz and Finney (2006) for a more extensive discussion of culturally appropriate models of heritage management.

Chapter 7: Rise of the Apprentice

1. Stone, Kowata, and Joash (2000, 2).
2. Interview with Binton Daniel, June 25, 2015.
3. Interview with Alson Kelen, July 24, 2014.
4. Interview with Captain Korent Joel, August 2, 2014.
5. Huth's (2013) interest in traditional navigation began with the death of two young kayakers in fog-obscured Nantucket Sound off the coast of Cape Cod and developed into an experiential course at Harvard University.
6. Journalist Kim Tingley and photographer Mark Peterson accompanied the 2015 voyage from Majuro to Aur, and the resulting story was featured as "The Secrets of the Wave Pilots" in the online edition and "Sixth Sense" in the hardcopy version of the *New York Times Magazine* (Tingley 2015).
7. Interview with Alson Kelen, June 25, 2015.
8. Interview with Binton Daniel, June 25, 2015.

9. Interview with Elmi Juonraan, June 25, 2015.
10. Interview with Alson Kelen, June 25, 2015.
11. Low (2013) captures the shifting dynamics on board *Hōkūleʻa* and Nainoa Thompson's spiritual journey.
12. Recorded by Kim Tingley, June 20, 2015, and transcribed and translated by Alson Kelen.

Epilogue: Return of the Canoe

1. Barker (2013); Jetnil-Kijiner (2012).
2. Blair (2011).
3. Carucci (2012) focuses on the Enewetakese in Ocean View and Genz et al. (2016a) concentrate on the Marshallese community in Hilo.
4. Australian Bureau of Meteorology and CSIRO (2014); Nurse et al. (2014).
5. Campbell (2014).
6. Majuro Declaration (2013).
7. Sustainable Sea Transport Research Programme (2015).
8. Newell et al. (2016); Nuttal (2015); Sustainable Sea Transport Research Programme (2015).
9. Polynesian Voyaging Society (2016).

Glossary

Adjokḷā	our northern wind (lit.); the atolls of Rongelap, Rongerik, Ailinginae, and Bikini
Aelōñ Kein Ad	these islands of ours (lit.); an older term for the Marshall Islands
bwebwenato	story, conversation, tale, history, episode (*bwebwenato*); legend (*bwebwenatoon etto*); biography (*bwebwenato mour*); chat (*bwebwenato budjek*)
dilep	backbone, spine (lit.); wave path
ekjab	spiritual beings associated with marine and bird life
Etao	a demigod trickster
iroij	chief
Iroijrilik	a god (also a post or pillar) from the time of creation demarcating the direction west
Jebrọ	youngest son of Lōktañūr; the star η Tauri in the Pleiades cluster located in the constellation Taurus
jeljeltae	third zone of currents, from *jeljelat* (loosening or unraveling) and *ae* (current)
Jineer ilo Koba	goddess who created the sun, moon, tides, currents, winds, and directions
Jitdaṃ Kapeel	seeking knowledge (lit.); name of an outrigger voyaging canoe
jukae	first zone of currents, from *juk* (going into or jumping into) and *ae* (current)
jur in okme	pole for breadfruit harvesting (lit.); navigational sign windward of an island
kāāj in rōjep	fishhook (lit.); navigational sign windward of an island
Kapinmeto	bottom of the ocean (lit.); the atolls of Ujae, Lae, and Wotho
Lainjin	a navigator; Litarmelu's son and Ḷotop's father
Ḷajibwināṃōñ	a god (also a post or pillar) from the time of creation demarcating the direction north
Leoa	a man who co-constructed with Ḷōṃtal the first paddling outrigger canoe

Liṃaakak	kite asterism in the Southern Cross
Liṃanṃan	Polaris or North Star
Litarmelu	the first person to learn wave navigation in the Marshall Islands; mother of Lainjin
Ḷōkōṃraan	a god (also a post or pillar) from the time of creation demarcating the direction east
Lōktañūr	a woman who invented the sail and became deified as the mother of all the stars; the star Capella in the constellation Auriga
Ḷōṃtal	a god who created the seas; alternately a man who co-constructed with Leoa the first paddling outrigger canoe
Ḷōrōk	a god (also a post or pillar) from the time of creation demarcating the direction south
Ḷotop	a navigator; Litarmelu's grandson and Lainjin's son
Ḷowa	a god who created the islands (also spelled Lōwa)
mattang	navigation model
meddo	navigation model showing a region of the Marshall Islands
nit in kōt	pit for bird fighting (lit.); navigational sign leeward of an island
okar	root (lit.); wave path
rebbelib	navigation model showing all or most of the archipelago of the Marshall Islands
ri-meto	person of the sea (lit.); navigator
rubukae	second zone of currents, from *rubuk* (crossing) and *ae* (current)
ruprup jọkur	breaking the shell, breaking out of the turtle shell (lit.); to initiate; intellectual transformation to becoming a navigator
Tūṃur	eldest son of Lōktañūr; the star Antares in the constellation Scorpius
Waan Aelōñ in Majol	a nongovernmental organization (Canoes of the Marshall Islands)
Waan Aelōñ Kein	former name of governmental organization (Canoes of These Islands)
wapepe	floating canoe (lit.); navigational model
Wūllep	a diety, variously a supernatural worm that lived in a shell in the depths of the ocean or emerged from a boil of Ḷowa

Bibliography

Abo, Takaji, Byron Bender, Alfred Capelle, and Tony DeBrum. 1976. *Marshallese-English Dictionary.* Honolulu: University of Hawai'i Press.

Ae'a, Hezekiah. 1947. "The History of Ebon." In *Fifty-sixth Annual Report of the Hawaiian Historical Society,* 9–19. Honolulu: Hawaiian Historical Society (original manuscript written 1862–1863; unpublished).

Agrawal, Arun. 1995. "Dismantling the Divide between Indigenous and Scientific Knowledge." *Development and Change* 26:413–439.

Alessio, Dennis F. 1989. *Waan Aelon Kein Report 1: The Jaluit Malmel.* Majuro: Historic Preservation Office, Alele Museum Report.

———. 1990. *Waan Aelon Kein Report 2: The Likiep Taburbur.* Majuro: Historic Preservation Office, Alele Museum Report.

———. 1991a. *Waan Aelon Kein Report 3: Traditional Measuring, Lashing and Construction Techniques of the Outrigger Canoes of Namdik (Namorik) Atoll.* Majuro: Historic Preservation Office, Alele Museum Report.

———. 1991b. *Waan Aelon Kein Report 4: The Construction of a Traditional Outrigger Canoe Using a Combination of Traditional and Contemporary Materials on Namdik (Namorik) Atoll.* Majuro: Historic Preservation Office, Alele Museum Report.

———. 1991c. *Waan Aelon Kein Report 5: Traditional and Contemporary Measuring, Lashing and Construction Techniques of the Outrigger Canoes of Ailuk Atoll.* Majuro: Historic Preservation Office, Alele Museum Report.

———. 1991d. *Waan Aelon Kein Report 6: Economic Survey of Boat Use and Construction Costs of Traditional Marshallese Sailing Outrigger Canoes on Ailuk Atoll.* Majuro: Historic Preservation Office, Alele Museum Report.

———. 1993. *Waan Aelon Kein Report 7: Walap in Enewetak: Measuring, Lashing and Construction Techniques of the Voyaging Canoes of Enewetak Atoll.* Majuro: Historic Preservation Office, Alele Museum Report.

Alessio, Dennis F., and Alson J. Kelen. 1995. *Waan Aelon Kein Report 8: "LANIN-MANTOL": The Flight of the Shearwater—Traditional Construction Techniques of an Outrigger Voyaging Canoe of Ujae Atoll in the Marshall Islands, Micronesia.* Majuro: Historic Preservation Office, Alele Museum Report.

———. 2004. "Waan Aelōñ in Majōl: Canoes of the Marshall Islands." In *Life in the Republic of the Marshall Islands,* edited by Anono L. Loeak, Veronica C. Kiluwe, and Linda Crowl, 192–225. Majuro and Suva: Institute of Pacific Studies.

Alkire, William H. 1965. *Lamotrek Atoll and Inter-Island Socio-Economic Ties.* Urbana: University of Illinois Press.

———. 1970. "Systems of Measurement on Woleai Atoll, Caroline Islands." *Anthropos* 65:1–73.

———. 1978. *Coral Islanders.* Arlington Heights, IL: AHM Publishing Corporation.

Ammarell, Gene. 1999. *Bugis Navigation.* New Haven: Yale University, Southeast Asia Studies.

Anderson, Atholl. 2000. "Slow Boats from China: Issues in the Prehistory of Indo-Pacific Seafaring." In *East of Wallace's Line: Studies of Past and Present Maritime Cultures of the Indo-Pacific Region,* edited by Sue O'Connor and Peter Veth, 13–50. Rotterdam, Netherlands: A. A. Balkema.

———. 2001. "Towards the Sharp End: The Form and Performance of Prehistoric Polynesian Voyaging Canoes." In *Pacific 2000, Proceedings of the Fifth International Conference on Easter Island and the Pacific,* edited by Christopher M. Stevenson, Georgia Lee, and F. J. Morin, 29–36. Los Osos, CA: Bearsville Press.

Anderson, Atholl, John Chappel, Michael Gagan, and Richard Grove. 2006. "Prehistoric Migration in the Pacific Islands: A Hypothesis of ENSO Forcing." *The Holocene* 16 (1): 1–6.

Anderson, Atholl, and Gerard O'Regan. 2000. "To the Final Shore: Prehistoric Colonization of Subpolar Polynesia." In *Australian Archaeologist: Collected Papers in Honor of Jim Allen,* edited by Atholl Anderson and Tim Murray, 440–454. Canberra, Australia: Coombs Academic Publishing.

Ascher, Marcia. 1995. "Models and Maps from the Marshall Islands: A Case in Ethnomathematics." *Historia Mathematica* 22:347–370.

Australian Bureau of Meteorology and CSIRO. 2014. *Climate Variability, Extremes and Change in the Western Tropical Pacific: New Science and Updated Country Reports.* Pacific-Australia Climate Change Science and Adaptation Planning Program Technical Report. Melbourne, Australia: Australian Bureau of Meteorology and Commonwealth Scientific and Industrial Research Organisation.

Avis, Chris, Alvaro Montenegro, and Andrew Weaver. 2008. "Simulating Island Discovery during the Lapita Exploration." In *Canoes of the Grand Ocean,* edited by Anne Di Piazze and Erik Pearthree, 121–142. Oxford, UK: British Archaeological Research (BAR) Archaeopress.

Barclay, Robert. 2002. *Meḷaḷ: A Novel of the Pacific.* Honolulu: University of Hawai'i Press.

Barker, Holly M. 2013. *Bravo for the Marshallese: Regaining Control in a Post-*

Nuclear, Post-Colonial World. Second edition. Case Studies on Contemporary Social Issues. Belmont, CA: Thomson Wadsworth (original: 2004).

Beaglehole, John C., ed. 1955. *The Journals of Captain James Cook on his Voyages of Discovery,* vol. 1: *The Voyage of the Endeavour, 1768–1771.* Cambridge, UK: Hakluyt Society.

Beardsley, Felicia R. 1994. *Archaeological Investigations on Kwajalein Atoll, Marshall Islands.* Honolulu: International Archaeological Research Institute, Inc.

Beckwith, Martha W. 1951. *The Kumulipo: A Hawaiian Translation Chant.* Chicago: University of Chicago Press.

———, ed. 2007. *Kepelino's Traditions of Hawaii.* Honolulu: Bishop Museum Press (originally published in 1932).

Bellwood, Peter S. 2000. "Formosan Prehistory and Austronesian Dispersal." In *Austronesian Taiwan: Linguistics, History, Ethnology, and Prehistory,* edited by David Blundell, 337–365. Berkeley, CA: Hearst Museum of Anthropology.

Bernarik, Robert G., Bob Hobman, and Pater Rogers. 1999. "Nasih Tasih 2: Journey of a Middle Pleistocene Raft." *International Journal of Nautical Archaeology* 28 (1): 25–33.

Biggs, Bruce G., and Mary Veremaluma Biggs. 1975. "No Ciri Kalia." Working Papers in Anthropology, Archaeology, Linguistics and Maori Studies No. 42. Auckland, NZ: Department of Anthropology, University of Auckland.

Blair, Chad. 2011. "No Aloha for Micronesians in Hawaii." *Civil Beat,* June 11. Accessed June 17, 2016. http://www.civilbeat.org/2011/06/11650-no-aloha-for-micronesians-in-hawaii/.

Blust, Robert. 1995. "The Prehistory of the Austronesian-Speaking Peoples: A View from Language." *Journal of World Prehistory* 9 (4): 453–510.

———. 1999. "Subgrouping, Circularity and Extinction: Some Issues in Austronesian Comparative Linguistics." In *Selected Papers from the Eighth International Conference on Austronesian Linguistics,* edited by Elizabeth Zeitoun and Paul Jen-kuei, 80–82. Taipei: Academia Sinica.

Byran, Edwin H. 1972. *Life in the Marshall Islands.* Honolulu: Pacific Scientific Information Center.

Campbell, John R. 2014. "Climate-Change Migration in the Pacific." *The Contemporary Pacific* 26 (1): 1–28.

Carucci, Laurence M. 1989. "The Source of the Force in Marshallese Cosmology." In *The Pacific Theater: Island Representations of World War II,* edited by Lamont Lindstrom and Geoffrey M. White, 73–96. Honolulu: University of Hawai'i Press.

———. 1995. "Symbolic Imagery of Enewetak Sailing Canoes." In *Seafaring in the Contemporary Pacific Islands: Studies in Continuity and Change,* edited by Richard Feinberg, 16–33. DeKalb: Northern Illinois University Press.

————. 1997a. *Nuclear Nativity: Rituals of Renewal and Empowerment in the Marshall Islands.* DeKalb: Northern Illinois University Press.

————. 1997b. "Irooj Ro Ad: Measures of Chiefly Ideology and Practice in the Marshall Islands." In *Chiefs Today: Traditional Pacific Leadership and the Postcolonial State,* edited by Geoffrey M. White and Lamont Lindstrom, 197–210. Stanford, CA: Stanford University Press.

————. 2001. "Elision or Decision: Lived History and the Contextual Grounding of the Constructed Past." In *Cultural Memory: Reconfiguring History and Identity in the Postcolonial Pacific,* edited by Jeannette M. Mageo, 81–101. Honolulu: University of Hawai'i Press.

————. 2012. "You'll Always Be Family: Formulating Marshallese Identities in Kona, Hawai'i." *Pacific Studies* 35 (1/2): 203–231.

Cassels, Richard. 1979. "Early Prehistoric Wooden Artefacts from the Waitore Site (N136/16), near Patea, Taranaki." *New Zealand Journal of Archaeology* 1:85–108.

Chamisso, Adelbert von. 1836. *Reise um die Welt mit der Romanzofischen Entdeckungs-Expedition in den Jahren 1815–1818 auf der Brigg Rurik, Kapitain Otto von Kotzebue.* Leipzig: Weidmannsche Buchhandlung. English translation: *A Voyage around the World with the Romanzov Exploring Expedition in the Years 1815–1818, in the Brig Rurik, Captain Otto von Kotzebue,* translated by Henry Kratz. Honolulu: University of Hawai'i Press, 1986.

Choris, Louis. 1822. *Voyage pittoresque autour du monde, avec des portraits de sauvages d'Amérique, d'Asie, d'Afrique, et des îles du Grand océan: des paysaes, des vues maritimes, et plusiers objects d'histoire naturelle; accompagné de descriptions par m. le baron Cuvier, et m. A. de Chamisso, et d'observations sur les crânes humains, par m. le docteur Gall. Par m. Louis Choris, peintre.* Paris: Imprimé de Firmin Didot. English translation: *Picturesque Voyage around the World,* in *History of Micronesia: A Collection of Source Documents,* translated by Leonard Mason. In *History of Micronesia: A Collection of Source Documents,* vol. 18: *Russian Expeditions, 1808–1877,* edited by Rodrigue Levasque, 435–456. Quebec: Levasque Publications, 1992.

————. 1826. *Vues et paysages des régions équinoxiales recueillis dans un voyage autour du monde.* Paris: Imprimé Chez Paul Renouard. English translation: *Views and Sceneries of Tropical Regions, Collected during a Voyage around the World,* translated by Leonard Mason. In *History of Micronesia: A Collection of Source Documents,* vol. 18: *Russian Expeditions, 1808–1877,* edited by Rodrigue Levasque, 458–487. Quebec: Levasque Publications, 1992.

D'Arcy, Paul. 2006. *The People of the Sea: Environment, Identity, and History in Oceania.* Honolulu: University of Hawai'i Press.

Davenport, William. 1953. "Marshallese Folklore Types." *Journal of American Folklore* 66 (261): 219–237.

———. 1960. "Marshall Island Navigational Charts." *Imago Mundi* 15:19–26.

deBrum, Raymond. 1959. "Calling the Waves." *Micronesian Reporter* 7 (1): 3.

———. 1961. "The Marshallese 'Sticks'." *Micronesian Reporter* 9 (3): 27.

———. 1962. "Marshallese Navigation (as told to C. R. Olson)." *Micronesian Reporter* 10 (3): 18–23.

de Laubenfels, Max W. 1950. "Ocean Currents in the Marshall Islands." *Geographical Review* 40 (2): 254–259.

DeLisle, Christina T., and Vicente Diaz. 1997. *Sacred Vessels: Navigating Tradition and Identity in Micronesia.* Documentary film. Color with black-and-white sequences, 28 minutes. Guam: Moving Islands Production.

Dobin, Jay. 2011. *Summoning the Powers Beyond: Traditional Religions in Micronesia.* Honolulu: University of Hawai'i Press.

Downing, Jane, Dirk H. R. Spennemann, and Margaret Bennet, eds. 1992. *Bwebwenatoon Etto: A Collection of Marshallese Legends and Traditions.* Marshallese Culture and History, Series E: Legends, Changes and Proverbs, vol. 1. Majuro: Historic Preservation Office.

Eisenhart, Otto. 1888. "Acht Monate unter den Eingeborenen auf Ailu (Marshall-Gruppe)." *Aus allen Welttheilen* 19:207–208, 223–226, 250–252.

Emory, Kenneth P. 1965. *Kapingamarangi: Social and Religious Life of a Polynesian Atoll.* Honolulu: Bernice Pauahi Bishop Museum.

Erdland, August P. 1906. *Wörterbuch und Grammatik der Marshallsprache nebst ethnographischen Erläuterungen und kürzen Sprachubungen.* Archiv für das Studium deutscher Kolonialsprachen. Berlin: Druck und Kommissionsverlag von Georg Reimer.

———. 1910. "Die Sternkunde bei den Seefahren der Marshallinseln." *Anthropos* 5:16–26.

———. 1914. *Die Marshallinsulaner: Leben und Sitte, Sinn und Religion eines Südsee-Volkes.* Anthropos Ethnologische Bibliothek 2. Münster: Aschendorffsche Verlagsbuchhandlung.

Falgout, Suzanne, Lin Poyer, and Laurence M. Carucci. 2008. *Memories of War: Micronesians in the Pacific War.* Honolulu: University of Hawai'i Press.

Falstad, Paul. 2016. "Ripple Tank Applet." http://www.falstad.com/ripple/index.html. Accessed June 16, 2016.

Feinberg, Richard. 1988. *Polynesian Seafaring and Navigation: Ocean Travel in Anutan Culture and Society.* Kent, OH: Kent State University Press.

Feinberg, Richard, and Marianne George. 2008. "Seafaring in the Polynesian Outliers." In *Encyclopedia of the History of Science, Technology, and Medicine in*

Non-Western Cultures, edited by Helaine Selin, 1,983–1,989. Berlin, Heidelberg, and New York: Springer-Verlag.

Field, Les W., and Richard G. Fox. 2007. "Introduction: How Does Anthropology Work Today?" In *Anthropology Put to Work*, edited by Les W. Field and Richard G. Fox, 1–19. Oxford, UK: Berg.

Finney, Ben R. 1979. *Hokule'a: the Way to Tahiti*. New York: Dodd, Mead & Company.

———. 1994. *Voyage of Rediscovery*. Berkeley: University of California Press.

———. 1998. "Traditional Navigation and Nautical Cartography in Oceania." In *Cartography in the Traditional African, American, Arctic, Australian, and Pacific Societies*, edited by David Woodward and G. Malcolm Lewis, *The History of Cartography*, vol. 2, book 3: 443–492. Chicago: University of Chicago Press.

———. 2003. *Sailing in the Wake of the Ancestors: Reviving Polynesian Voyaging*. Honolulu: Bishop Museum Press.

———. 2007. "Ocean Sailing Canoes." In *Vaka Moana: Voyages of the Ancestors: The Discovery and Settlement of the Pacific*, edited by K. R. Howe, 100–153. Honolulu: University of Hawai'i Press (originally published in 2006).

Finney, Ben, Paul Frost, Richard Rhodes, and Nainoa Thompson. 1989. "Wait for the West Wind." *Journal of the Polynesian Society* 98 (3): 261–302.

Finney, Ben, and Bernard Kilonsky. 2001. "Closing and Opening the Polynesian Triangle: *Hōkūle'a's* Voyage to Rapa Nui." In *Pacific 2000, Proceedings of the Fifth International Conference on Easter Island and the Pacific*, edited by Christopher M. Stevenson, Georgia Lee, and F. J. Morin, 353–363. Los Osos, CA: Bearsville Press.

Finney, Ben R., Bernard J. Kilonsky, Stephen Somsen, and Edward D. Stroup. 1986. "Re-learning a Vanishing Art." *Journal of the Polynesian Society* 95 (1): 41–90.

Finney, Suzanne S., Mary Mostafanezhad, Guido Carlo Pigliasco, and Forrest Wade Young, eds. 2015. *At Home and in the Field: Ethnographic Encounters in Asia and the Pacific Islands*. Honolulu: University of Hawai'i Press.

Finsch, Otto. 1893. "Ethnographische Erfahrungen und Belegstücke aus der Südsee." *Annalen des K. & K. Naturhistorischen Hofmuseums* 8 (2): 375–438. Vienna: K. & K. Naturhistoriches Hofmuseum.

Frake, Charles. 1995. "A Reinterpretation of the Micronesian 'Star Compass'." *Journal of the Polynesian Society* 104 (2): 147–158.

Garrison, Tom. 2001. *Oceanography: An Invitation to Marine Science*. Pacific Grove, CA: Brooks/Cole-Wadsworth.

Gegeo, David W., and Karen A. Watson-Gegeo. 2001. "'How We Know': Kwara'ae Rural Villagers Doing Indigenous Epistemology." *The Contemporary Pacific* 13 (1): 55–88.

Genz, Joseph H. 2008. "Marshallese Navigation and Voyaging: Re-learning and Reviving Indigenous Knowledge of the Ocean." PhD diss., University of Hawaiʻi at Mānoa.

———. 2011. "Navigating the Revival of Voyaging in the Marshall Islands: Predicaments of Preservation and Possibilities of Collaboration." *The Contemporary Pacific* 23 (1): 1–34.

———. 2014. "Complementarity of Cognitive and Experiential Ways of Knowing the Ocean in Marshallese Navigation." *Ethos* 42 (3): 332–351.

———. 2015. "From Nuclear Exodus to Cultural Reawakening: A Navigator's Journey." In *At Home and in the Field: Ethnographic Encounters in Asia and the Pacific Islands,* edited by Suzanne S. Finney, Mary Mostafanezhad, Guido Carlo Pasciali, and Forrest Wade Young, 201–208. Honolulu: University of Hawaiʻi Press.

———. 2016. "Resolving Ambivalence in Marshallese Navigation: Relearning, Reinterpreting, and Reviving the 'Stick Chart' Wave Models." *Structure and Dynamics* 9 (1): 8–40.

———. 2017. "Without Precedent: Shifting Protocols in the Use of Rongelapese Navigational Knowledge." *Journal of the Polynesian Society* 126 (2): 209–232.

Genz, Joseph, Jerome Aucan, Mark Merrifield, Ben Finney, Korent Joel, and Alson Kelen. 2009. "Wave Navigation in the Marshall Islands: Comparing Indigenous and Western Scientific Knowledge of the Ocean." *Oceanography* 22 (2): 234–245.

Genz, Joseph H., Mylast Bilimon, Conny Livai, Jr., and Attok Nashon. 2016a. " 'We Are Like Wandering Birds Looking for Our Nest': Marshallese Voices on Ethnic Tensions in Hilo, Hawaiʻi." Paper presented at the annual meeting for the Society for Applied Anthropology, Vancouver, British Columbia, March 28–April 2.

Genz, Joseph H., and Ben R. Finney. 2006. "Preservation and Revitalization of Intangible Cultural Heritage: A Perspective from Cultural Anthropological Research on Indigenous Navigation in the Republic of the Marshall Islands." *Micronesian Journal of the Humanities and Social Sciences* 5 (1/2): 306–313.

Genz, Joseph H., Noelani Goodyear-Kaʻōpua, Monica C. LaBriola, Alexander Mawyer, Elicita N. Morei, and John P. Rosa. 2016b. *Militarism and Nuclear Testing.* Vol. 1 of *Teaching Oceania Series*, edited by Monica LaBriola. Honolulu: Center for Pacific Islands Studies, University of Hawaiʻi at Mānoa.

George, Marianne. 2012. "Polynesian Navigation and Te Lapa—'The Flashing'." *Time and Mind: The Journal of Archaeology, Consciousness and Culture* 5 (2): 135–174.

Giesberts, Leo. 1910. "Die Seefahrerkunst der Marshallaner." *Hiltruper Monatshefte* 27:55–60.

Gladwin, Thomas. 1970. *East Is a Big Bird: Navigation and Logic on Puluwat Atoll.* Cambridge, MA: Harvard University Press.

Goodenough, Ward. 1953. *Native Astronomy in the Central Carolines.* Philadelphia: University of Pennsylvania Press.

Green, Roger C. 1991. "Near and Remote Oceania: Disestablishing 'Melanesia' in Culture History." In *Man and a Half: Essays in Pacific Anthropology and Ethnography in Honor of Ralph Bulmer,* edited by Andrew Pawley, 491–502. Auckland, NZ: The Polynesian Society.

Grimble, Arthur. 1931. "Gilbertese Astronomy and Astronomical Observances." *Journal of the Polynesian Society* 40 (4): 197–224.

Gulick, Luther H. 1862. "Micronesia of the Pacific Ocean." *Nautical Magazine and Naval Chronicle* 31:169–182, 237–245, 298–308, 408–417.

Haddon, Alfred C., and James Hornell. 1975. *Canoes of Oceania.* Bernice Pauahi Bishop Museum Special Publications. Honolulu: Bishop Museum Press (originally published 1936–1938).

Hambruch, Paul. 1912. "Die Schiffahrt auf den Karolinen- und Marshallinseln." *Meereskunde Sammlung Volkstumlicher Vortrage zum Verstandis der Nationalen Bedeutung von Meer und Seewesen* 66:1–40.

Hanlon, David. 2003. "Beyond 'the English Method of Tattooing': Decentering the Practice of History in Oceania." *The Contemporary Pacific* 14 (1): 19–40.

———. 2009. "The 'Sea of Little Islands': Examining Micronesia's Place in 'Our Sea of Islands'." *The Contemporary Pacific* 21 (1): 91–110.

———. 2014. *Making Micronesia: A Political Biography of Tosiwo Nakayama.* Honolulu: University of Hawai'i Press.

Hau'ofa, Epeili. 1994. "Our Sea of Islands." *The Contemporary Pacific* 6 (1): 148–161.

———. 2001. "The Ocean in Us." *The Contemporary Pacific* 10 (2): 392–410.

Hein, James R., Florence L. Wong, and Dan L. Mosier. 1999. *Bathymetry of the Republic of the Marshall Islands and Vicinity.* U.S. Geological Survey, Miscellaneous Field Map Studies Map. MF 2324, Version 1.3. Accessed June 16, 2016. http://pubs.usgs.gov/mf/1999/2324/.

Heyerdahl, Thor. 1953. *American Indians in the Pacific.* Chicago: Rand McNally.

Hezel, Francis X. 1983. *The First Taint of Civilization: A History of the Caroline and Marshall Islands in Pre-Colonial Days, 1521–1885.* Pacific Islands Monograph 1. Honolulu: University of Hawai'i Press.

———. 1995. *Strangers in Their Own Land: A Century of Colonial Rule in the Caroline and Marshall Islands.* Pacific Islands Monograph 13. Honolulu: University of Hawai'i Press.

Hill, John, and Andrew Williamson. 2012. *The Land of Eb.* Film. Color. 88 minutes. Kailua, HI: Kona Film Group.

Horridge, Adrian. 2008. "Origins and Relationships of Pacific Canoes and Rigs." In

Canoes of the Grand Ocean, edited by Anne Di Piazze and Erik Pearthree, 85–106. Oxford, UK: British Archaeological Research (BAR) Archaeopress.

Hutchins, Edwin. 1995. *Cognition in the Wild.* Cambridge, MA: MIT Press.

Huth, John E. 2013. *The Lost Art of Finding Our Way.* Cambridge, MA: Belknap Press.

Ingold, Tim. 2000. *The Perception of the Environment: Essays in Livelihood, Dwelling and Skill.* London and New York: Routledge.

Irwin, Geoffrey. 1992. *The Prehistoric Exploration and Colonization of the Pacific.* Cambridge, UK: Cambridge University Press.

———. 2004. *Kohika: The Archaeology of a Late Maori Lake Village in the Ngati Awa Rohe, Bay of Plenty, New Zealand.* Auckland: Auckland University Press.

———. 2007. "Voyaging and Settlement." In *Vaka Moana: Voyages of the Ancestors: The Discovery and Settlement of the Pacific,* edited by K. R. Howe, 55–91. Honolulu: University of Hawai'i Press (originally published in 2006).

———. 2008. "Pacific Seascapes, Canoe Performance, and a Review of Lapita Voyaging with Regard to Theories of Migration." *Asian Perspectives: Journal of Archaeology for Asia and the Pacific* 47 (1): 12–27.

———. 2011. "Sailing from Polynesia to the Americas." In *Polynesians in America: Pre-Columbian Contacts with the New World,* edited by Terry Jones, Alice A. Storey, Elizabeth A. Matisoo-Smith, and José Miguel Ramírez-Aliaga, 395–417. Lanham, MD: Alta Mira Press.

Jetnil-Kijiner, Kathy. 2012. "History Project." Accesed June 16, 2016. https://www.youtube.com/watch?v=DIIrrPyK0eU.

Johnson, Giff. 2013. *Don't Ever Whisper: Darlene Keju, Pacific Health Pioneer, Champion for Nuclear Survivors.* Charleston, SC: CreateSpace Independent Publishing Platform.

Johnston, Barbara R. 2016. "Climate Change, Migration, and Biocultural Diversity—Emerging Trends, D/volutionary Tipping Points? Michael J. Kearney Distinguished Lecture." Paper presented at the annual meeting for the Society for Applied Anthropology, Vancouver, British Columbia, March 29–April 2, 2016.

Johnston, Barbara R., and Holly M. Barker. 2008. *Consequential Damages of Nuclear War: The Rongelap Report.* Walnut Creek, CA: Left Coast Press, Inc.

Jones, Terry, Alice A. Storey, Elizabeth A. Matisoo-Smith, and José Miguel Ramírez-Aliaga, eds. 2011. *Polynesians in America: Pre-Columbian Contacts with the New World.* Lanham, MD: Alta Mira Press.

Kabua, Mike. 2004. "Iaekwoj Eo An Jebro: Jebro's Race and Liberation Celebrations." In *Life in the Republic of the Marshall Islands,* edited by Anono L. Loeak, Veronica C. Kiluwe, and Linda Crowl, 15–30. Majuro and Suva: Institute of Pacific Studies.

Kirch, Patrick V. 2000. *On the Road of the Winds: An Archaeological History of the*

Pacific Islands before European Contact. Berkeley: University of California Press.

———. 2010. "Peopling the Pacific: A Holistic Anthropological Perspective." *Annual Review of Anthropology* 39:131–148.

Kirch, Patrick V., and Marshall Sahlins. 1992. *Anahulu: The Anthropology of History in the Kingdom of Hawaii.* Chicago: University of Chicago Press.

Kiste, Robert C. 1974. *The Bikinians: A Study in Forced Migration.* The Kiste and Ogan Social Change Series in Anthropology. Menlo Park, CA: Cummings.

Knappe, Wilhelm. 1888. "Religiöse Anschauungen der Marshall-Insulaner." *Mittheilungen von Forschungsreisenden und Gelehrten aus den Deutschen Schutzgebieten* 1:63–81.

Knight, Gerald. 1999. *A History of the Marshall Islands.* Third edition. Majuro: Micronitor News and Printing Company (original edition: *Man This Reef,* Majuro: Micronitor, 1982).

Kotzebue, Otto von. 1821. *Entdeckungs-Resie in die Südsee und nach der Berings-Strasse zur Erforschung einer nordöstlichen Durchfahrt, unternommen in den Jahren 1815–1818, auf Kosten Sr. Erlaucht des Herrn Reichs-Kanzlers Grafen Romanzoff auf dem Schiffe Rurick.* Vol. 2. London: Longman, Hurst, Rees, Orme, and Brown. Three vols. English translation: *A Voyage of Discovery, into the South Seas and Bering's Straits, for the Purpose of Exploring a North-East Passage, Undertaken in the Years 1815–1818, at the Expense of His Highness the Chancellor of the Empire, Count Romanzoff, in the Ship Rurick, under the Command of the Lieutenant in the Russian Imperial Navy, Otto von Kotzebue,* translated by H. E. Llyod. New York: Da Capo Press, 1967.

———. 1830. *Neue Reise um die Welt, in den Jahren 1823–1826.* London: Henry Colburn and Richard Bently. Two vols. English translation: *New Voyage Round the World in the Years 1823–1826,* translated by J. Brief. New York: Da Capo Press, 1967.

Kovach, Margaret. 2009. *Indigenous Methodologies: Characteristics, Conversations, and Contexts.* Toronto: University of Toronto Press.

Kowata, Kinuko, Terry L. Mote, Donna K. Stone, and Bernice Joash. 1999. *Inọñ in Ṃajōl: A Collection of Marshallese Folktales.* Majuro: Alele Museum, Library and National Archives.

Krämer, Augustin, and Hans Nevermann. 1938. "Ralik-Ratak (Marshall-Inseln)." In *Ergebnisse der Südsee-Expedition, 1908–1910 II. Ethnographie, B: Mikronesien,* vol. 11, edited by Georg Thilenius, 215–232. Hamburg: Friedrichsen, de Gruyter & Co.

Lagerloef, Gary S. E., Gary T. Mitchum, Roger B. Lukas, and Pearn P. Niiler. 1999. "Tropical Pacific Near-Surface Currents Estimated from Altimeter, Wind, and Drifter Data." *Journal of Geophysical Research* 104 (C10): 23,313–23,326.

Lassiter, Luke E. 2005. *The Chicago Guide to Collaborative Ethnography.* Chicago: University of Chicago Press.

Lauer, Matthew, and Shankar Aswani. 2009. "Indigenous Ecological Knowledge as Situated Practices: Understanding Fishers' Knowledge in the Western Solomon Islands." *American Anthropologist* 111 (3): 317–329.

Lauer, Peter K. 1976. "Sailing with the Amphlett Islanders." In *Pacific Voyaging and Navigation*, edited by Ben R. Finney, 71–89. Polynesian Society Memoir 39. Wellington, NZ: The Polynesian Society.

Lessa, William A. 1961. *Tales from Ulithi Atoll: A Comparative Study in Oceanic Folklore.* Folklore Studies 13. Berkeley: University of California Press.

Lewis, David. 1978. *The Voyaging Stars: Secrets of the Pacific Island Navigators.* New York: W. W. Norton & Company, Inc.

———. 1994. *We, the Navigators: The Ancient Art of Landfinding in the Pacific.* 2nd ed. Honolulu: University of Hawai'i Press (originally published in 1972).

Lili'uokalani (Queen). 1978. *The Kumulipo: An Hawaiian Creation Myth.* Kentfield, CA: Pueo Press (originally published in 1897).

Low, Sam. 2013. *Hawaiki Rising: Hōkūle'a, Nainoa Thompson, and the Hawaiian Renaissance.* Waipahu, HI: Island Heritage Publising.

Majuro Declaration. 2013. "Majuro Declaration for Climate Leadership." Accessed June 16, 2016. http://www.majurodeclaration.org/.

Malo, David. 1951. *Hawaiian Antiquities (Moolelo Hawaii).* Honolulu: Bishop Musuem Press (first published in Hawaiian ca. 1838; first English edition, trans. Nathaniel B. Emerson, published in 1898).

Mara, Ratu Sir Kamisese. 1997. *The Pacific Way: A Memoir.* Honolulu: University of Hawai'i Press.

Marck, Jeffrey C. 1986. "Micronesian Dialects and the Overnight Voyage." *Journal of the Polynesian Society* 95 (2): 253–258.

Marshall, Mac. 2004. *Namoluk beyond the Reef: The Transformation of a Micronesian Community.* Boulder, CO: Westview Press.

Mason, Leonard. 1948. *Rongerik Report: Summary Findings and Recommendations.* Guam: Office of the High Commissioner of the Trust Territory of the Pacific Islands.

McArthur, Phillip H. 2000. "Narrating to the Center of Power in the Marshall Islands." In *We Are a People: Narrative and Multiplicity in Constructing Ethnic Identity*, edited by Paul Spickard and W. Jeffrey Burroughs, 85–97. Philadelphia: Temple University Press.

Meachem, W. 1984. "On the Improbability of Austronesian Origins in South China." *Asian Perspectives* 26:89–106.

Meinicke, Carl E. 1863. "Die Gilbert- und Marshall-Inseln." *Zeitschrift für Allgemeine Erkunde: Mit Unterstützung der Gesellschaft für Erkunde zu Berlin* 2:369–417.

Metzgar, Eric. 2006. "Carolinian Voyaging in the New Millennium." *Micronesian Journal of the Humanities and Social Sciences* 5 (1/2): 293–305.

Meyer, Manulani A. 2001. "Our Own Liberation: Reflections on Hawaiian Epistemology." *The Contemporary Pacific* 13 (1): 124–148.

Miller, Rachel L. 2010. "Wa Kuk Wa Jimor: Outrigger Canoes, Social Change, and Modern Life in the Marshall Islands." MA thesis, University of Hawai'i at Mānoa.

Nakayama, Masao, and Fredrick L. Ramp. 1974. *Micronesian Navigation, Island Empire and Traditional Concepts of Ownership of the Sea.* Saipan: Fifth Congress of Micronesia.

Newell, Alison, Peter Nuttal, Biman Prasad, and Joeli Veitayaki. 2016. "Turning the Tide: The Need for Sustainable Sea Transport in the Pacific." *Marine Policy.* Accessed July 1, 2016. http://dx.doi.org/10.1016/j.marpol.2016.01.009.

Niedenthal, Jack. 2001. *For the Good of Mankind: A History of the People of Bikini and Their Islands.* Majuro: Bravo Press.

Nurse, Leonard A., Roger F. McLean, John Agard, Lino Pascal Briguglio, Virginie Duvat-Magnan, Netatua Pelesikoti, Emma Tompkins, and Arthur Webb. 2014. "Small Islands." In *Climate Change 2014: Impacts, Adaptation, and Vulnerability.* Part B: *Regional Aspects. Contribution of Working Group II to the Fifth Assessment Report of the Intergovernmental Panel on Climate Change,* edited by V. R. Barros, C. B. Field, D. J. Dokken, M. D. Mastrandrea, K. J. Mach, T. E. Bilir, M. Chatterjee, K. L. Ebi, Y. O. Estrada, R. C. Genova, B. Girma, E. S. Kissel, A. N. Levy, S. MacCracken, P. R. Mastrandrea, and L. L. White, 1,613–1,654. Cambridge, UK, and New York: Cambridge University Press.

Nuttal, Peter. 2015. "The Case for Immediate Priorization of a Transition to a Low Carbon Freight Future for Pacific Islands States." Paper presented at the United Nations Conference on Trade and Development, the Multi-Year Expert Meeting on Transport, Trade Logitsics and Trade Facilitation, fourth session (sustainable freight transport), Geneva, October 14–16.

Olopai, Lino M., with Juliana Flinn. 2005. *The Rope of Tradition: Reflections of a Saipan Carolinian.* Saipan: Northern Mariana Islands Council for the Humanities.

Pawley, A., and M. Pawley. 1994. "Early Austronesian Terms for Canoe Parts and Seafaring." In *Austronesian Terminologies: Continuity and Change,* edited by A. K. Pawley and M. D. Ross, 329–361. Canberra: Australian National University.

Peattie, Mark R. 1993. *Nan'yō: The Rise and Fall of the Japanese in Micronesia, 1885–1945.* Pacific Islands Monograph 4. Honolulu: University of Hawai'i Press.

Peterson, Glenn. 1993. "Kanengamah and Pohnpei's Politics of Concealment." *American Anthropologist* 95 (2): 334–352.

———. 2009. *Traditional Micronesian Societies: Adaptation, Integration, and Political Organization*. Honolulu: University of Hawai'i Press.

Petrosian-Husa, Carmen C. H. 2004. "Activities of the Alele Museum in 2004." *Micronesian Journal of the Humanities and Social Sciences* 3 (1–2): 87–89.

Polynesian Voyaging Society. 2016. "The Malama Honua Worldwide Voyage." Accessed June 16, 2016. http://www.hokulea.com/worldwide-voyage/.

"Project 4.1 Morphs to Haunted House." 2012. *Marshall Islands Journal* 43 (41): 8.

"Project 4.1 Zombieland." 2012. *The Rockville High School Rampage*, October 23. Accessed June 16, 2016. http://www.rockvillerampage.com/features/project -4-1-zombieland/#.

Rainbird, Paul. 2004. *The Archaeology of Micronesia*. Cambridge, UK: University of Cambridge.

Rehg, K. 1995. "The Significance of Linguistic Interaction Spheres in Reconstructing Micronesian Prehistory." *Oceanic Linguistics* 34 (2): 305–326.

Riesenberg, Saul H. 1976. "The Organization of Navigational Knowledge on Puluwat." In *Pacific Voyaging and Navigation*, edited by Ben R. Finney, 91–128. Polynesian Society Memoir 39. Wellington: The Polynesian Society.

Rieth, Timothy M., Terry L. Hunt, Carl Lipo, and Janet M. Wilmshurst. 2011. "The 13th Century Polynesian Colonization of Hawai'i Island." *Journal of Archaeological Science* 38:2,740–2,749.

Rubinstein, Donald H. 2009. "Cultural Preservation of Traditional Textiles on Fais Island in Micronesia: Problems and Paradoxes." Paper presented at the second ASEAN Textile Symposium, Manila, February 2–3.

Rubinstein, Donald H., and Sophiano Limol. 2007. "Reviving the Sacred Machi: A Chiefly Weaving from Fais Island, Micronesia." In *Material Choices: Refashioning Bast and Leaf Fibers in Asia and the Pacific*, edited by Roy W. Hamilton and B. Lynn Milgram, 154–165. Los Angeles: Fowler Museum, University of California–Los Angeles.

Salmond, Anne. 2005. "Their Body is Different, Our Body is Different: European and Tahitian Navigators in the 18th Century." *History and Anthropology* 16 (2): 167–186.

Sarfert, Ernst G. 1911. "Zur Kenntnis der Schiffahrtskunde der Karolliner." *Korrespondenz-Blatt der Deutschen Gesellschaft für Anthropologie, Ethnologie und Urgeschichte* 42:131–136.

Schück, Albert. 1884. "Die Entwicklung Unseres Bekanntwerdens mit den Astronomischen, Geographischen und Nautischen Kenntnissen der Karolineninsulaner nebst Erklärung der Medos oder Segelkarten der Marshall-Insulaner, im Westlichen Grossen Nord-Ocean." *Tijfschrift van het Koninklijke Nederlandsch Aardrujkskundig Genootschap te Amsterdam* 1 (2): 226–251.

———. 1902. *Die Stabkarten der Marshall-Insulaner.* Hamburg: Kommissionsverlag von H. O. Persiehl.

Schwartz, Jessica A. 2012. "A 'Voice to Sing': Rongelapese Musical Activism and the Production of Nuclear Knowledge." *Music and Politics* 6 (1): 1–21.

Sharp, Andrew. 1956. *Ancient Voyagers in the Pacific.* Memoir 32. Wellington, NZ: Polynesian Society.

Siers, James. 1977. *Taratai: A Pacific Adventure.* Wellington, NZ: Millwood.

———. 1978. *Taratai II: A Continuing Pacific Adventure.* Wellington, NZ: Millwood.

"Signs and Weather." 1959. *Micronesian Reporter* 7 (2): 19–24.

Simpson, Audra. 2007. "On Ethnographic Refusal: Indigeneity, 'Voice' and Colonial Citizenship." *Junctures: The Journal for Thematic Dialogue* 9:67–80.

Sinoto, Yoshi. 1983. "The Huahine Excavation: Discovery of an Ancient Polynesian Canoe." *Archaeology* 36 (2): 10–15.

Smith-Norris, Martha. 2016. *Domination and Resistance: The United States and the Marshall Islands during the Cold War.* Honolulu: University of Hawai'i Press.

Solheim, Wilhelm G. 1984–1985. "The Nusantao Hypothesis: The Origin and Spread of Austronesian Speakers." *Asian Perspectives* 26 (1): 77–88.

Spennemann, Dirk H. R. 1992. "Historic Preservation Legislation." Majuro: Ministry of Internal Affairs, Historic Preservation Office.

———. 1993. *Ennannin Etto: A Collection of Essays of the Marshallese Past.* Marshall Islands Culture and History. Series F: Technical Studies and Miscellaneous, vol 1. Majuro: Historic Preservation Office.

———. 1999. "No Room for the Dead: Burial Practices in a Constrained Environment." *Anthropos* 94:35–56.

———, ed. 2004. *The First Descriptions of the Southern Marshalls: The 1778 Accounts of Thomas Gilbert, Edward Home, and John Marshall.* Majuro: Micronitor Press.

———. 2005. "Traditional and Nineteenth Century Communication Patterns in the Marshall Islands." *Micronesian Journal of the Humanities and Social Sciences* 4 (1): 25–52.

Stone, Donna K. 2001a. *Ri-Jedjed Iju in Majel: Stars and Constellations of the Marshall Islands.* Traditional Lifeways English Series 2001/01. Majuro, Alele Museum, Library and National Archives.

———. 2001b. "Changing View, Cultural Survival: Knowledge and Power in the Marshall Islands." *Cultural Resource Management* 5:39–40.

Stone, Donna K., Kinuko Kowata, and Bernice Joash. 2000. *Jabōnkōnnaan in Majel̗: Wisdom from the Past: A Collection of Marshallese Proverbs, Wise Sayings and Beliefs.* Majuro: Alele Museum, Library and National Archives.

Sundt, Richard A. 1973. "The Fallout on Rongelap Atoll and Its Social, Medical and Environmental Effects." Unpublished manuscript on file at the Nuclear Claims Tribunal, Majuro.

Sustainable Sea Transport Research Programme. 2015. "Micronesian Sustainable Transport Center: A Catalyst for Change." Suva, Fiji: Pacific Center for Environment and Sustainable Development and University of the South Pacific.

Teaiwa, Katerina M. 2015. *Consuming Ocean Island: Stories of People and Phosphate from Banaba.* Bloomington and Indianapolis: Indiana University Press.

Teaiwa, Teresia K. 1994. "Bikinis and Other S/Pacific N/Oceans." *The Contemporary Pacific* 6 (1): 87–109.

Thomas, Nicholas. 1992. "The Inversion of Tradition." *American Ethnologist* 19 (2): 213–232.

Thomas, Steve. 1987. *The Last Navigator.* New York: Henry Holt and Company.

Thorne, Alan, and Robert Raymond. 1989. *Man on the Rim: The Peopling of the Pacific.* Sydney: Angus and Robertson.

Tingley, Kim. 2015. "Sixth Sense." *New York Times Magazine*, March 20. Also published as "The Secrets of the Wave Pilots." Accessed June 16, 2016. http://www.nytimes.com/2016/03/20/magazine/the-secrets-of-the-wave-pilots.html?_r=0.

Tobin, Jack A. 1953. *The Bikini People: Past and Present.* Guam: District Administrator, U.S. Trust Territory of the Pacific Islands.

———. 1956. *Land Tenure in the Marshall Islands.* Washington, DC: National Research Council, Pacific Science Board.

———. 2002. *Stories from the Marshall Islands: Bwebwenato Jān Aelōñ Kein.* Honolulu: University of Hawai'i Press.

Turnbull, David. 2000. *Masons, Tricksters, and Cartographers: Comparative Studies in the Sociology of Scientific and Indigenous Knowledge.* Studies in the History of Science, Technology and Medicine. Amsterdam: Hardwood Academic Publishers.

Walker, Isaiah H. 2011. *Waves of Resistance: Surfing and History in Twentieth-Century Hawai'i.* Honolulu: University of Hawai'i Press.

Walsh, Julianne M. 2003. "Imagining the Marshalls: Chiefs, Tradition, and the State on the Fringes of U.S. Empire." PhD diss., University of Hawai'i at Mānoa.

Weibel, Elizabeth. 2012. "Zombies are Coming to Rockville." *The Gazette*, August 27. Accessed June 16, 2016. https://www.washingtonpost.com/local/zombies-are-coming-to-rockville/2012/08/27/828b61c2-f072-11e1-b74c-84ed55e0300b_story.html.

Weisler, Marshall I. 1997. "Prehistoric Long-Distance Interaction at the Margins of Oceania." In *Prehistoric Long-Distance Interaction in Oceania: An Interdisci-*

plinary Approach, edited by Marshall I. Weisler, 149–172. Auckland: New Zealand Archaeological Association Monograph.

———. 2000. "Burial Artifacts from the Marshall Islands: Description, Dating and Evidence for Extra-Archipelago Contacts." *Micronesica* 33 (1/2): 111–136.

———. 2001. *On the Margins of Sustainability: Prehistoric Settlement of Utrok Atoll, Northern Marshall Islands.* Oxford, UK: Archaeopress.

Wilmshurst, Janet M., Terry L. Hunt, Carl P. Lipo, and Atholl J. Anderson. 2011. "High-Precision Radiocarbon Dating Shows Recent and Rapid Initial Human Colonization of East Polynesia." *Proceedings of the National Academy of Sciences* 108 (5): 1,815–1,820.

Winkler (Captain). 1898. "Über die früheren Zeiten in den Marshall-Inseln gebrauchten Seekarten, mit einigen Notizen über die Seefahrt der Marshall-Insulaner im Allgemainem." *Marine Rundschau* 10:1,418–1,439. English translation (1901): "On Sea Charts Formerly Used in the Marshall Islands, with Notices on the Navigation of These Islanders in General." *Smithsonian Institute Report for 1899* 54:487–508.

Wood-Ellem, Elizabeth. 1999. *Queen Sālote of Tonga: The Story of an Era, 1900–1965.* Honolulu: University of Hawai'i Press.

Wright, L. Donelson. 1995. *Morphodynamics of Inner Continental Shelves.* Boca Raton, FL: CRC Press.

Index

Page numbers in italics refer to figures.

About the Author

Joseph H. Genz teaches anthropology at the University of Hawai'i at Hilo. After serving as a U.S. Peace Corps Volunteer in Samoa (1997–1999), he earned a PhD in anthropology from the University of Hawai'i at Mānoa (2008). In partnership with the Majuro-based community organization Waan Aelōñ in Majol (Canoes of the Marshall Islands) and an international team of scientists from the fields of oceanography and physics, he has collaboratively chronicled, researched, and facilitated the cultural revival of voyaging and wave navigation in the Marshall Islands for over a decade.